PRAISE FOR *MAN ON FIRE*

"It seems that Steven Raichlen has 'been on fire' for most of his life. A great collector of tales and travel, Steven has twined his years of adventure with some of his most iconic and meaningful dishes. *Man on Fire* is a deeply personal look at how the magic of food and cooking can nurture our souls, shape our lives, and feed a lifetime of exploration."

—Aaron Franklin, owner of Franklin's Barbecue and *New York Times* bestselling author of *Franklin Barbecue: A Meat-Smoking Manifesto*

"Raichlen takes readers on a rich and engaging journey from curious food lover to world-renowned grilling expert, sharing personal memories, travels, and decades of culinary wisdom along the way. Filled with heart, flavor, and insight, *Man on Fire* is an inspiring and deeply enjoyable read for anyone who appreciates the everyday joys that food and shared experiences can offer."

—Emeril Lagasse

"Steven is a master who makes fire feel both ancient and new, teaching that barbecue is not just technique but a culture, a journey, and a joy."

—Francis Mallmann

"*Man on Fire* is a masterclass in living boldly from one of the true pioneers of live-fire cooking. It's honest, heartfelt, and packed with the kind of stories only a life spent chasing flavor and purpose can deliver. Steven Raichlen is a true legend."

—Derek Wolf, Over the Fire Cooking

"In *Man on Fire*, you find out how a French literature scholar from Baltimore ended up traveling to 75 countries, winning five James Beard Awards, and landing in the Barbecue Hall of Fame right alongside the rest of us. That's one hell of a journey, and Steven tells it the way he does everything—with class, with honesty, and with a deep respect for the craft."

—Myron Mixon, five-time World Barbecue Champion
and *New York Times* bestselling author

"Steven's heart and spirit come through in this fine-tuned memoir. From his birth in Japan to his Iron Chef battle in Tokyo, from his literary adventures on Chappaquiddick to an awesome streak of recipes, Raichlen never misses!"

—Amy Ephron, novelist, screenwriter, film producer,
and author of *Unseasonably Cold*

"Baseball has Babe Ruth, basketball Michael Jordan, hockey Wayne Gretzky and for BBQ, Steven Raichlen . . . He has been barbecue's cheerleader, sage, and high priest, and if there is one man responsible for the modern barbecue revolution, it's *The Barbecue Bible* author and longtime PBS TV host. Now he has pivoted to the personal, and in this gripping memoir tells how he overcame childhood tragedy and a chronic fear of the camera to become an internationally bestselling author and popular TV host—in three different languages! With lots of entrepreneurial advice, inside wisdom about barbecue, and 25 previously unpublished recipes, *Man on Fire* has something for every reader, from barbecue buffs to literature lovers, history geeks, armchair travelers, and anyone who wants to be his or her own boss."

—Larry Olmsted, award-winning journalist, *New York Times* bestselling
author of *Real Food, Fake Food*, and senior columnist for Forbes.com

MAN ON FIRE

ALSO BY STEVEN RAICHLEN

Nonfiction

Boston's Best Restaurants

A Taste of the Mountains Cooking School Cookbook

A Celebration of the Seasons

Healthy Jewish Cooking

Miami Spice

The Caribbean Pantry

The Barbecue! Bible

Barbecue! Bible Sauces Rubs and Marinades

How to Grill

BBQ USA

Best Ribs Ever

Planet Barbecue

Bold & Healthy Flavors

Man Made Meals

Project Smoke

Project Fire

The Brisket Chronicles

How to Grill Vegetables

Project Griddle

Fiction

The Hermit of Chappaquiddick

MAN ON FIRE

Of Life, Love, Literature, and *Really Good* Barbecue

A Memoir

STEVEN RAICHLEN

BENBELLA
BenBella Books, Inc.
Dallas, TX

The events, locations, and conversations in this book, while true, are re-created from the author's memory. The essence of the story and the feelings and emotions evoked are intended to be accurate representations. In certain instances, names, persons, organizations, and places have been changed to protect an individual's privacy.

BenBella

BenBella Books, Inc.
8080 N. Central Expressway
Suite 1700
Dallas, TX 75206
benbellabooks.com
Send feedback to feedback@benbellabooks.com

Printed in the United States of America
10 9 8 7 6 5 4 3 2 1

Library of Congress Control Number: 2026021480
ISBN 9781637749609 (hardcover)
ISBN 9781637749616 (electronic)

Editing by Rebecca Pillsbury and Claire Schulz
Copyediting by Karen Wise
Proofreading by Michael Fedison and Jill Kramer
Text design and composition by Aaron Edmiston
Cover design by Morgan Carr
Cover image Image © Adobe Stock / malashkos
Author photograph on page 335 by Gary N. Blum, reproduced with permission
Printed by Lake Book Manufacturing

To family past:

Frances Raichlen

Sonny Raichlen

Ethel and Sam "Dear" Raichlen

Sarah and Jack Goldman

Family future:

Ella

Mia

Julian

And above all:

To my wife, Barbara

CONTENTS

RECIPES

The truth, the whole truth, and nothing but the truth . . .
—the oath for witnesses in United States courtrooms

Why ruin a good story with the truth?
—Barbara Raichlen

Introduction

IN THE BEGINNING

I never set out to become the "Barbecue Guru" or "Gladiator of the Grill" (as Oprah called me), or any of the other sobriquets bestowed on me over the years (my favorite being the "Shakespeare of Barbecue").

I majored in French literature at Reed College in Portland, Oregon, and figured I would lead a quiet, scholarly life as a professor of comparative literature. Instead, I became a food writer, TV host, the author of more than thirty books, and dare I say, the man who launched the barbecue revolution. Most people know me for my work with live-fire cooking, but I've also been a translator, cooking teacher, restaurant critic, wine and spirits columnist, healthy food evangelist, product designer, and consultant. Oh, and I've never worked in an office or had a "real" job or a steady paycheck.

I battled the Iron Chef in Tokyo; hosted TV shows in English, French, and Italian; and consulted on several restaurants, including one in Hong Kong and one for a cruise line. I've written for *The New York Times, GQ,*

Esquire, and all the major food magazines. I wrote a novel called *The Hermit of Chappaquiddick* (yes, *that* Chappaquiddick)—a foodie love story set on the island where I've lived for two decades. I even translated a Marquis de Sade short story for *Playboy*.

I've spent time with Julia Child and James Beard. I've broken bread at the White House and grilled with Oprah and Howard Stern. I've tasted wine with Stanley Tucci, swapped watch stories with Nicolas Hayek (founder of Swatch—I'm a watch guy), and interviewed legions of chefs from Alain Ducasse to José Andrés to Jean-Georges.

The lecture circuit has taken me to Harvard University, the Library of Congress, the Smithsonian Institution, and the National Press Club. My restaurant reporting has led me to meals at hundreds of Michelin-starred restaurants and thousands of casual grill shacks around the world. Along the way, I've won five James Beard Awards and three IACP–Julia Child Awards, and was inducted into the Taste and Barbecue Halls of Fame.

On a darker note, I survived my mother's drug addiction and death when I was seventeen years old.

I've had an unconventional career (that's putting it mildly) and have led a kaleidoscopically varied life. What follows are the highs and lows, the smoke and sizzle, with plenty of inside baseball about book writing, television, history, language, travel, and of course, barbecue. It's not a cookbook—I've written enough of those already—but you will find twenty-five of my favorite recipes, created over the years to mark my passage from my childhood in Japan and Baltimore to my apotheosis at the grill. It's all been fascinating for me, and I hope it will be of interest to people around the world (grill enthusiasts and not) who have bought my books, read my articles, and watched my TV shows.

This is the story of a man on fire.

Chapter One

THE BATTLE OF THE BARBECUE GODS

1953, 2003

Preparing to battle Iron Chef Rokusabura Michiba.

There are many places I could begin this book.

With my childhood, growing up in a decidedly non-foodie household in Baltimore. With the publication of my first cookbook or my induction into the Barbecue Hall of Fame. But the best place to start might be the least likely place I ever expected to find myself considering my academic background in French literature: on the set of a TV show in Tokyo about to battle the Iron Chef.

Now, I'm a writer, not a chef. Sure, I cook, and I certainly know my way around a grill. But I could no more run a restaurant kitchen on a busy Saturday night (my definition of a true chef) than I could pilot an F-16.

The Iron Chef adventure began a few months earlier with a phone call from Mainichi Broadcasting in Tokyo. Would I be willing to appear on a Japanese television show about American barbecue? They proposed sending a TV crew to my home in Martha's Vineyard to film a traditional American barbecue for the Fourth of July.

Of course, I said yes. If I could serve as an ambassador for American barbecue, well, for a man bent on global domination in grilling, it was an opportunity I couldn't refuse. The film crew arrived with a surprise guest: a musically inclined chef named Kumahachi Morino. Famed for singing his recipes on Japanese television, Morino brought a bag of mystery ingredients from Japan.

"Let's see what the American grill master can do with preserved cod roe, red bean paste, gobo [burdock root], and dried sea cucumber ovaries," he said with friendly defiance as we shook hands.

Over the course of my career, I've grilled just about everything, including foods you'd never expect to grill. (The short list includes seaweed and ice cream.) Mystery ingredients? Bring them on.

Morino inspected our house, marveling at the height of our pillow-top bed (a far cry from a Japanese on-the-floor futon) and our Sub-Zero

March 11, 1953—my arrival on Planet Barbecue.

refrigerator, which he quipped was "half the size of a Tokyo apartment." After much bowing and *kinichiwas,* he changed into his whites, his apron more crisply starched than the shirt I wore on my wedding night. I fired up the grill.

I sliced the cod roe into some freshly shucked oysters, which I smoke-roasted over charcoal. Not bad. I stuffed the red bean paste into cored apples (Fujis, no less), adding brown sugar, cream cheese, and butter, and smoked them over applewood. I direct-grilled the sea cucumber ovaries, which came out like caviar-flavored potato chips. These I could get to like. The grilled burdock root was a bust (too fibrous), but Chef Morino seemed to enjoy the apples. As he gesticulated fiercely at the camera, I could almost sense a smile.

I must have done something right, because one of the producers—Shiori Suzuki—had a surprise for me.

"How would you like to come to Tokyo to battle the Iron Chef on Japanese television?" she asked. "We'll pay all the travel expenses for you and your wife."

How could I say no to that?

I ALWAYS WELCOME A CHANCE to return to Japan. I was born there, in the historic city of Nagoya, on March 11, 1953. My father was stationed in Nagoya during the Korean War, running the pharmacy at a United States Air Force hospital. My mother came for an extended visit, and I arrived nine months later.

My father spoke glowingly of his years in Nagoya. As a lieutenant, he earned seventy-five dollars a month, but that was enough to pay for a housekeeper, nanny, driver, and membership at a local country club. He dined in the homes of Japanese co-workers, awed by the food and their hospitality. Until, that is, he learned that the vegetables he ate with such relish had been fertilized by the "honey bucket man" (charged with emptying outhouses and selling their contents to local gardeners). Until his friends explained that the "pancakes" he so savored one evening were actually pan-fried pig brains.

I spent nine months in Japan; unfortunately, they were the first nine months of my life, so I don't remember my sojourn. Apparently, this Caucasian baby in his white jumpsuit, with his stylish blond mother and handsome uniformed young father, impressed the locals mightily.

I didn't return to the land of my birth until 1996, when I went there to research Japanese barbecue for my first book on grilling, *The Barbecue! Bible.* I was impressed by the delicacy and refinement of Japanese grilling—the way small is beautiful (as opposed to the plate-burying largesse of American barbecue)—and how grill masters achieved explosive flavors with just a

An American baby in Nagoya, Japan.

few primal seasonings, such as sesame oil, soy sauce, and mirin. One Tokyo master chef, Masaki Saito, put it to me this way: "Japanese grilling is minus food, not plus food. It's about what you leave out, not what you put in."

No ten-ingredient barbecue rubs for Mr. Saito.

A few years later, I traveled to Tokyo again for the publication of a Japanese Raichlen grill book. My books have been translated into many languages, but none posed quite the challenge of the Japanese edition. The typical Japanese grill, the hibachi, isn't much wider than an American shoebox. That eliminated porterhouse steaks and beef tomahawks. And Japanese grills don't generally come with lids, which cut out indirect grilling and smoking. (No pork shoulders or beer can chicken.) We culled through the recipes in three of my books to come up with small-format dishes, like kebabs and satays, that one could direct grill over charcoal. The publisher was gracious enough to include my American versions of yakitori and teriyaki.

The ensuing book tour included interviews with Japanese *GQ* and *Playboy* and an appearance on Japan's top-rated morning TV show. I chose to demonstrate that American campfire classic: s'mores. The hosts looked horrified as they attempted to eat the sticky, gooey mess of charred marshmallow and melted chocolate with chopsticks. Everywhere I was asked how my sojourn in Nagoya had influenced my grilling. I didn't have the heart to explain that, during that time, I hadn't yet graduated to solid food.

NOW HERE I WAS, IN 2003, in the Tokyo studio of a popular variety show called *Baribari World Values*. In a few days, I would face off with the toughest, winningest chef in Japanese TV history—Rokusaburo Michiba—in a contest extravagantly titled "The Battle of the Barbecue Gods."

Mere mention of the name Michiba was enough to strike fear into the hearts of most chefs, much less food writers. He was the first Iron Chef in Japan, and he's still known as "The God of Japanese Cuisine." Born into a family of tea-ceremony masters, he presides over some of the hardest-to-get-into restaurants in Tokyo. His predilection for warrior robes, wooden platform sandals, and hand-forged knives made him the culinary equivalent of a samurai. Oh, and his official biography includes this sentence: "He is known for being particular about the types of porcelain used to plate his food for service."

I arrived with my family in Tokyo on a steamy August afternoon and promptly convened a war council. We resolved to follow the advice of another great Asian warrior, Sun Tzu: "Know your enemy." For the next three days, we visited as many Japanese grill restaurants as we could.

When it comes to barbecue, the Japanese are at least as grill crazy as we Americans are. Japanese grilling turns up everywhere: at street festivals and by riversides, in rough-and-tumble yakitori shops near train stations, at elaborate kaiseki (tea ceremony–inspired) meals, and at exclusive grill restaurants where dinner for four costs more than I paid for my first car.

On the third day, we reviewed our observations about Japanese barbecue:

- Small is beautiful.
- Simple is beautiful.
- Delicate is beautiful.
- Traditional is beautiful.
- And theatrics don't hurt, either.

But in the end, it was my wife who had the best advice: "Don't try to compete with the Japanese on their own terms."

According to the Battle of the Barbecue Gods rules, each contestant would prepare a three-course meal. After prep time in the afternoon, there would be thirty minutes of grilling time in the studio. The judging would be done by the two *Baribari* hosts, plus eight professional actors onstage and an audience of forty (mostly teenage girls). Ballots took the form of pink ping-pong balls to be piled in tall Lucite tubes. The contestants with the most, er, balls would win.

I decided to start with a dish that no tradition-minded Japanese grill master would ever conceive of: barbecued soup, a sort of gazpacho made with smoked tomatoes, peppers, and onions. The main course would be quintessentially American: grilled chicken and barbecued ribs, both seasoned with a pepper, brown sugar, and paprika-based rub and slathered with sweet, smoky Kansas City–style barbecue sauce. For theatrics, I would grill the chicken breasts as they do in Tuscany—under bricks. (This keeps the meat moist and helps crisp the skin.) The chicken and ribs would be served with a shocking lack of Japanese delicacy—in whole plate-burying slabs—with homemade coleslaw on the side.

I also planned to drop in an extra dish, a dessert inspired by my hometown, Miami: wedges of pineapple brushed with coconut milk, dipped in cinnamon sugar, then caramelized on the grill. Which brought me to my first setback: the grill. I had requested a charcoal-burning American-style kettle. What I got was barely a grill at all. Picture a gas-fired ring burner topped by a wire cake rack. The contraption looked more like an oversize Bunsen burner than a grill.

At 9 PM, a production assistant came to collect us. Time slowed down. I had heard the theme music to the *Iron Chef* show dozens of times, and now I was marching into the studio to its cadence.

Baribari World Values wasn't quite the traditional *Iron Chef* TV show. It turned out to be a cross between an evening magazine and a quiz show, with a dash of Oprah and Letterman. During the show, the actors were asked questions about American barbecue, and their ludicrous responses added to the general hilarity of the show. The humor did little to relieve the pressure I was feeling, as I don't speak Japanese.

Dead ahead stood Chef Michiba, unsmiling, in his platform sandals and indigo robe. We locked eyes and bowed, and the bell for the battle rang. I began by rigging up a smoker in a wok to smoke the tomatoes for the gazpacho. I massaged barbecue rub into the chicken breasts and arranged them on the grill, placing a foil-wrapped brick on top. As I worked, I explained what I was doing. After all, when you cook on American television, you talk.

Mistake number one: "Why is the American chattering so much?" the host asked the audience, seated on risers to our left.

Come time to prepare the ribs, I summoned the cohost, a timid young woman, motioning for her to turn her back to the audience. I pointed to her spine to explain where baby back ribs come from (literally "high on the hog")—a gesture that never fails to break the ice with television hosts in the United States. Mistake number two: The young woman froze like a deer in the proverbial headlights, and the host snarled at me again.

Mr. Michiba, meanwhile, had not uttered a word. His cleaver spoke for him, magisterially whacking live spiny lobsters in half. He placed a sheet of metal on a bowl of hot charcoal (so much for direct grilling), heaped it with seaweed, piled on lobsters and fresh abalone, and threw in some pricey matsutake mushrooms for good measure. He placed seaweed on top, then another metal plate, then a layer of glowing charcoal and a bunch of fresh fern fronds. In a matter of minutes, the whole thing hissed and fumed like Mount Etna.

So much for the theatrics of grilling under a brick.

But then something remarkable happened. The host came over to my table. I offered him a tiny taste of barbecued chicken, which he ate hot off the grill with his fingers. He asked for another piece, then a rib, then a forkful of coleslaw.

"Michiba is using the most expensive ingredients he can find," the host mused. "The American is cooking with inexpensive, commonplace ingredients like chicken, pork, and cabbage." Suddenly, everyone seemed interested in tasting my ribs. I smiled for the first time in twenty-four hours.

It's not polite to gloat, so I will not tell you the final score, but I will tell you that my ping-pong balls towered over Michiba's, and that the humble American barbecue bested the Iron Chef's lobster and matsutakes—gallery-quality serving platter notwithstanding.

The host wrapped up a half rack of ribs in foil to take home. Mr. Michiba bowed graciously and uttered the first English word I heard him say all evening: "Rematch."

But I knew a lucky night when I had it. I told him I was retired and hung up my tongs.

THE RIBS THAT BEAT THE IRON CHEF

Yes, it's true. I battled Japanese Iron Chef Rokusaburo Michiba on Japanese television. And won! I did so, in part, with a dish completely alien to Japanese grilling: American barbecued ribs. Like all great American barbecue, these ribs owe their appeal to multiple layers of flavor: the peppery sting of the rub, the fruity tang of the cider spray, the apple-y sweetness of the barbecue sauce, and of course the haunting smoke flavor of slow-smoldering applewood. Not surprisingly, the baby back ribs in Japan are tiny by American standards: A rack weighs barely a pound. Their equivalent in the US would be the Danish baby backs you sometimes see at the supermarket. But battle-winning ribs can also be made with conventional American baby backs, which weigh 2 to 2 1/2 pounds. That's what I call for here.

Makes 2 to 4 racks, enough to serve 2 really hungry people or 4 as part of a large meal

1 tablespoon dark brown sugar

1 tablespoon shichimi togarashi (Japanese pepper rub—see Note)

1 tablespoon coarse salt (kosher or sea)

1 tablespoon freshly ground black pepper

1 tablespoon sweet paprika

1 teaspoon dry mustard

½ teaspoon celery seed

2 (2- to 2 ½-pound) racks American baby back ribs or 4 (1-pound) racks Danish baby back ribs

½ cup apple cider

1 ½ cups Smoky Apple Barbecue Sauce (recipe follows) or your favorite barbecue sauce

You'll also need:

1 ½ cups applewood chips, soaked in water for 30 minutes, then drained

1. To make the rub, combine the brown sugar, shichimi togarashi, salt, pepper, paprika, mustard, and celery seed in a small bowl and mix with your fingers, breaking up any lumps. Season the ribs with the rub on all sides, reserving 1 tablespoon rub for serving.
2. Meanwhile, set up your grill (ideally a charcoal grill) for indirect grilling and heat to medium (325°F). Place a large drip pan in the center of the grill under the grate. Brush or scrape the grill grate clean and oil it well. Place the apple cider in a spray bottle and set it near the grill.
3. Place the ribs, meat side up, in the center of the grate over the drip pan and away from the heat. If cooking on a charcoal grill, add half of the wood chips to each mound of coals. If using a gas grill, place all the chips in the grill's smoker box.
4. Lower the grill lid and cook the ribs for 45 minutes. Spray on both sides with apple cider. Lower the lid again and continue cooking until the ribs are darkly browned and cooked through, and the meat has shrunk back from the ends of the bones by ¼ to ½ inch. The total cooking time will be 1½ to 2 hours. The ribs should be tender enough to pull apart with your fingers. If using charcoal, replenish the coals as needed.
5. Just before serving, brush each rack of ribs on both sides with 3 to 4 tablespoons of the barbecue sauce. Move the ribs directly over the fire and grill until the barbecue sauce is browned and sizzling, 2 minutes per side.
6. Transfer the ribs to a large platter and sprinkle with the reserved 1 tablespoon rub. Cut into half racks or individual bones for serving, with the remaining barbecue sauce on the side.

Variation: How to cook these ribs in a smoker. Set up and light the smoker according to the manufacturer's instructions and heat to 250°F. Place the ribs in the smoker meat side up and smoke until cooked through, 3½ to 4 hours. Spray the ribs with apple cider after 1 hour and after 2 hours. Brush the ribs with the barbecue sauce the last 30 minutes of cooking. Replenish the charcoal and wood as needed.

Note: Shichimi togarashi, Japanese seven spice, is a peppery blend of ginger, red pepper flakes, sesame seeds, orange peel, and other spices. If it's unavailable, substitute 1 teaspoon each hot red pepper flakes and sesame seeds.

SMOKY APPLE BARBECUE SAUCE

Completing our apple theme is this smoky apple barbecue sauce. Apple butter makes it fruity; Tabasco cranks up the heat.

Makes 2 cups

¾ cup ketchup
¾ cup chili sauce
½ cup water
6 tablespoons apple butter
3 tablespoons cider vinegar
2 tablespoons dark brown sugar
1 tablespoon molasses
1 tablespoon Worcestershire sauce
1 teaspoon Tabasco or other favorite hot sauce
1 teaspoon liquid smoke
½ teaspoon freshly ground black pepper

1. Combine all the ingredients in a large, heavy saucepan and whisk to mix. Bring the sauce to a simmer over medium-high heat. Reduce the heat to medium-low and gently simmer the sauce until thick, richly flavored, and reduced to about 2 cups, 8 to 12 minutes, whisking occasionally.
2. Transfer the sauce to a clean jar and let cool to room temperature, then refrigerate until serving. The sauce can be made several days ahead.

Chapter Two

GROWING UP ON CODDIES AND CRAB

1954–1970

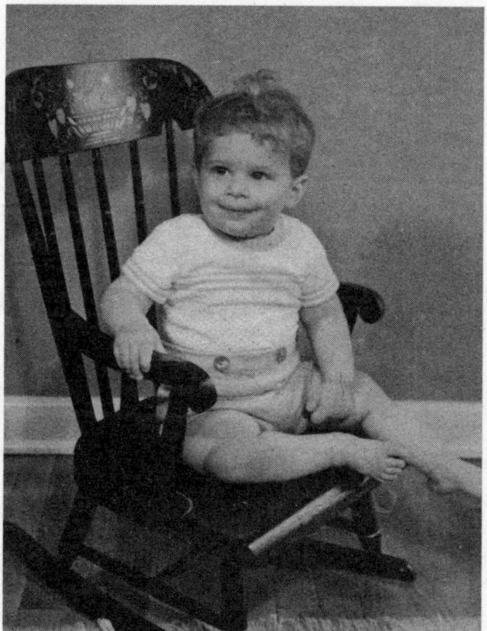

Growing up in Baltimore.

I grew up in a second-tier city with first-rate food.

The city was Baltimore—Charm City to you, Hon—birthplace of "The Star-Spangled Banner," the Orioles, and the Colts. (I never forgave the Colts for moving to Indiana.) But when I lived there, Charm City wasn't particularly charming. There was no Harbor Place, no Camden Yards, and no Maryland Museum of Science.

There was, however, a working harbor that on good days smelled like mace and curry powder, thanks to the proximity of the McCormick Spice Company. (It was a sad day when the company moved its headquarters to Hunt Valley in the 1970s.) On bad days, the harbor smelled like spoiled fish. Baltimore didn't have the swanky restaurants of New York or the celebrity chefs of Los Angeles. It didn't have the farm-to-table ethos of Berkeley, California. But we had something better: crab. Not just any crab, but *Callinectes sapidus*, the "beautiful, tasty swimmer"—that feisty crustacean of the Chesapeake we Marylanders know and love as the blue crab.

Living in Miami half the year, I eat my fair share of stone crab and enjoy it. I've feasted on king crab in Alaska during a book tour, sampled hairy crab in Singapore (not worth the fifty-dollars-per-crab price tag), and devoured Venice's bite-size *moeche* (softshell crabs—worth whatever the price, and then some). But nothing compares to the sweet, briny, buttery flavor of blue crab—the taste that defines Baltimore.

Blue crab was responsible for several of the hometown delicacies I enjoyed growing up, not to mention a Baltimore rite of passage. First, the crab cake—misunderstood and dare I say mangled by almost anyone who doesn't come from Charm City. A proper crab cake, I learned growing up, does not contain onion or garlic. It does not contain bell peppers or corn. And it certainly doesn't contain jalapeños. The only permissible flavorings are dry mustard and Old Bay Seasoning. You bind these ingredients together with cracker crumbs (or sometimes milk-soaked bread), beaten egg, and a

Mayland steamed crabs: the iconic food of my childhood.

generous measure of mayonnaise (we ate a lot of Hellmann's in Baltimore). Health-conscious folks broil crab cakes; the not-so-health-conscious deep-fry them. A few fire-obsessed people even grill them. That would be me.

A lot has changed on the Baltimore food scene, but you can still experience a classic crab cake at Faidley's Seafood at the historic Lexington Market. Four generations of Raichlens have shopped there, and I always make a pilgrimage to Faidley's when I'm in Baltimore. The crab cakes are always as I remember them: tall as they are wide, crammed with sweet, snowy backfin lump crabmeat, and served the old-fashioned way, on saltine crackers.

The ultimate dish for any self-respecting Baltimorean is steamed crabs. You start with wriggling live blue crabs piled into a large pot, then layered with coarse salt, Old Bay Seasoning, and palate-blasting doses of black pepper. Boiling beer and vinegar provide the steam. When the crabs turn fire-engine red, you dump them without ceremony onto a table covered with newspaper (preferably *The Baltimore Sun*) and devour them with your bare hands.

It was my grandfather, Dear, who taught me how to eat steamed crabs. (My grandmother called him "Dear" as a term of affection; I thought that was his name.) "To start, twist off the claws," explained Dear. "Smash them with a mallet, then pry out the meat with the point of a paring knife." (At a proper Baltimore crab house, a knife and mallet are the only utensils provided.) Next, lift the "apron" (the tab on the crab's underbelly—it's a little like opening a can of beer) to remove the carapace. "Using a knife," Dear continued, "scoop out the mustard [buttery yellow fat] in the points of the shell. Discard the inedible 'feathers' [gills] and 'spaghetti' [intestines], then crack the body in half to extract the sweet meat."

Each morsel of crab would get seasoned by the salty, fiery spice paste on our hands. Shell shards nicked our fingers, adding a masochistic sting. When I was young, I could polish off a couple dozen crabs at a sitting, with Dear watching over my shoulder to make sure I didn't waste a single strand of meat. We partook of this feast at landmark restaurants, like the now sadly closed Obrycki's Crab House, in the then rough-and-tumble (and now gentrified) neighborhood of Fells Point. Obrycki's reigned as Baltimore's premier crab house from 1944 to 2011.

I'm often asked what I would choose for my last meal. People seem disappointed when I don't say barbecue. No, for my last meal, give me Maryland steamed crabs. They taste like home and my childhood—and they take forever to eat.

Another Baltimore delicacy was coddies, and these fried cakes of mashed potato and salt cod marked a second Raichlen rite of passage. Codfish cakes turn up around the planet, of course, and I've sampled my fair share—from *bolinhos de bacalhau* in Lisbon to *accras* in St. Barts. But only in Baltimore did we eat them cold, slathered with ballpark mustard on saltine crackers, and usually standing up.

The rite of passage involved Milford Mill, a swim club at an old granite quarry, long filled with water from an underground spring, a mile from where we lived. When I turned thirteen, my parents deemed me old enough to walk to the quarry by myself. I would watch with admiration as daredevil divers plunged off the high cliffs surrounding the quarry. They got the girls. I dove in from the safety of a considerably lower diving board. I did not get the girls. But I did get coddies at the snack bar, with its greasy concrete floor, sixties pop music blaring from the jukebox, and bikinied teenage girls I was too timid to ask to dance.

Baltimore had a ugly side in those days. The swim club remained segregated through much of my childhood. When Blacks were finally admitted, the Ku Klux Klan protested at the entrance. I remember asking my father why the Baltimore zoo had separate bathrooms and water fountains for "Whites" and "Coloreds." His answer was awkward for both of us. It was a blemish on a great food city that leaned more toward the South than the North.

A third childhood "C" food was corned beef—sliced so paper-thin that the pink meat shone with pearly iridescence. Corned beef turned up at all our local delis, but no one served it better than Attman's Delicatessen on Lombard Street. In the early 1900s, Lombard Street was the heart of immigrant Jewish Baltimore, our Lower East Side. My grandfather remembered shopping there with his family as a kid. Opened in 1930 by Harry and Ida Attman from Ukraine, Attman's is the last surviving vestige of immigrant Jewish Lombard Street. I go there whenever I visit Baltimore. They still slice the corned beef paper-thin and pile it improbably high on soft rye bread with a smear of mustard.

Which brings us to the fourth Charm City "C" food: chocolate tops, a.k.a. Berger cookies, created by a German baker in the 1830s. Mr. Berger's innovation was to top a sugar cookie with a thick layer of fudge-like chocolate icing. The chocolate top paled in comparison, however, to the sugar cookies and fudge made by my grandmother, Ethel Lee Fribush Raichlen. Grammie Ethel piped the batter in ridged ribbons from an ancient cookie press and baked them on an equally ancient cookie sheet. They were sweet, they were buttery, they were vanilla-scented and toasty (especially at my favorite part, the dark edges). She kept them in a red Snyder's of Hanover pretzel tin, which miraculously never went empty.

As for fudge, Grammie Ethel made hers with unsweetened Baker's chocolate, which kept it free of the sickly sweetness that mars most commercial fudge. She would beat the mixture by hand until it fell from a raised spoon the right way (no candy thermometers for Grammie Ethel) and set it to harden in a time-blackened pie pan. She always made sure to have fudge on hand when I returned to Baltimore from college, and long after.

MY GRANDFATHER, DEAR

My grandfather was a smallish man with an oversize personality. His role as family patriarch made him a giant. His parents gave him the name Samuel Israel Raichlen (the initials of which became the name of his company, SIR Sales), but everyone knew him by the name I gave him: "Dear."

Born in Baltimore in 1905 to Latvian parents, Dear personified the Jewish immigrant experience at the turn of the last century. His father, Isidor, eked out a living as a tailor before starting a modest uniform cap company. His parents were socialists; Dear would boast how they took him to Eugene V. Debs rallies when he was a kid. His family moved a lot (to stay one step ahead of creditors, Dear would quip); he remembered moving men packing the family's belongings in barrels to be hauled in a horse-drawn wagon to the next rented apartment. He lived long enough to board a 747 airliner to Israel for his fiftieth wedding anniversary with my grandmother, and to watch Neil Armstrong walk on the moon.

When Dear's father died at the age of forty-three, his mother, Sarah, took over the cap business. Thanks to the demands of military uniforms during World War II, she built it into one of the largest uniform cap companies on the East Coast.

Dear and his generation experienced the sort of anti-Semitism I thought was dead—until recently. His family would show up at hotels and resorts where they had booked rooms months earlier, but with one look at their Jewish features, the desk clerk would be "unable" to find their reservation. Dear wrote letters to President Franklin Roosevelt during World War II, urging him to bomb Auschwitz and the other concentration camps. We now know how that worked out.

Dear owned a drugstore on Keswick Road in the working-class Baltimore neighborhood of Hampden. He practiced pharmacy in an age when druggists still compounded medicines, rather than simply transferring pills from large bottles to small ones. He'd mix powders from hand-painted pharmaceutical jars and pack them into gelatin capsules. He'd pound ointments to a paste in a marble mortar and pestle, to be stuffed into silvery foil squeeze tubes with handwritten labels.

Dear ran the pharmacy for more than three decades. But the real love of his life and purpose for living was his family. In 1925, he married my grandmother. She came from a wealthy family of furriers, and her parents looked down on this brash upstart pharmacist. Until the Depression, that is, when his in-laws lost everything. Dear shamelessly reminded them of their reduced circumstances for the rest of their years. He was always a hero in my eyes, but he never forgot a slight.

Like most women of her generation, my grandmother, Grammie Ethel, played a subservient role to her husband. Her favorite words (or at least her most repeated words) were "Yes, Dear." She would listen to a story Dear had repeated a hundred times, nodding her head as though she was hearing it for the first time. She was a gentle soul who always assumed the best in people. Her personality cleaved less to the eye-for-an-eye sternness of the Old Testament than the turn-the-other-cheek forgiveness of the New.

My grandparents, Ethel and Samuel "Dear" Raichlen.

The kitchen was Grammie's domain, but occasionally she'd let Dear take a turn at the stove. On Sunday mornings, he'd prepare scrambled eggs with smoked salmon and sautéed onions. He'd insist on lox "wings" (the strong-flavored fin section of the salmon)—the cheapest cut of the fish for which he acquired a taste when money was tight. He swore to the end that lox wings tasted the best.

Dear used to say of me: "You're Sonny's son, but you're my boy."

Amen!

IF BALTIMORE FED MY BELLY, Friday-night dinners with Grammie Ethel and Dear fed my soul. Grammie would light the Shabbos candles in brass candlesticks handed down from her grandmother. Beyond that, we weren't particularly religious. We lived our Judaism through our food. (But as crab eaters, we didn't keep kosher.)

Invariably, Dear and my father talked business while my mother helped Grammie Ethel in the kitchen. On the menu? Chopped liver, ethereal in texture, which Grammie put through an old hand-cranked grinder. Chicken soup the color of pale gold, with marrow bones and crunchy *mandelech* (soup nuts). I would watch with delight as my Aunt Linda squirted a ketchup smiley face into her chicken soup. When my great-grandmother was still alive, we feasted on freshly baked pirogi, oniony meat turnovers that shattered into a million tasty shards when you took a bite. Grandma Fribush also made a killer chocolate roll, a yeasty, flaky, cocoa- and sugar-stuffed pastry today better known as a babka.

So, what's any of this have to do with barbecue? Nothing. And everything. Enter a final Baltimore delicacy I knew nothing about when I was growing up. Pit beef originated at rough-and-tumble grill parlors nestled among the truck stops, strip joints, and cheap motels along an industrial thoroughfare called Pulaski Highway. And that explains why I never heard of it. The Baltimore I grew up in was an extremely parochial city, where Jews lived with other Jews in certain neighborhoods, Gentiles in others, Blacks in yet others, and so on. There was relatively little interaction between them. When I was a kid, my family would never think of going to Pulaski Highway.

Which meant that I missed out on eating one of America's best beef sandwiches for three decades. I have tried to make up for that lost time. Some years ago, I wrote a story about Baltimore pit beef for *The New York Times*. I've since prepared it at Barbecue University and on several of my TV shows.

Pit beef starts as top round. Unlike most regional American barbecue, it's grilled, not smoked, so it lacks the heavy smoke flavor found in Kansas

City. It's also served rare—like the rarest of roast beef—which would be unthinkable for Texas brisket. The secret to making it tender is to shave it paper-thin on a meat slicer. The bread is different too—no white bread, as you'd get in Texas, nor the hamburger bun in the Carolinas, but a crusty kaiser roll or seeded rye. Both breads reflect the German heritage of many Baltimoreans in this part of town. The traditional condiment for Baltimore pit beef is horseradish sauce—as much as you can take without wincing. A slice or two of raw onion raises the sandwich to the level of art.

Looking back, I grew up at an extraordinary moment in American gastronomy. Both of my great-grandmothers—Grandma Fribush and Bubbe Marks—were born in Eastern Europe. I was lucky enough to have them in my life well into my twenties. When they were young, they'd ride the streetcar to Lexington Market to buy poultry with the feathers still on and pluck the birds at home, just as they had in the Old Country. Everything was made from scratch.

Equally made from scratch and equally multigenerational were our family holiday dinners. They were noisy, crowded, and joyous. Twenty, thirty, sometimes forty people squeezed at tables doglegged from dining room to living room to den. Yes, you got your cheeks pinched and smeared with lipstick. But in today's fragmented society, where extended family members seldom live in the same city, I look back on those huge family dinners as indescribably precious. I'm sad that their time has passed.

THE CRAB CAKES I GREW UP ON

Crab figured prominently in my childhood food world, as it did for almost anyone who grew up in Baltimore. There was crab imperial—a sort of crab gratin flavored with sherry, paprika, and mayonnaise. There were softshell crabs, which we Marylanders ate pan-fried long before their current ubiquity in sushi rolls. But the dish that most defines Baltimore is the crab cake. I've already told you what *not* to put in a crab cake (see page 16). The real McCoy contains chiefly crab—preferably meaty chunks of backfin lump—with a whisper of Old Bay Seasoning and dry mustard and just enough mayonnaise and cracker crumbs to hold it all together.

Makes 4, enough to serve 4 as a starter or 2 as a main course

1 pound jumbo lump crabmeat
1 large egg
2 teaspoons Old Bay Seasoning
1 teaspoon dry mustard
⅓ cup mayonnaise (preferably Hellmann's)
¼ cup saltine cracker crumbs
2 tablespoons unsalted butter
1 tablespoon extra-virgin olive oil or more butter
Saltine crackers and lemon wedges, for serving

1. Pick through the crab, removing and discarding any bits of shell.
2. Crack the egg into a mixing bowl and whisk in the Old Bay and dry mustard until smooth. Whisk in the mayonnaise. Lay the crab on top and sprinkle with the cracker crumbs. Using a rubber spatula or your hands, gently fold the crab and cracker crumbs into the egg mixture. Work with a light touch and fold just long enough to mix.

3. Wet your hands and divide the crab mixture in four portions. Form each one into a patty 1 to 1½ inches thick. (Good crab cakes are supposed to be thick.) Place on a plate lined with plastic wrap and chill for at least 30 minutes.
4. Just before serving time, melt the butter with the oil in a large skillet over medium heat. (The oil helps raise the burning temperature of the butter.) When the oil is the right temperature, bubbles will dance around a dipped piece of crab. Gently lower the crab cakes into the fat and pan-fry until golden brown on both sides and cooked through, 3 to 5 minutes per side. Lower the heat as needed to keep the crab cakes from burning.
5. Serve the crab cakes with saltines and lemon wedges. Many people like to eat crab cakes with tartar sauce—homemade, please!

Chapter Three

THE WORST DAY OF MY LIFE

1970

Mother and son in 1960.

Spring break of my junior year in high school started the way any holiday would for a seventeen-year-old longhair living in the Baltimore suburbs in 1970. I gathered with some buddies at the home of my friend Bruce and fired up a joint. We ordered pizzas (pepperoni and olives for me) and pilfered some of Bruce's dad's beer. As we lit another reefer, we debated whether Ginger Baker, drummer of the English rock band Cream, would survive long enough to complete his next album or overdose on speed. We wondered whether Jethro Tull (the rock band, not the eighteenth-century British agronomist) would really play a concert in Baltimore. We bought tickets, but Jethro never showed.

I don't remember the rest of our conversation, but it probably had something to do with how lucky we were to be the Fabulous Five (nod to the Beatles deliberate)—five friends inextricably bound by our love of music and marijuana. We spent the night at Bruce's, sleeping on the floor, crashing around midnight.

I walked the half mile home the next morning, arriving at 4117 Ronis Road, a 1960s split-level house with white asbestos shingles and green trim, on a block of nearly identical houses in the Baltimore suburb of Pikesville. The lawn was freshly mowed—one of the ways I earned my allowance. I had carved a peace symbol into the grass with our lawn mower. If my father noticed, he didn't say anything. Maybe he was used to the eccentricities of his hippie musician son.

I entered the house. My Fender bass guitar and Vox amplifier stood by the door; I had band practice later that day.

"Mom?" I called. No answer. I ascended the stairs to the Formica table in the kitchen.

"Mom?" Still no answer. She must be home—her blue Mustang convertible was still in the driveway. Of course, it was only 10 AM, and my mom rarely awoke before noon.

"Mom," I called again, rounding the dry sink in the living room, bounding up the stairs to the bedroom level. The house was oddly quiet, the door to my parents' bedroom ajar.

My mother was a ballet dancer. I didn't get my passion for food from her; she was a lousy cook. She taught me something far more important: an unwavering dedication to one's craft. While other moms were baking cookies and brownies for classroom parties, her life was an endless sequence of classes, rehearsals, and performances pursued with a dedication that bordered on manic. This truth, as much as any subsequent culinary training, shaped my career as a food writer.

Frances Raichlen: prima ballerina.

Even if my mother had liked cooking, her devotion to ballet would have kept her out of the kitchen. Like most dancers, she had tortured attitudes about food. Despite her petite size (four feet, eleven inches tall and ninety pounds), she was always on some sort of diet. She scooped bagels long before the arrival of Dr. Atkins. She once subsisted on leathery, paprika-dusted, oven-broiled veal breast for a solid month.

"Delight for some, starvation for others," she wrote in one of her notebooks. "Blessed are those who can eat without worry."

She was born Frances Helene Miller in Baltimore on August 19, 1933.

Her mother—my Grammie Sarah—was an auburn-haired beauty whose parents owned a liquor store and a movie theater. The latter, Grammie Sarah would quip, made her popular with her classmates.

My mother's father, Carson Miller, was a handsome ne'er-do-well with a bad-boy swagger. A photo on my desk shows the family in 1938, my aunts and uncles seated on the steps of their house on Brooks Lane. (It's strange to see them looking younger than my own step-kids do today.) My mother—five or six years old at the time—sits on my Uncle Irv's lap, her ringlet curls golden in the sunlight. Everyone faces the camera and smiles. Everyone except Carson, his jaw set defiantly, looking off in the distance to his next hustle.

That next hustle did him in. Around this time, he took a job selling life insurance. Instead of depositing the premiums in the company's bank account, he spent them at Pimlico racetrack. Eventually, his employers discovered the shortfall. As the police closed in, Carson locked himself in the garage and ran a hose from the exhaust pipe through his car window. Grammie Sarah found him dead at the wheel the next morning, and found herself, at the age of thirty-three, a widow.

Happily, my mother was away at summer camp at the time. Unhappily, when my grandmother remarried a year later to my Grandpa Jack Goldman, she sat young Frances down with a warning: "Don't do anything to jeopardize this marriage," she said. "If it comes to a choice between you or Jack, you'll go to live with your grandmother."

How much of my mother's subsequent troubles came from her father's suicide or her mother's ultimatum? How much came from the genes that made Carson sneer instead of smile in the family photo?

I've made Grammie Sarah sound coldhearted. She wasn't. Back then, few men would have married a woman with a child. She counted herself lucky and was determined to keep her new husband happy. She was a devoted grandmother who played an oversize role in my life growing up.

She often picked me up after school, sat by my bedside when I was sick, and prepared hot homecooked meals for us once a week. When I turned eighteen, Grammie Sarah asked me what I wanted for my birthday. "Eggs Benedict for breakfast," I told her. (Even back then, I was food obsessed.) Damned if I didn't find her hunched over a cookbook, whisking egg yolks in a double boiler, to make the hollandaise sauce.

Normally in the 1960s, the task of cooking would have fallen to my mother. But Fran, as I sometimes called her, was busy dancing her heart out. She'd miss PTA meetings and parent-teacher conferences, and on occasion forgot to pick me up after school. As an only child, I'd usually come home to an empty house.

Dinners at home often came courtesy of the Swanson company in a newly developed meal format called the TV dinner. Each compartment in the aluminum foil tray held a different part of the meal: Salisbury steak topped with gluey mushroom gravy, for example, with limp green beans and mealy mashed potatoes on the side. You'd peel the top foil off the last compartment while heating the tray so the contents would brown. My favorite part of a TV dinner was a dessert like apple brown betty or blueberry cobbler.

Over the years, my mother's behavior became more erratic—especially after she started taking a pep pill/weight loss aid called Dexedrine. She'd badger doctors for pills, then take the same prescription to a half dozen different drugstores to procure more, bringing me along to lend her the air of a respectable suburban housewife.

In 1966, my mother moved to New York for a year to train with a Russian ballet master named Madame Swaboda. "I am going for a crack at the title!" she scrawled in a note to us. "We all three will win!" She regaled us with stories of her successes in our weekly phone calls but never asked us to watch her perform.

Six months into her year in New York, my father received a phone call from Bloomingdale's. A Mrs. Raichlen had embarked on a $3,000 shopping spree and didn't have the means to pay for it. She rambled incoherently to the desk clerk at her hotel. My father drove to Manhattan to get her, then brought her to Phipps Psychiatric Hospital in Baltimore. She spent several weeks being treated for a nervous breakdown—her second.

I remember visiting her at Phipps and trying to strike up a friendship with another patient, a teenage drummer. I thought it was normal for a kid to have a mother in a mental hospital, just like I thought it was normal to have a mother who took drugs and slept all day and couldn't seem to remember to pick up her son after school.

Apparently, my mother was just a little too short and a little too old to have a successful career in dance in New York. Giving up ballet finally broke her.

"To have been a part of the world of dance—to have been heralded as a bright star, to have known intimately all the beauty and light, and sound and sight and movement," she wrote in one of her notebooks, "it is a world from which you can't exit. My soul cries out in anguish. What price? What price?"

Deprived of dancing, during the last year of her life my mother took up drawing. She pursued it with the same ferocious passion she brought to ballet. Unfortunately, she had no real talent. I still have her sketchbooks—some of the few physical keepsakes of her that remain. Chronicling her desperation, she wrote a prose poem:

Loneliness is like a lone sparrow in the cold bleak winter.
It is like a single leaf clinging to a tree in a gale.

It is like a little child accidentally separated from his mother in a crowd, and to whom ten minutes seems an eternity. It is like being hungry in the presence of food.

WHICH BRINGS US BACK to that sunny April morning in 1970, when I returned home after that night of music, pot, pizza, and hanging with my pals.

The door to my parents' bedroom was ajar. I went in.

And there was my mother—lying on the bed, covers awry, her legs bent at odd angles. Her eyes were open, the corneas clouded over. A slick of saliva dribbled from her open mouth down her cheek. Her breathing was shallow and labored.

"Mom," I said. No reaction. I said it louder and touched her arm. No reaction. I shook her and shook her again. No reaction. I got a cup of cold water from the bathroom and poured some on her face. No reaction.

At the time, my father worked at the headquarters of the Read's Drug Store chain (motto: "Run right to Read's").

I called to tell him: "Mom is asleep. I can't wake her."

"Call an ambulance and wait for me at home," he said.

I walked out of the bedroom, pretending this wasn't happening. I walked back in and shook her. No, I couldn't wake her. I walked in and out of the bedroom several times.

Minutes later, siren blaring, the ambulance arrived. The attendants (they hadn't yet come to be called EMTs) knocked on the door and came upstairs carrying a stretcher. One took my mother's arm; she still had a pulse. The other motioned to her nightgown and asked me to pull it down. It must have ridden up during the night, leaving her privates exposed. I lowered the nightgown as he asked, feeling oddly guilty. They lifted her onto the stretcher and brought her down the stairs.

My father's office was twenty-five minutes away. His car screeched up to our house ten minutes after I called him. He must have run every red light on the way. As we got into the ambulance, neighbors gathered in their driveways to watch. We sped to Mount Sinai Hospital, where generations of Raichlens have been treated—including Grandpa Jack, who had died there a few years earlier from a heart attack.

As we rode to the hospital, sirens blaring, my dad kept squeezing my hand. If he said something to me, I don't remember it. They wheeled the gurney into the emergency room and that was the last time I saw my mother.

The next three days were a roller coaster of hope and despair, of boredom and extreme emotion. Sometimes family members waited with us; sometimes it was just me and my dad. At first, there was hope. Maybe they pumped her stomach in time. Then the doctor warned my father that even if she survived, there would likely be irreversible brain damage.

The second day, I went to band practice. At the time, I played bass guitar in a rock group called Syrup. (It was a time when kids in Baltimore would drink Robitussin AC to get high.) My dad wanted me to have some vestige of normalcy, so he thought band practice would be good for me.

My fellow musicians were surprised to see me. Having heard about my mother, they hadn't expected me to show up for practice. Later that evening, they came to our house. Our drummer, Pete, a kid from a rough neighborhood on the wrong side of Park Heights Avenue, perennially dressed in ripped T-shirts, showed up wearing a sports coat and tie. My friend Bruce also showed up in a tie. It was surreal—like they knew something I didn't.

It took her three days to die. My dad, trying to protect me from the vision of this limp rag of a body hooked up to tubes and monitors, kept me out of the intensive care unit. Gradually, her vital signs weakened. On the final day, my father put his arms around me and hugged me.

"It's over," he said and sobbed.

The cause of death was an overdose of a sleeping medication called chloral hydrate. She took something on the order of eighty pills. The normal dose was one or two. She was thirty-eight years old.

Had I been paying attention, the warning signs would have been obvious. A week earlier, while driving at sixty miles an hour on the Baltimore Beltway, my mom turned and asked, "If I jump out of the car, do you think I would die?" A few days after that, my dad discovered strange bruises and marks on her forearms. But by then, we were so used to her erratic behavior, neither of us paid any heed.

After her death, I insisted to everyone I was fine. Your mother commits suicide? No big deal. You were the one who found her? So what? Looking back on it, I was a wreck. I stopped smoking pot. I gave up playing music, left the band, and sold my guitars and equipment. My dad offered to arrange for me to speak with my mother's psychiatrist.

"I'm fine," I said. "I don't need it."

I came to regard suicide as a heroic act—a fitting end for geniuses like van Gogh and Ernest Hemingway. Years later, on my first date with my now-wife, I felt obliged to tell her my mother committed suicide.

"Oh my God," she screamed. "When?"

"Eleven years ago," I said.

I guess a mother's suicide stays with you. I finally realized that killing yourself and leaving your son behind isn't really heroic at all.

I often wonder what would have happened had my mother lived long enough for the advent of modern antidepressants, like Zoloft or Prozac. (The drugs available during the worst of her illnesses are now regarded as barbaric.) I wonder if she would have engaged with the women's liberation movement.

"Where can I find something that I can contribute to life, some small responsibility which will give me some dignity," she wrote in her journal.

That was a cause she could have thrown herself into that didn't require the body of an eighteen-year-old, as did ballet, to succeed.

I HAVE A CONFESSION TO MAKE and it's really, really painful. Three days prior to her overdose, driving home from dinner at Grammie Sarah's, my mother asked me—no, begged me—to take her to the movies. "Please," she asked over and over. Selfish seventeen-year-old that I was, mindful of some stupid homework assignment, or maybe just embarrassed to be seen at the movies with my mother, I refused.

As I think about it now—and I have for most of my life—that was the single most cruel, hurtful act I've ever done. Here was a woman—my mother—so desperately unhappy, she was about to take her life. She hungered for just one simple pleasure, one small gesture of kindness and compassion. Perhaps it would have saved her life.

Of course, that's Steven's guilty conscience talking, because as my father explained and as countless family members, friends, and therapists have told me, it wasn't my fault. My mother was mentally ill. (Schizophrenia was the diagnosis.) She would have killed herself eventually, regardless of what I did or did not do. And yet, I'll go to my grave feeling responsible for her sad, lonely death.

In a weird way, the guilt hasn't been all bad. Over the years, it's made me feel like I had to do more than anyone else to make up for it. That's led to my writing thirty-plus books—many of them five hundred pages and more. To being in constant motion (I spend four months of the year on the road). To taking on more projects and speaking engagements than any reasonable person would do, simply because I can't say no. I said no once when I was young, and look what happened.

No matter how many books I write, how many TV shows I make, how many classes I teach, or audiences I entertain, it will never be enough. I will always carry the weight of my mother's suicide on my shoulders.

My family on the day of my bar mitzvah.

I have painted a rather dark portrait of my mother. I fear I've sold her short. When she wasn't in the throes of mental illness, which was often, she was warm, bright, and endearing. She was smart—Mensa smart—and when childhood dilemmas arose, she always gave me good advice. I have no doubt my mother loved me—dare I say, fiercely. I certainly loved her back.

One last note on my mother's death. If there's an afterlife, maybe it brought her some comfort. Her funeral would have exceeded her wildest expectations. Here was a woman whose favorite song lyric was "I'm a little petunia in an onion patch." She often complained that no one would show up at her funeral.

Well, the cortege of cars stretched for three city blocks, and the hundreds of attendees included her childhood pals, dance friends (among them a pre-Hollywood Goldie Hawn—one of her dance mates at the Wally Saunders Dance Studio), and a long-haired hippie contingency for yours truly. The rabbi eulogized her aptly. My mother's Hebrew name was Fegeleh ("sparrow").

"A precious little bird has flown," he said.

MY MOTHER THE GRILL MASTER

Despite her dancer's diets and conflicted attitudes toward food, my mother did make a few dishes I still hunger for. One of them had an eerie foreshadowing of the activity I'm best known for today.

My mother's chief specialty involved a piece of cooking equipment that few women would have touched in the 1960s: a barbecue grill. She was our family grill master and brought to this activity an impetuousness that characterized her dancing and her life. She'd load it with charcoal briquets and douse it with gasoline. (Do not try this at home!) That lit the grill in a hurry, imparting a subtle, but not completely unpleasant petroleum scent to the food. For many years, that's what I thought barbecue was supposed to taste like!

I remember only one of my mom's specialties on that grill, but it was a killer: a sirloin steak that she charred jet black on the outside, while leaving the center blood-red and virtually still mooing. We called it "Pittsburgh rare," a reference to the coal-fed blast furnaces in Steel Town. I can still taste that charred exterior and the sweet, sanguine tang of the bloody meat in the center. From what I can remember, my mother never made a sauce. Her idea of a condiment was an astringent relish of raw cranberries and kumquats. Extreme cuisine before it was fashionable.

My mother died long before I became a food writer and TV host. I suspect she would have regarded my career with no small amazement. In our family, the apple fell very far from the tree.

MY MOTHER'S PITTSBURGH RARE STEAK

Fearless. Impetuous. Passionate. Impatient. Extreme. These may be odd words to use to describe a steak. But they certainly described my mother. Whatever she undertook, she did boldly, even recklessly. Whether executing a complicated ballet routine or grilling a simple steak, she did so with grand gestures and a blithe disregard for convention. No handsome crosshatch of grill marks. No carefully monitored cooking times or instant-read meat thermometers. She'd throw the meat on the grill, char it until the outside was the color of coal and the inside was barely warm, then slap it onto a plate. We called the steak "Pittsburgh rare"—the black evoking the smoke or perhaps coal from the Pittsburgh steel mills. Yeah, it was rare—even still raw in the center—but for any diehard steak lover, it's nirvana.

Serves 2

2 (8- to 10-ounce) sirloin steaks, 1 inch thick

Coarse salt (kosher or sea) and freshly ground black pepper

Garlic powder

1. Set up your grill for direct grilling and heat to high. Ideally, you'll be using a charcoal grill. Brush or scrape the grill grate clean and oil it well. (Note: My mom would never have done this—she just threw the meat on the grill.)
2. Very generously season the steaks on both sides with salt, pepper, and garlic powder. Arrange on the grate over the hottest part of the fire and grill until very darkly browned, dare I say charred black on the outside,

but still very rare in the center. You'll want to cook a 1-inch-thick steak about 2 minutes per side (or to taste).

3. Transfer the steak to plates or a platter and let rest for 1 minute, then slice and serve.

Chapter Four

JAMES BEARD WAS ALSO AN ALUM

1971–1975

A longhair from Baltimore enrolls at Reed College in Portland, Oregon.

I chose to attend Reed College for all the wrong reasons. It turned out to be one of the best decisions of my life.

The first reason was distance. My mother had committed suicide. I wanted to get as far away as possible from what I morbidly joked was the scene of the crime. You can't get much farther from Baltimore than Portland, Oregon.

The second reason was hair. Back in 1970, I had a lot of it, and so did the guys pictured in the Reed College catalog. Male hair length marked a sharp cultural divide in those turbulent years of the 1970s. Longhairs played psychedelic music. Longhairs opposed the war in Vietnam. I was a longhair, so I figured I'd fit right in at Reed.

Reed College was founded in 1908 with a lofty mission: "To promote the life of the mind through the intrinsic value of intellectual pursuit." Note the word "intrinsic." Reed's raison d'être—now as then—is learning for its own sake.

One of the school's first students was John Reed (no relation to the school's founder, Simeon Reed), the communist activist who chronicled the Russian Revolution in the book *Ten Days That Shook the World,* subsequently immortalized by Warren Beatty in one of my all-time favorite movies, *Reds.*

Another of Reed's illustrious alums was James Beard, who, like John Reed, dropped out before graduating. (More on him later.) He foreshadowed yet another famous Reed dropout: Steve Jobs. In fact, most of my classmates did not graduate four years after enrollment; workaholic that I was (and still am), I was the oddball. People took their time about getting their education—if they graduated from Reed at all.

Today, Reed is celebrated for its academic rigor. Back when I attended, it was considered a hotbed of anarchism and sin. Despite the conservative look of its Tudor Gothic architecture, Reed's unofficial motto—emblazoned on sweatshirts and pennants—read "Communism, Atheism, and

Free Love." There were no exams or grade-point averages at Reed. Grades, such as they were, were based on class participation and essays.

The core of the Reed education was the Humanities program (Hum 110 and 210 in Reed-speak), a two-year interdisciplinary course on Western civilization. We learned by reading history's great books and intellectual trend-setters, starting with Homer, Hesiod, and Plato. In year two, we worked up to "modern" thinkers such as Sigmund Freud and Karl Marx. Despite its unstructured social life (no fraternities, and our egghead athletes competed against local high school teams), Reed demanded academic excellence. It still does.

If you've read my cookbooks, you may have noticed how I always try to put recipes in their cultural context—their history, who created them, and what they say about the society where they're cooked. I acquired this historical perspective at Reed. For me, recipes tell a larger story about people and their culture, and I came to care about this at Reed too. Fun fact: It turns out that the oldest written barbecue recipe in Europe—beef wrapped in fat and grilled with sea salt, retsina wine, and olive oil—appears in Homer's *Iliad*, a sacred meal eaten the night before Achilles battles Hector. As for how it was cooked, it was our old Hum 110 friend Hesiod who penned the myth of how Prometheus gave man the gift of fire.

I came to Reed as an art major but quickly realized that the soul of a tortured artist does not a master draftsman or painter make. Next, I contemplated a major in English literature. I studied Anglo-Saxon (the language of the British Isles before the Norman Invasion in 1066), reading England's first great literary masterpiece, *Beowulf*, in the original language. This was considerably more challenging than it sounds; the opening lines of the poem read:

Hwæt! Wē Gār-Dena in geārdagum
þēodcyninga þrym gefrūnon

("Yo! We Spear-Danes in days of old
Heard of the glory of kings.")

Reading *Beowulf* was one of my weirdest accomplishments at Reed, and I've been something of a literary nerd ever since.

One evening, I attended a lecture by a recent PhD in English literature who was applying for a teaching position at Reed. I don't recall his subject, but I do remember watching the poor guy light one cigarette on the burning stub of another for one hour straight. He was one of more than a hundred candidates applying for that single post at Reed. I realized that future employment prospects for an English major weren't so promising.

So, I switched to a subject with even poorer future employment prospects: French literature. I figured that if I couldn't find a teaching post in French literature after graduation, at least I could become a translator.

I had fallen in love with France when my father took me there my junior year of high school—a sort of male bonding / healing trip after my mother's death. (I've returned to France every year since.) I loved everything about Paris—the architecture, the cafés, the bicycle-jammed streets, and especially the food. We dined at all the top restaurants of the day: Maxim's, Fouquet's, Lasserre—the last with a ceiling that opened to the stars. We met up-and-coming young chefs, like Roger Vergé and Michel Rostang, long before they earned their first Michelin stars. I returned the following year after graduating from high school, backpacking through France with one of my classmates. At the bottom of my backpack was a crumpled corduroy sports coat—to be excavated for a dinner at Maison Rostang.

I DECIDED TO WRITE my senior thesis on a writer virtually no one had ever heard of, not even in the French department: the fourteenth-century poet

Christine de Pisan. I picked Christine not on account of her sublime style or profound message. No, what really grabbed me was the fact that so little had been written about her. At the time, I couldn't find a single book of literary criticism on Christine.

Christine de Pisan was born in Venice in 1363 and spent her childhood in the court of King Charles V in Paris. She married when she was fifteen and was widowed by the age of twenty-four. She became the foremost woman of letters in medieval Europe and the first to earn her living by her pen (a necessity after being cheated out of her husband's estate). Her sheer volume of work (more than three hundred ballads and poems) made her the medieval equivalent of Nora Roberts; her feminist message put her on par with Erica Jong.

I focused my analysis on two of Christine's master works—*The City of Women* and *The Book of the Three Virtues*—in the context of the medieval tradition of courtly love. Why the Middle Ages? I had come to be fascinated by the stark contrasts of that distant age: the splendor of the rich, the wretchedness of the poor; the sublime art, the monstrous violence; the flourishing of a great literary tradition in an age when books had to be "published" one by one, each copied by hand. Looking back, on a psychological level, I was probably trying to escape the present. An

Christine de Pisan: medieval woman of letters and subject of my thesis.

obscure medieval poet, writing in the French equivalent of Chaucer's English, certainly kept me remote.

My thesis defense went reasonably well until one of the female committee members gently pointed out that as a fledgling medieval French scholar—and clueless male—I had missed the entire feminist message of Christine's work. But the thesis experience did give me a taste for writing about subjects without a large body of existing scholarship. Twenty years later, I would do so again with *The Barbecue! Bible.* I like forging my own path.

My on- and off-campus jobs were as educational as my studies. My father paid my tuition; I thought it only fair that I should work for my living expenses. My first year at Reed, I landed a job with the Art Department, photographing art books so the professors could use slides of the great paintings to illustrate their lectures. (Obviously, this was back before we could download an image online—the internet didn't exist.) I learned a lot about art history with that job—a subject that still enthralls me today.

I also picked up a gig loading firewood into a dump truck for a man who had recently gotten out of prison. That lasted three weekends and cured me of my romantic proletariat notions about physical labor. I worked as a dishwasher at a local hospital and as a "slopper" (dishwasher) at the Reed College Commons (our food service facility). It was in this capacity that I met another famous Reed College dropout: Steve Jobs.

As I recall, Jobs belonged to a group of "scroungers," students who would position themselves by the window where other students deposited their dirty dish trays for sorting and washing. There were always some edible leftovers—an uneaten roll, a piece of fruit, a cookie, or a mini carton of milk. A clever scrounger could put together an entire dinner without paying for Reed's meal program. And one of those scroungers was Jobs.

One class Jobs took at Reed would profoundly influence his vision for the personal computer. The Art Department at the time employed two world-famous calligraphy professors: Lloyd Reynolds and Robert Palladino. The elegant lettering they taught graced flyers and bulletin boards across the campus. Their scripts became the inspiration for the multiple typefaces Steve Jobs made available on the first Macintosh computer.

My junior year, I landed one of the most coveted jobs at Reed: babysitting the boilers in the campus power plant. If I pulled the swing shift, I got paid to study for eight hours. If I pulled the graveyard shift, I worked for a while, slept for a while, and likely fell asleep in class the next morning.

But my best job was off campus: I became a clerk at Otto's Sausage Kitchen and Meat Market, a half mile up "the hill" (Woodstock Boulevard) from Reed. Otto's was the go-to gourmet market / sandwich shop for generations of Reedies. Founded in 1921 by German-born Otto Eichentopf, Otto's specialized in sausages stuffed and smoked on the premises. My favorites included the beefy summer sausages, intensely smoky frankfurters, and peppery *jägerwurst* (hunters' sausages) that crunched when you took a bite.

Over the years, the meat market became a deli, with the Bronleewee family running the front of the house and the Eichentopfs manning the sausage factory in the back. The Bronleewees introduced me to wine tasting and European cheeses. I've never looked back.

The 1970s were a terrific time to discover wine. Robert Mondavi had established California as a serious viticultural region. Château Montelena and Stag's Leap beat the pants off French wines in a famous blind tasting in Paris—drolly commemorated in the movie *Bottle Shock*. The first wineries opened in Oregon's Willamette Valley and Washington's Columbia and Yakima Valleys—wineries like Eyrie, Erath, and Sokol Blosser. Our damp Pacific climate—so depressing in daily life—helped produce pinot noirs of cedary softness that could hold their own against French Burgundies.

When I was growing up, cheese meant Velveeta (really), so Otto's cheese case came as another revelation. There was Bel Paese, a soft, mild, creamy cow's milk cheese from northern Italy with a pleasant edge of bitterness. (Italians appreciate bitter flavors—perhaps more than anyone else on the planet.) There was Havarti, a soft, buttery Danish cheese we sliced thin on a meat slicer. There was Jarlsberg, a Swiss-style cheese from Norway with large, moist "eyes" (holes) and a sweet, nutty finish. Also from Norway came a strange, hard, sweet goat cheese called *gjetost* that tasted like sour caramel.

Of course, with today's global cheese trade, when an incredible selection of cheese from all over the world can be found at your local supermarket, Otto's selection in the 1970s seems quaint. But my two years working at Otto's opened me to a world of food and wine I didn't know existed, and propelled me to a career in food at least as much as did my subsequent travels in Europe.

Unfortunately, things did not work out in the long run for my employers, the Bronleewee family. Some years later, the Eichentopfs, who owned the building, decided they wanted to take over the deli, not just the sausage shop. After three decades of running Otto's, the Bronleewees were forced to leave the business. I learned a lesson I've practiced ever since: Own your own business and be your own boss.

I ATTENDED REED AT A TIME of great upheaval in both college education and American gastronomy. On the educational side, there were politics—Nixon's invasion of Cambodia; Reedie marches on the statehouse in Salem; student strikes that shuttered Eliot Hall and forced the temporary suspension of classes. On the culinary side, there was a jovial lady with a wake-the-dead voice who showed us how to bone ducks, roll out puff pastry, and beat egg whites into a snowy cloud with a whisk in a copper bowl. (Julia Child, of course.)

Taking a break from my studies.

Like most Reedies at the time, I lived in a group house off campus, where I became the de facto cook, working my way through *Mastering the Art of French Cooking*—although with considerably less aplomb than Julie Powell in *Julie & Julia*. We baked honey whole wheat bread from the *Tassajara* cookbook. When one of my roommates became vegetarian, we cooked soybean stroganoff from *Recipes for a Small Planet*. We made yogurt from scratch in the newly invented Salton yogurt machine. We brewed beer in the basement. From time to time, a bottle or two would explode, turning the basement into a minefield for the house felines. I don't remember how the beer tasted, but I know we drank a lot of it, and home brewing certainly cut down on the house grocery bill.

When our parents or other deep-pocketed relatives passed through Portland, we dragged them to the two marquee restaurants in town at the time: Indigene and L'Auberge. The former served high-style Italian food; the latter, French. Sometimes we'd thrill at seeing our professors dining at adjacent tables. When we were paying, we ate at the Russian Renaissance or Heavy Number Taco or Rosie's Deli. We couldn't afford to eat the pricey continental fare at the Benson Hotel, but when we wanted to feel sophisticated, we'd go for drinks at the Benson Bar.

In 1975, I graduated from Reed with honors—and that degree in French literature. My father, grandparents, and my Aunt Annette flew out to Portland to attend the ceremony. Our commencement speaker was *The New Yorker* film critic at the time, Pauline Kael, and she perplexed the audience (or at least my grandparents) by delivering a lecture on the history of the movies, without a single reference to how we students might boldly venture out into the world to face our future. The woman who received her diploma right before me wore a hat with a bird's nest pinned to it. Another student wore face paint. Another came in shorts. It was, indeed, a typical Reed graduation.

Reed's most famous foodie alum was James Beard. I had the good fortune to meet him in person at a cooking class in Ohio. He was an old man by then; he oversaw the class from a barstool, letting his assistants do the actual teaching. I mentioned to him that I, too, attended Reed College. I can't say he seemed particularly impressed to meet me; then again, I hadn't really accomplished anything yet in the food world. I didn't know at the time that his departure from Reed was involuntary.

James Beard was gay—unrepentantly so—and he attended Reed in an age when homosexuals were expected to hide in the closet. He was discovered committing an act of "oral indecency" with a professor. He was promptly expelled. But he doesn't seem to have harbored resentment; when he died, he bequeathed his townhouse in Greenwich Village to Reed.

The college, in an act of stupendous shortsightedness, promptly sold the property. They could have kept it and turned it into a culinary research center. They could have hired another Reed foodie to run that center—I would have loved a job like that. Instead, Reed sold it to the newly formed James Beard Foundation. I would return to the Beard House many times to do book launches and special events. The kitchen was wallpapered with world maps; an open shower stood in the living room. The house was as eccentric as its occupant, who was as eccentric as Reed College itself.

Which brings me back, in an indirect way, to my thesis on that obscure medieval poet. While looking for books on Christine de Pisan, I stumbled upon a medieval cookbook. *The Forme of Cury* (*cury* being the Middle English term for "cookery") was written around 1390 by a master cook in the court of Richard II. Thumbing through its pages, I found such strange-sounding dishes as *mawmenee* (a game stew flavored with honey, wine, and cinnamon), *furmente with porpays* (porpoise wheat porridge), and *payn ragoun* (a sticky candy flavored with ginger and galangal). The ingredients were equally perplexing: What the heck are spikenard, cubeb, and verjus? I experimented with some of the recipes for my housemates, even if I had to replace the galangal with pedestrian ginger. I had no idea how that experience would change my life.

The Forme of Cury played a much bigger role in my evolution as a food writer and TV host than medieval poetry ever did. Improbable as it seems, I owe it all to that seemingly impractical degree in French literature.

STARVING-STUDENT SPAGHETTI

College students eat a lot of spaghetti. It was true when I attended Reed. It's true now. Back in those days, one of our favorite restaurants was the Old Spaghetti Factory—first because we could afford it, and second because it served really good food. A half century later, I still make one of their specialties—spaghetti with brown butter and myzithra cheese. In a nutshell, you cook butter until it turns brown, thereby endowing it with a toasty, nutty flavor, then toss it with spaghetti and finely grated myzithra cheese. The latter is a Greek sheep milk grating cheese—tangy and salty—which goes great with the nutty brown butter. It's one of the world's truly great pasta dishes, and the fact that it requires only three ingredients (four if you count salt for the pasta pot) saves you both time and money. Look for myzithra at a Greek market or a well-stocked supermarket. If unavailable, substitute Pecorino Romano, ricotta salata, or even a nice, well-aged Parmigiano-Reggiano.

Serves 2 to 3

½ teaspoon salt
8 ounces spaghetti
6 tablespoons unsalted butter
1 cup finely grated myzithra cheese, divided
Freshly ground black pepper, for garnish (optional)

1. Bring 3 quarts of water to a boil in a large pot. Add the salt and spaghetti and boil until cooked to taste, 6 to 8 minutes for al dente. (No, contrary to popular belief, throwing a noodle up to the ceiling to see if it sticks is not a reliable test for doneness—much as we believed so when I was in college.)
2. When the spaghetti is nearly done, melt the butter in a saucepan over medium-high heat. Cook it, swirling the pan until it starts to brown, 2 to 3 minutes.
3. Drain the spaghetti in a colander and transfer it to a large serving bowl. Pour the brown butter over it and sprinkle with ¾ cup of the cheese. Toss to mix. Serve at once, sprinkling the remaining ¼ cup cheese on top of each serving. A good grinding of black pepper is optional but welcome.

Chapter Five

ALIMENTARY, MY DEAR WATSON

1975–1976

My Watson Fellowship year offered a bird's-eye view of history.

The announcement arrived in a stiff white envelope the week of my twenty-first birthday, during my senior year at Reed College. The sender lived on Benefit Street in Providence, Rhode Island. It certainly proved providential, because it came from the Thomas J. Watson Foundation, informing me that I had won a fellowship to study medieval cooking in Europe.

Watson Foundation? Medieval cooking? A note of explanation is in order. It involved a bottle of retsina. Okay, maybe two bottles.

Thomas J. Watson Sr. founded International Business Machines (later, simply "IBM") in 1914, which grew into one of the most important multinational corporations of twentieth-century America and beyond. In 1961, Watson's widow, Jeannette, launched a foundation to honor her late husband. Its stated mission called for the empowerment of students "to expand their vision, test and develop their potential, and gain confidence and perspective to do so for others." Its unofficial goal was to do soft diplomacy for America, sending enterprising young college graduates as ambassadors around the world.

At the time, Reed College was one of thirty-five schools invited to nominate students for a Watson Fellowship. At the urging of my thesis advisor, Bill Ray, I applied—one of a dozen or so Reedies to do so. I was a chronic procrastinator back then and hadn't really given much thought to my proposal. Then I flashed on *The Forme of Cury*, that fourteenth-century cookery book I discovered while researching my thesis on Christine de Pisan.

That was it: Medieval Cooking in Europe. Serious enough to show my bona fides as a scholar. Whimsical enough to fit the Watson model—the foundation had no interest in sending a student abroad to do graduate-level academics at a foreign university.

The night before the proposal was due, I dined with friends at a Greek restaurant. The retsina flowed (retsina being a resin-flavored wine Greeks have drunk since the age of Homer—I knew that thanks to Reed College's Hum 101 class). After two bottles, my inspiration flowed too.

Thanks to my thesis, I knew something about the Middle Ages. My knowledge of medieval cooking was limited, but I was familiar with three medieval cookbooks: the English *The Forme of Cury* and the French *Le Viandier* and *Le Ménagier de Paris*. I could throw around the names of some weird ingredients used in the Middle Ages, like grains of paradise and mugwort. With a little embroidering, I could whet appetites by describing iconic medieval dishes, such as *hypocras* (spiced wine), *flaumpeyns* (flame-patterned meat pies), and *cokentryce* (a fantastical banquet dish made by joining the front half of a roasted capon to the back half of a similarly cooked piglet).

That's where the retsina came in—because nothing spurs the imagination like wine and a looming deadline. I completed the Watson application around midnight and mailed it off, nursing a fierce hangover the next morning. My application made the first cut, and a few weeks later, the director of the Watson Foundation at the time, Daniel Arnaud, arrived at Reed to interview candidates. Curiously, he seemed less interested in the particulars of medieval cooking than in how I would proceed with the project.

"A Watson Fellowship comes with two conditions," Dr. Arnaud explained. "It must take place abroad. And you can't be affiliated with a university."

Twist my arm! I told Arnaud I planned do my research in two countries.

"I'll make France, specifically Paris, my home base," I said. Then as now, France enjoyed the reputation for having the world's most sophisticated cuisine. I explained how Paris was home to the Cordon Bleu cooking school, where I intended to learn about modern French cuisine, and the Bibliothèque Nationale, which houses one of the world's best collections of medieval manuscripts. "As for England," I said, "the British Library has the original manuscript of *The Forme of Cury*, and the Bodleian Library in Oxford possesses a medieval book collection unparalleled in Europe."

"How good is your French?" Dr. Arnaud asked.

"*Convenable*," I replied. "Good enough."

"How do you plan to gain access to the rare manuscript collections?" Arnaud countered.

I mentioned Reed French Department head Sam Danon, who had volunteered to write me a letter of introduction.

"We're not interested in fellowship projects that are solely academic," Arnaud explained.

I told him how vague medieval recipes were when it came to measurements and cooking times, and that my plan was to study modern French cooking to help make sense of the medieval recipes I would find.

Arnaud's last question startled me: "Does my name have any special significance for you?"

It took me a moment to make the connection: His name was an anadrome (reversal) of Arnaut Daniel, a famous twelfth-century troubadour whom Petrarch called the "grand master of love." I reached in my backpack and pulled out an anthology of troubadour poetry. I'd been studying Dr. Arnaud's namesake earlier that week as background for my thesis.

I left the interview uncertain as to what Dr. Arnaud thought of me. I forgot about the Watson Fellowship until that stiff white envelope arrived. It presented me with a dilemma. In the interim, I had also applied for and received a Fulbright Fellowship to study paleography (the art of deciphering ancient writing) at the University of Bordeaux. The Watson involved travel, cooking, monastery kitchens, and medieval castles. The Fulbright would confine me to studying dusty old manuscripts in a rare-books room.

I didn't need retsina to resolve that one. I accepted the Watson. I finished my thesis, graduated from Reed cum laude, and spent the summer planning my departure.

Medieval cooking. The very notion evokes images of Rabelaisian lords ripping apart roasted ox haunches and tossing the bones over their shoulders to waiting mastiffs. Well, like so much about our notion of the Middle Ages, the image is both true and false. Yes, people ate with their hands in medieval times—widespread use of the fork would have to wait for the Renaissance—but they followed strict rules of etiquette laid out in manuscripts that circulated like *Miss Manners* does today. No, it was rare for people to eat whole animals. Meat was considerably tougher in those days than now, and given the level of medieval dentistry, few people had a full set of teeth. Instead, chefs often chopped, pounded, and pureed ingredients until their original state was unrecognizable.

So how does one study medieval cooking in Europe? I devised a four-pronged plan of attack:

- I would get my hands on as many medieval manuscripts and cookery books as I could find, and would scour medieval art for images of food, cooking, and dining.
- I would visit castles and monasteries—especially those with surviving kitchens and dining rooms—to get a feel for where people cooked and ate seven hundred years ago.
- I would spend time with vintners, charcutiers, and cheesemakers to learn about traditional production methods that originated in the Middle Ages.
- I would enroll in a modern cooking school in Paris to learn the fundamentals of cooking so I could extrapolate backward to how people in the Middle Ages cooked.

Extrapolation was sorely needed. It turned out that medieval recipes fell far short of the precision of modern cookbooks. The basic format ran something like this: "Take some of this, that, and the other, and combine in the customary fashion." There were no precise measurements, no cooking times or temperatures, and many of the ingredients would be incomprehensible to a modern cook.

There were also linguistic challenges. *The Forme of Cury* was written in Middle English—the language of Chaucer—and used an ancient letter called a thorn (þ) to signify the "th" sound. Culinary terms would sound strange to our ears. To "seethe," for example, meant to boil (we still use the expression "seething mad"). To "hewe" meant to slice or cut, and "gobbets" meant bite-size pieces.

My plan was to start my Watson year by enrolling at the Cordon Bleu cooking school in Paris. That would get me settled in the center of the world's culinary universe and give me a solid start in deciphering medieval recipes. Immediately, I encountered a setback. The Cordon Bleu was fully booked for the upcoming semester and wouldn't have any openings until January. The Watson Foundation was okay with setbacks. They believed that unforeseen challenges forced their fellows to grow.

At this point, I made a decision that still puzzles me now as much as it horrified my family then. I enrolled in a German language school, the Goethe-Institut, in Rothenburg ob der Tauber. "Red Town" (on account of the red-tile roofs of its half-timbered houses) is a village in northern Bavaria little changed, in outward appearance at least, from the Middle Ages. I couldn't have picked a more appropriate setting for medieval studies. The bedroom window faced a Gothic church steeple, whose bells began ringing at six in the morning. The apartment lacked central heating because the Hausfrau hadn't gotten around to renovating her centuries-old house.

Germany would turn out to be a rich source of medieval cookbooks, so from an intellectual perspective, learning German made sense. But Bavaria was also where Hitler rose to power in the 1930s. Had I lived in Germany at that time, I would surely have perished in a Nazi death camp. Thirteen of my cousins, among them Baruch, Rosa, and Simon Rochlin, met that fate after being deported from Riga, Latvia, to Auschwitz. Their names appear—along with those of 70,000 other Latvian Jews—on a memorial wall at the Holocaust Museum in Riga.

In fact, were it not for a vagary of timing, I myself might not be alive today. In 1938, my great-grandmother, "Grandma" Raichlen (she was such an imposing figure, no one called her by her first name), planned a family reunion trip to Riga. My father, who was sixteen years old at the time, volunteered to accompany her as her escort and driver. The invasion of Poland put an end to that trip, and my family remained safe in Baltimore.

Once settled in Rothenburg, I quickly established a routine. In the morning, I trod cobblestone streets to a local bakery for a breakfast of *Sonnenblumenbrot*—a whole-grain sunflower seed bread I still dream about today. From there, it was on to the Goethe-Institut for German classes. I spent afternoons at the Rothenburg Historical Center, where I did, indeed, find medieval recipes (including one for *Lebkuchen*—"love cookie"

Watson Fellows gather in Salzburg, Austria, in 1976. I'm third from the left in the front row.

literally—the ancestor of modern gingerbread). There were laws—lots of laws—regulating food safety and fair business practices. The archivists, Dr. Schnurrer and Herr Wild, generously helped me with my research. Herr Wild walked with a limp—the result of a battle wound and his harsh years in a Soviet reeducation camp after the war. That, of course, meant that the helpful Herr Wild had been a soldier in Hitler's Nazi army.

A few months later, the Watson Foundation organized a meeting for European-based fellows in Salzburg, Austria. We stayed at Schloss Leopoldskron, a sumptuous eighteenth-century castle. The final banquet concluded with *Salzburger Nockerln*—a sort of free-form vanilla soufflé dusted with powdered sugar. I was asked to thank the chef and hotel staff in my newly acquired German. It was a weird conclusion to six months in a place I rightly should have hated, but where I found much to learn and admire.

•

I ARRIVED IN PARIS IN JANUARY 1976 to enroll at the Cordon Bleu. Finally, I'd get some practical culinary knowledge to help me make sense of those medieval recipes. At the time, the CB (as we called it) was run by a stern Frenchwoman named Madame Brassard. We students (especially we Americans) couldn't be trusted not to ruin expensive ingredients, Madame reasoned, so she provided us with cheap meat, plebeian fish such as mackerel and whiting, and lowbrow vegetables like rutabagas and cabbage. We never saw a truffle or foie gras. There were no printed recipes and a lot of repetition in the menus. Food-wise, I was underwhelmed. On the plus side, I was learning to cook in French.

All the while, I continued my research on medieval cooking. I discovered that, in many ways, the food scene in the Middle Ages, at least for the upper classes, resembled our own. There were celebrity chefs like Guillaume Tirel, better known by his nickname Taillevent ("Wind Slicer" on account of his dazzling knife skills), who rose from lowly *happelapin* (scullery lad) to become master chef to kings Charles V and Charles VI. Along the way, he acquired a mansion, an equestrian travel escort, and even a coat of arms featuring three kettles.

There were internationally bestselling cookbooks, like *Le Viandier* ("The Victualer"), first "published" (handwritten) in the 1380s. The book went through twenty printed editions between 1486 and 1615 alone, and it's still in print today. (May my *Barbecue! Bible* enjoy such longevity!)

There were status-symbol ingredients, but instead of being caviar and truffles, they were spices. Cooking, for the rich at least, relied on a global trade network that imported cubebs (long peppers) from Java, asafetida (a malodorous but flavorful seasoning nicknamed "devil's dung") from India, and saffron from Iran. A pound of black pepper would have cost the equivalent of a day laborer's yearly wages, yet an astonishing number of medieval recipes call for it. Ditto for another "seasoning" that was equally rare and costly in the Middle Ages: sugar.

Medieval cooking in Europe. The original prints hang in our dining room.

There were cult dishes that went viral, like blancmange (from the French words for "white" and "eat")—a mousse-like pudding made with chicken, rice, almond milk, and sugar. The dish turned up in cookbooks across Europe and reflected the medieval blurring of savory and sweet. (Blancmange survives today as an English dessert.)

Then, as now, food had a strong theatrical component. Chefs crowned spit-roasted chickens with paper helmets and skewered them on lances to ride to the table on the backs of spit-roasted pigs. Peacocks and swans—top poultry choices in the Middle Ages on account of their lush plumage—were roasted, then cunningly redecorated with their feathers. The shenanigans of Salt Bae would have been right at home.

There were rigorous dress codes and rules of etiquette. (One book advised diners not to scratch their fleas at the table.) Come to think of it, given the tank tops and flip-flops that some of today's crass diners wear to nice restaurants, I wish there was more etiquette now.

Of course, in other ways, medieval cuisine would have seemed unimaginably alien. There was no refrigeration to keep food cold and safe. There was no propane to fire ovens and ranges. There was no electricity to power appliances like mixers and food processors. (The latter would have been much appreciated, as a vast number of medieval recipes called for reducing meats and nuts to a puree.) Spit-roasting was a popular cooking method, but the rotisserie had to be turned by hand (a miserable job done by a boy as young as eight—although sometimes the spit was turned by a dog on a treadmill). For that matter, the only way to illuminate a kitchen was by torchlight.

If a chef wanted to record or publish a recipe, he (or his scribe) had to write it out by hand. (Maybe that's one reason medieval recipes were so terse.) Yet publish chefs did; during my Watson year, I discovered more than a hundred medieval cookbooks. ChatGPT puts that number at 250, with forty extant manuscripts in French, fifty in English, and eighty in

German. Then, as now, chefs resorted to plagiarism. For centuries, Taillevent was assumed to be the author of *Le Viandier*, but scholars recently found a similar text written thirty years earlier (when the chef would have been at most ten years old). Similarly, and more recently, French chef Paul Bocuse took two-thirds of his bestselling 1977 book *French Cooking* verbatim from a 1953 book authored by one Alfred Guérot.

Taillevent's recipes are laconic by modern standards. We could think of them as "tweets"—written by a professional for professionals in the sort of culinary shorthand used by chefs throughout the ages. His seasoning may strike us as heavy-handed, if not downright exotic. More than half the recipes in *Le Viandier* call for saffron, for example, and Taillevent routinely reached for galangal, spikenard, borage, and purslane. He eschewed simplicity, subjecting most meats to spit-roasting, boiling, frying—or sometimes all three—in a single recipe, reducing whole birds and roasts to small pieces, mincemeats, or puree.

FOUR AND TWENTY BLACKBIRD BAKED IN A PIE

Ever since our emergence as *Homo sapiens*—and perhaps even earlier—human beings have felt a need to create art. In prehistoric times, this took the form of cave paintings and ivory sculptures. In the Middle Ages, as today, the urge often took a culinary turn. Medieval chefs built castles out of "marchpane" (marzipan), surrounded by moats of spiced wine. They dyed their food orange with saffron, red with sandalwood, and yellow with turmeric—all obtained at great expense from Asia. They "baked" live birds in mammoth pies—ready to fly out when the crust was opened. A 1549 version of the recipe read:

> *To make Pies that the Birds may be alive in them, and fly out when it is cut up . . . Make the coffin [crust] of a great Pie . . . bake it hollow with bran [straw] inside. After baking, remove the bran, then put in . . . as many small live birds as the empty coffin will hold. Sending it to table, on cutting the lid the birds will fly out, delighting the company.*

DURING THAT PARIS YEAR, my girlfriend at the time, Susan, and I lived in a studio apartment on the Rue du Mont Tabor, around the corner from the Place de la Concorde. The "kitchen" consisted of a closet with a toy-box range the size of a toaster oven. The setup was too small to attempt to cook the medieval recipes I unearthed in my research.

Fortunately, friendships come easily in one's twenties, and invitations were offered at the drop of a hat. During spring break, I found myself in a farmhouse near Chinon leased by a friend of a friend. I finally had a kitchen large enough to try out some of the medieval recipes. The first dish I tackled was *capouns in councys* (capon in spiced sauce) from *The Forme of Cury*. The original recipe ran like this:

> *Take Capons and rost hem right hoot þat þey be not half y nouhz and hewe hem to gobettes and cast hem in a pot, do þerto clene broth, seeþ hem þat þey be tendre; take brede and þe self broth and drawe it up yferer; take strong Powdour and Safroun and Salt and cast þer to. take ayrenn and seeþ hem harde; take out þe zolkes and hewe þe whyte*

þerinne, take the Pot fro þe fyre and cast þe whyte þerinne. messe þe disshes þerwith and lay þe zolkes hool and floure it with clowes, & serue hit forth.

In modern English, it would read:

Take capons and roast them until very hot, but not completely cooked, then cut them into bite-size chunks. Place them in a pot and add clear broth and simmer until tender. Mix bread into the broth and stir it well. Add a strong spice blend, plus saffron and salt. Take eggs and boil them until hard. Take out the yolks and chop the whites. Remove the pot from the fire and stir in the whites. Lay the whole egg yolks on top and stud the surface with cloves and serve it forth.

The recipe speaks volumes about medieval cooking. First, a capon is a castrated rooster—bigger and meatier than a chicken and much beloved in the Middle Ages. Curiously, when I was growing up, my great-grandmothers would roast capons. The bird has virtually disappeared from American tables today.

The bread was used as a thickener, and in the Middle Ages, slices of stale bread would be used as plates. (The French word for "slice" is *tranche*—origin of our term "trencher," a flat plate.) "Strong spice" would have been a blend of black pepper, cloves, ginger, nutmeg, and grains of paradise. Think of it as a proto-barbecue rub. Saffron provided both color and flavor. Cloves may seem like an odd spice for chicken, until you think of the modern clove-studded Easter ham.

Lacking a capon, I used chicken, which I partially roasted whole in the oven (a medieval chef would have used a turnspit in the fireplace). I cut the chicken into pieces, which I then simmered in homemade chicken stock. For strong spice I substituted modern French *quatre épices* (a mix of white pepper, cloves, nutmeg, and ginger). The overall effect seemed more Moroccan than English or French, but my taster guinea pigs devoured it to the last bite.

It turns out that besides making a living—at least in part—by writing cookbooks, Taillevent and I had two additional connections. By an amazing coincidence, Christine de Pisan's father, Thomas de Pisan, served as Royal Physician and Astrologer to Charles V at about the time that Taillevent was hired to run the kitchen. So it's highly likely that his daughter Christine—subject of my Reed thesis—met the great chef and experienced his cooking.

And like most cooks in the Middle Ages—indeed, most cooks until the Industrial Revolution—Taillevent did most of his cooking over an open wood fire. You could say he was a grill master two and a half centuries before the word "barbecue," from the Taíno Indian *barbacoa,* entered Europe's lexicon, and six centuries before I experienced my own baptism by barbecue fire.

My plan following my fellowship year was to write a book on medieval cooking. Two scholars beat me to it. *To the King's Taste: Richard II's Book of Feasts and Recipes* by Lorna Sass, and *Fabulous Feasts* by Madeleine Cosman came out the same year and took the wind out of my sails. Besides, I had no idea how hard it really is to write a book. I wouldn't learn that for another five years, and like many women after childbirth, I still repress how arduous it is today.

Many years later, I served on the Watson Foundation board, interviewing candidates for future fellowships. The board members were still shaking their heads about the guy who managed to convince the foundation to fund a year of eating and drinking through Europe under the guise of studying medieval cooking.

YPOCRAS (HIPPOCRAS)

Medieval Spiced Wine

People drank a lot of wine during the Middle Ages. And beer. And hard cider, perry (pear cider), and hydromel (mead). The one thing they didn't drink much of was water. Alcohol was relatively safe to drink back then, while water—especially in cities—was crawling with maleficent microbes. Which brings us to a popular medieval beverage that provided both pleasure and health: ypocras. That's a fancy name for red wine spiced with ginger, cinnamon, black pepper, and sugar (given its high price, sugar was used more as a spice than a sweetener in the Middle Ages). Ypocras often turned up at the end of a meal; the spices were believed to stimulate digestion. As for its curious (and curiously familiar-sounding name), it was short for a Hippocratic sleeve or hippocras bag—a cloth strainer through which you passed the wine to remove the spice pieces. (Hippocrates, of course, was the ancient Greek physician considered to be the father of Western medicine.) Note: Grains of paradise (*Aframomum melegueta*) are a spice in the pepper family with a flavor that hints at black pepper and allspice.

Here's the Middle English version (from a fourteenth-century manuscript):

To make Ypocras:

Take gynger, synamome, graynes, and sugur;
take a quarte of red wyne, and do þerto;
and medle all þis togedur, and let it stonde half a day;
and then clense it thorow a bagge of Ipopotys,
and kepe it in a clene vessel, and serve it forth.

Here's a modern English version:

To make Hippocras:

Take ginger, cinnamon, grains [of paradise], and sugar.

Add a quart of red wine to these ingredients.

Mix all together and let stand for half a day.

Then strain it through a hippocras bag [a cloth filter],

and store it in a clean vessel. Serve it forth.

And here's a modern recipe inspired by a fourteenth-century English recipe:

Serves 4

1 (750 mL) bottle dry red wine

2 cinnamon sticks, broken

1-inch piece fresh ginger, peeled and thinly sliced

1 teaspoon black peppercorns

½ teaspoon allspice berries

4 to 5 tablespoons sugar (white, light brown, or dark brown—your choice), or to taste

1. Combine all ingredients in a nonmetallic bowl or jug. Whisk well to dissolve the sugar. Cover the mixture and let stand for 8 hours or overnight in a cool corner of your kitchen.
2. Strain the mixture through cheesecloth, a fine-mesh strainer, or a coffee filter. Correct the sweetness, adding more sugar as needed to taste, and serve.

Chapter Six

MY MOVEABLE FEAST

1976–1977

With La Varenne pastry chef Albert Jorant.

I went to the newly opened La Varenne cooking school at 34 rue Saint Dominique in Paris one icy morning in February 1976 to interview its founder, Anne Willan, about the history of cooking. I left an hour later, signed up as a stagiaire.

Anne greeted me with a trademark English formality that would intimidate me for months. She was a stately woman with upswept brown hair and a widow's peak. Her accent belied her upper-class upbringing in Newcastle Upon Tyne in Yorkshire in northern England.

"Please sit," Anne said—as much an order as an invitation. "Tell me about this Watson project on medieval cooking."

What brought me to Anne's book-filled office was her current editorial project: *Great Cooks*. The book—still one of my go-to references—traced the history of cooking through its foremost practitioners—from the ancient Roman epicure Apicius to the epochal twentieth-century chef Auguste Escoffier.

When we finished discussing medieval cooking, Anne asked me if I wanted to join La Varenne's stagiaire program. I said yes without knowing what a stagiaire was.

A stagiaire, I quickly learned, is a cross between an intern and a galley slave. My job involved translating the live cooking demonstrations of La Varenne's French chefs into English for our primarily American students. I also wrote instructional booklets, proofread manuscripts, and did a dozen other tasks besides. Every morning, I donned La Varenne's signature brown-and-white-checkered shirt and dark pants. Every night, I couldn't wait for the next day to begin.

Anne Willan was one of the leading educators, food writers, and cookbook authors of my generation—a close friend of Julia Child and an indispensable link between French gastronomy and the burgeoning new American cuisine. (At age eighty-seven, she lives in London and still writes about food.) At its height, La Varenne was the most sought-after cooking school in the world.

Julia had a larger-than-life personality, and Madeleine Kamman had the bona fides of being a native-born Frenchwoman. But Anne brought to French cuisine an intellect forged at Cambridge University, where she earned a master's degree in economics. The author of thirty books, she had done stints as culinary advisor at the Château de Versailles and associate editor at *Gourmet* magazine. What inspired me was how she integrated serious journalism and meticulous historical research into practical, hands-on French cuisine. She is the intellectual of the food world. Over the decades, Anne would become my teacher, mentor, employer, landlord, and friend. She's also, indirectly, the reason I decided to pursue a career writing cookbooks.

The École de Cuisine La Varenne opened the year I embarked on my Watson Foundation Fellowship, occupying the first two floors of a nineteenth-century building that previously housed a bistro. Two blocks to the left stood the École Militaire—Louis XV's monumental military school and hospital, today the site of Napoleon's tomb. A short walk south was the Rodin Museum, dedicated to France's most famous sculptor. The neighborhood is home to foreign embassies and French ministries, not to mention the most beautiful bridge in Paris, the Pont Alexandre III. Approaching La Varenne from the east, I could see the tip of the Eiffel Tower soaring above the rooftops.

Anne named her school after François-Pierre de la Varenne (1615–1678), the chef considered to be the father of modern French cuisine. In 1651 La Varenne published *Le Cuisinier François,* the first French cookbook to extol the virtues of stocks, essences, and sauces. He broke with the excessive spicing and blurring of savory and sweet in the Middle Ages. He introduced reduction-based sauces and roux as a thickener and offered the first written recipe for *pâte feuilletée* (puff pastry).

Some years ago, I bought a third edition of La Varenne's book (a far cheaper version than the first edition owned by Anne), and while by today's standards, *Le Cuisinier François* is short on precise measurements and cooking times, it represented a giant leap forward from the vague instructions of the handwritten medieval cookbooks I studied for my Watson Fellowship. Several of the recipes, such as *bœuf à la mode* (wine-braised pot roast), *duxelles* (a mushroom pâté named for one of La Varenne's employers, the Marquis d'Uxelles), and *œufs à la neige* ("snow eggs," a milk-poached meringue dessert), remain part of the French culinary repertoire today.

I couldn't have dreamed of a more perfect graduate school than La Varenne. From Anne, I learned an enormous amount about food history—not only what happened, but how to research it. Anne and her husband, World Bank communications director Mark Cherniavsky, had amassed a world-class collection of antique cookbooks and reference works. "Feel free to use any of our books for your research," they graciously offered.

Equally important, Anne taught me how to draft recipes and write cookbooks. She used La Varenne as her test kitchen, developing recipes for both classes and her books. She tested recipes as many as a dozen times—often using ingredients smuggled back from the United States. American flour and bacon, for example, cook very differently than their French counterparts. Anne wanted to make sure her recipes would work in American kitchens.

La Varenne founder Anne Willan: employer, mentor, and friend.

During my tenure at La Varenne, Anne wrote her James Beard Award–winning *The Country Cooking of France*. Her *La Varenne Pratique* and seventeen-volume *Look and Cook* series set a new standard for culinary pedagogy.

She also taught me a great trick about editing that I use to this day (including for this book).

"When you proofread a book or article for the last time, start on the last page and work to the first," Anne explained. "You'll catch errors you glossed over because you've read the text from front to back so many times."

At the heart of the La Varenne educational experience was a team of extraordinary French chefs. First in command was Fernand Chambrette, former chef-owner of La Boule d'Or restaurant in Paris, which earned two Michelin stars in the 1950s. Chambrette shuffled around in checkered trousers and bedroom slippers, and could ream you out with swear words that would make a sailor blush. (He commonly referred to Anne as *la taulière,* "the warden.") The same man possessed an extensive library of rare books and once gave me a leather-bound edition of the poetry of the great medieval bad-boy poet, François Villon. Chambrette's food was exquisite in the sort of no-holds-barred butter-, cream-, and egg-yolk-centric style of old-time French cuisine. He could coax flavors out of trimmings and vegetable scraps that would normally be discarded. He could take the toughest, orneriest cut of meat and make it tender enough to cut with the side of a fork.

Albert Jorant was La Varenne's pastry chef, and he came to the school from the Cordon Bleu via yours truly. (He asked me to pass a message to Anne that he was interested in jumping ship to her new school.) A successful pastry-shop owner and caterer, Jorant could make puff pastry from scratch in minutes and pipe baking sheets full of *langue de chat* (cat's tongue) cookies and *biscuits à la cuillère* (ladyfingers) with the rapidity and precision of a machine. He'd intersperse his pastry demonstrations with magic tricks—making balls of brioche dough disappear only to pull them from my ear moments later. He was an unrepentant ladies' man, but his warm smile and gentle demeanor kept him from being too obnoxious.

Chambrette and Jorant were old-school chefs who began their culinary apprenticeships—schooled in blows and abuse—at the age of thirteen. They lived and cooked through the Nazi occupation of Paris. Jorant would tell us how he would add acorn flour to bulk up his loaves during the war. Understandably, under their watch, absolutely no food went to waste.

The third culinary musketeer was Claude Vauguet, considerably younger than Chambrette, but a master in his own right. Claude became a close friend and would often invite me and other stagiaires to dinner at his apartment with his wife, Suzanne. That itself was an education in how the French eat at home, with meals beginning with the aperitif (often a gentian-flavored liqueur called Suze) and, oddly, packaged peanuts. By the time we made it through the first course, main course, salad course, cheese course, dessert, and post-prandial Armagnac, it was well past midnight. More than a few times, I spent the night on their couch.

Anne Willan believed that the best way to learn French cuisine was through classical French recipes made with top-notch ingredients purchased several times a week at Rungis, the great food market outside Paris. I had never seen a chicken with its head, feet, and entrails intact, but those were the birds we worked with. Lobsters and eels arrived in wooden crates live and wriggling. The overriding message: Buy food in its natural state and leave your squeamishness at the door.

The La Varenne education unfolded in three phases. First were the "demos"—cooking demonstrations executed by one of the chefs and simultaneously translated into English by me and other stagiaires. Translation is an intoxicating activity: When you're in the groove, your mind occupies two spaces and two cultures at once. I quickly discovered I loved standing

La Varenne chef instructor Claude Vauguet.

in front of an audience—even if it was just to translate for the real star of the show, the chef. One day, a family friend sobered me up.

"Translating someone else's thoughts is admirable. But wouldn't you rather think important thoughts of your own and have someone else translate for you?" he said. That would occur many years later, as I came to give classes and lectures around the world.

A Chambrette demonstration might start with one of his La Boule d'Or specialties: *billi-bi,* for example, a mussel soup enriched with staggering quantities of *crème double* (heavy cream) and butter. He'd follow that with a *mousseline de coquilles St. Jacques,* an ethereal scallop mousse. Dessert might be another artery-clogging Chambrette specialty, *petits pots de crème*—vanilla, coffee, and chocolate custards thickened with a dozen egg yolks and served in tiny ceramic pots.

Meanwhile, a hands-on class with Chef Claude would take place downstairs. The students split into teams, each tasked with preparing part of the menu. One team would sauté fresh morels and *trompettes de la mort* (ominously named but innocuous "death's trumpet" mushrooms) to make a creamy mushroom soup called *velouté forestier*. A second team would transform a Rouennais duck (again with head, feet, and entrails intact) into a flambéed *canard à l'orange*. The third team might tackle a *feuilletée aux fraises*, a fruit tart constructed from hand-rolled puff pastry, made-from-scratch pastry cream, and strawberries more flavorful than any I had ever tasted in the US. As class drew to a close, the students would platter their masterpieces and, with no small pride, sit down to sample them at lunch.

Lunch was the third part of the La Varenne education, because each dish was dissected, analyzed, and critiqued by La Varenne director Gregory Usher. Gregory was an interesting man. Like James Beard, he came from Portland, Oregon, and like Beard, he was gay. He moved to Paris, drawn by the nonjudgmental lifestyle and especially by the food. Gregory knew more about Paris restaurants than most Parisians. You could count on him to take you to the bistro that served the best *pieds panés* (pan-fried pigs' feet) or *rognons à la moutarde* (kidneys with mustard sauce) in town.

Eventually, Gregory left La Varenne to become the first director of the Ritz-Escoffier cooking school at the Hotel Ritz on the Place Vendôme. Over the years, Gregory became a close friend, and we looked forward to seeing him whenever we visited Paris. Unfortunately, when the AIDS epidemic struck in the 1980s, he was one of its first victims. We think about him often and miss him to this day.

La Varenne's alumni went on to become magazine editors, cookbook authors, cooking school owners, and chefs—not only in the United States but in Australia, South Africa, and Anne's native England. Amanda Hesser, for example, joined *The New York Times* as a food writer before creating the popular website *Food52*. Scientist-inventor Nathan Myhrvold founded the Cooking Lab and wrote the authoritative six-volume *Modernist Cuisine*. Yet another La Varenne alum would specialize in global grilling and become the author of this book.

A LOT OF MY LEARNING took place by trial and error. One of a stagiaire's duties was to skim the enormous stockpot that simmered for hours on the kitchen burner. Stock involves simmering vast quantities of veal bones with aromatic vegetables to extract the flavor and gelatin. Conscientious skimming removes the fat, which would otherwise emulsify in the simmering stock, making it, in one of Chambrette's favorite words, *dégueulasse* (disgusting). But genius stagiaire Steven Raichlen thought he could take a shortcut. Since fat rises to the surface, why not skip skimming and simply refrigerate the stock once it's ready? The fat would congeal on the top, then could be removed in a sheet and discarded. Only it didn't congeal. Instead, the fat homogenized, turning the stock cloudy and gross.

"*Fous-moi ça à la poubelle,*" Chambrette said. ("Dump this crap in the

Translating for Michelin-starred chef and La Varenne culinary director Fernand Chambrette.

trash.") Ten kilos of veal bones and vegetables wasted. He wasn't very happy with me that day.

Another time, Chambrette procured one of the first black truffles of the season. I had never tasted the fabled fungus, and I could scarcely contain my excitement. Chambrette sliced a small truffle and mixed it with scrambled eggs, which he cooked the classical French way—in a double boiler over simmering water. (The idea was to make a smooth mixture more akin to hollandaise sauce than the curd-like scrambled eggs we eat in the States.) Come time to serve, Chambrette spooned the truffle slices onto my plate, saving the straight scrambled eggs for himself. At first, I was honored by his largesse, but I didn't quite understand why people made so much fuss about truffles.

"*Pauvre con*" (poor idiot), he said. "The flavor passes from the truffle to the eggs." I had the truffles, but he had eaten the portion with the taste.

From time to time, Anne would invite celebrity chefs to teach at La Varenne. One of the most anticipated was Paul Bocuse. The self-styled "emperor of nouvelle cuisine" achieved international renown for a luncheon he served at the Élysée Palace (the French White House) for then-president Valéry Giscard d'Estaing. Highlighting that meal was Bocuse's *soupe aux truffes,* beef consommé flavored with black truffles and foie gras, baked under a magisterial puff-pastry dome.

At La Varenne, he prepared another legendary Bocuse specialty: *poularde de Bresse en vessie.* The Bresse region east of Lyons reputedly produces the best chickens in France. Bocuse slid thinly sliced black truffles under the bird's skin, then stuffed the chicken into a pig's bladder, which looked like a leathery tan balloon. He tied the bladder tight with string, then poached the whole shebang in a huge pot of simmering chicken broth. Anne Willan herself did the translating; and Bocuse, a master of self-promotion, went on to describe his numerous decorations and accolades. As for the pig's bladder, it was supposed to seal in the chicken-and-truffle flavor, to be released in a rush of aroma when carved tableside.

Come time to present the chicken, Bocuse fished it from the broth and fumbled with the bladder to open it. I stood in the back of the room with the other stagiaires—too far away to savor the aroma. I was not so far away, however, as to miss the fact that the chicken was still raw at the bone. Even Bocuse, his ego for once deflated, admitted that the bird could have used more cooking.

Poaching. Steaming. These time-honored techniques were part of what showed me the limits of French cuisine and, indirectly, led me to barbecue. They subtracted flavor, not added it, resulting in anemic-looking food.

Searing. Browning. Charring. This is how flavor develops and where it resides. Give me a grilled chicken with char marks or a flame-darkened rotisserie bird, and you can have all the pig's bladders you desire.

One thing we did not do at La Varenne—or pretty much anywhere else in France at the time—was grill. A popular technique in the Middle Ages, when just about everything was cooked over a wood fire, grilling seemed to have been forgotten in the 1970s. Today, in a return to French cuisine's roots, marquee chefs are opening grill restaurants, like the charcoal-fired Clover Grill by Michelin-starred Jean-François Piège.

Anne and Mark lived in a luxurious apartment adjacent to the Champ-de-Mars. The Eiffel Tower soared just outside their window. When the couple went to their vacation home in Normandy, and later to their château in Burgundy, they let me stay in the apartment.

When Anne toured the United States, I often accompanied her as her assistant. I had my first taste of real barbecue on one of those trips. We were in Longview, Texas, doing a class and dinner at the home—make that mansion—of an oil mogul. The man served two hundred people on museum-quality china. I mean real china—the sort brought back on clipper ships in the early nineteenth century, pieces so valuable that the oil mogul insisted on washing each hand-painted plate himself.

Wanting me to have an authentic Texas experience, he took me to a tack shop to buy Tony Lama cowboy boots and a Stetson hat. Then he put me on a horse that broke into a gallop so fast I didn't have time to be frightened. That evening, we feasted on slow-smoked brisket at a restaurant called Bodacious Bar-B-Q. It would be another twenty years before I came to understand the labor and time that went into that brisket—and master the technique for barbecuing it myself.

When Anne and Mark bought Château du Feÿ, a seventeenth-century château near Joigny in Burgundy, they brought me to France for the summer to help them move in. I organized their vast library, hung paintings and engravings, and did a hundred other tasks to turn the château into a place where Anne could work. I'd later visit Anne and Mark at the château, graduating from worker to houseguest.

As my year and a half at La Varenne drew to a close, Anne and Mark made an extraordinary gesture. Knowing my passion for culinary history and my intention to continue my research, they bought me a library—books including André Castelot's *L'Histoire à Table* (*History at the Dining Table*) and *Le Grand Dictionnaire de Cuisine* (*The Great Dictionary of Cuisine*) by Alexandre Dumas. (Yes, *that* Alexandre Dumas, author of *The Three Musketeers* and *The Count of Monte Cristo.*) Those books still occupy a place of honor in my library today.

Anne gave me three more gifts—less tangible but no less important. The first was a model for uniting mind and hand—the intellectual component of gastronomy and hands-on cooking—which she had woven into the DNA of La Varenne. I had a paradigm for my life's work: I would cook. I would teach. And above all, I would write. My beat would be the intersection of food, literature, and culture.

As I was about to leave Paris, Anne Willan gave me another gift, in the shape of a warning: "You know, Steve"—back then I was Steve, not Steven—"you'll never make a living writing cookbooks." Never underestimate the power of wanting to prove an authority figure wrong!

The third gift, years later, was a romance. But I'll share that story later.

NINE LESSONS I LEARNED FROM JULIA CHILD

I first met Julia Child at La Varenne cooking school in Paris, where I was working as a translator and editorial assistant. For weeks, La Varenne buzzed about the upcoming visit of the most important person in the food world. To get ready, we scrubbed the school from top to bottom and planned the most elaborate menu we could think of. The day she arrived, I wore an ugly brown sports coat and ghastly wide tie—the only "dressy" clothes I owned. Of course, one belly laugh and whiplash handshake from Julia and I realized that what anyone wore or looked like mattered to the great lady not one whit.

A few years later, I took Barbara (then my fiancée, now my wife) to visit Julia and Paul at La Pitchoune, their farmhouse in Provence. Without telling her where we were going, we drove on a series of switchbacks near the perfume-making town of Grasse, Barbara growing increasingly curious with each passing kilometer. We parked at the end of a long driveway. The minute the first "Yoo-hoo" rang out, Barbara understood our destination: lunch with Julia Child.

After introductions and hugs, Julia put us to work peeling tomatoes, snapping green beans, and shelling hard-cooked eggs to make a *salade niçoise*. Barbara promptly forgot everything she had learned at La Varenne, including incising an *X* in the tomatoes before plunging them in boiling water for a few seconds to loosen the skin. I fumbled with the can opener as I tried to extract dark oily tuna fish from the can—no grilled tuna for Julia's niçoise salad.

Lunch took place outside on a shady terrace. Julia asked about Barbara's studies at La Varenne, and Paul showed us his paintings. Gradually we relaxed as Julia served the cheese course, then the sweet Cavaillon melons we had brought for dessert. We almost forgot we were dining with a culinary superstar.

I was also lucky enough to spend time with Julia at her home in Cambridge, Massachusetts. We shopped at the same market, Savenor's, and often dined at the same restaurants. She once came to my home for a caviar tasting, gamely ascending the three flights of stairs to my apartment.

Over the years, Julia gave me lots of advice about writing and about life. Here are nine lessons I learned from the grand dame of French cuisine.

Start with your ultimate goal in mind. Julia Child set out to master the art of French cuisine. (Hum, what a perfect title for a cookbook!) She pursued that goal with single-minded purpose, first at the Cordon Bleu cooking school in Paris, then by writing her groundbreaking cookbooks, then by pioneering a new television medium—the cooking show. She continued to teach, inspire, and entertain for the rest of her life.

Earn your chops. Julia elbowed her way into one of the most closed, male-dominated arenas of Gallic culture: French cuisine. She worked shoulder to shoulder with battle-hardened male students (many of them ex–World War II GIs) under chauvinistic French chefs. She practiced chopping endless batches of onions and other basic techniques at her apartment on the Rue du Bac so she could keep up with her fellow classmates. Once she graduated, she never hesitated to don a toque and call herself a chef.

Whatever you do, make it original. Julia's *Mastering the Art of French Cooking* sparked a revolution in American cuisine. It changed how we cook and eat forever. My first cookbook, *A Taste of the Mountains Cooking School Cookbook*, focused on the classic French cuisine I learned in Paris. Julia graciously acknowledged the book, but in her forthright way urged me to make my next book about a subject that hadn't been written about ad nauseum already (including by Julia)—a subject I could make my own.

When you find your subject, own it. I wrote a lot of cookbooks—some of them award-winners. But it wasn't until I moved to Miami that I wrote what I consider to be my first truly original book, *Miami Spice*. (Original in the sense that no one had done it before.) It took leaving my comfort zone, meeting a fresh crowd of food professionals, and immersing myself in a whole new set of ingredients and cuisines in the Caribbean-Latino-Deep Southern melting pot that defines Miami. When I won an IACP–Julia Child Award for the book, Julia looked me in the eye as if to say, "*That's* what I was talking about." It was one of the proudest moments in my life.

Write it, revise it, and revise it again. Julia took great pains to get it right, testing recipes over and over (she reportedly did her French bread fifty times) until she was satisfied that her results could be replicated with ingredients readily available in a typical American kitchen. Good writing takes a *lot* of rewriting. This book, for example, went through six drafts!

If you *really* want to be successful as a cookbook author, pick a subject with wide appeal, but take an approach that you, and you only, can do. *Miami Spice* did well (100,000+ copies well), but it remained a niche book. It wasn't until I wrote *The Barbecue! Bible* that I had a global bestseller. I didn't realize it at the time, and it certainly wasn't intentional, but I had stumbled onto a subject of enormously broad appeal. Everyone loves barbecue and just about everyone grills. But my approach—a global perspective on grilling—was different from every other book out there. The research was grueling and expensive, but that's what Julia's "unique approach" demanded.

Don't be afraid to take risks and make mistakes. Whenever I dined at Julia's Cambridge home, she served dishes she was in the process of recipe testing. Maybe they worked and maybe they didn't. I remember an autumn soup served in a whole Hubbard squash that collapsed at the table. Fortunately, Julia served it on a platter with a high rim. Julia scooped the soup into bowls as best she could and served it. It was delicious! As the French say, "You can't make an omelet without breaking some eggs." Writing a novel took me away from higher-paying assignments, but I wouldn't have wanted to leave this planet without having tried it at least once.

Surround yourself with young people. I was honored to be invited to Julia's home for dinner, of course, but at the time I didn't understand why. I was a fledgling food writer with just a few freelance stories under my belt. Julia surrounded herself not only with the acknowledged experts of the day, but the up-and-comers. Young people help keep you young. Just ask Julia's great friend Jacques Pépin, who at age eighty-one launched a foundation to celebrate the next and future generations of chefs. As I write this, he just celebrated his ninetieth birthday. This is as true in medicine as it is in the food world; as we age, we want doctors who are substantially younger than we are!

Get receipts. One day, I was behind Julia in the checkout line at Savenor's in Cambridge. I noticed she had divided her groceries in two piles and paid for them with separate credit cards. On the back of each receipt, she wrote what ingredients she had purchased and the purpose and recipe for each. It turned out she was being audited by the IRS. She made sure every business expense was really for business. Some years later, I was also audited, and I actually got a larger tax refund thanks to my Julia-inspired recordkeeping. Her advice paid off!

PETITS POTS DE CRÈME

(Insanely Rich Cream Custards)

La Varenne founder Anne Willan was my mentor, but it was her head chef, Fernand Chambrette, who taught me how to cook. Apprenticed at the age of thirteen, Chambrette rose through the harsh ranks of French cuisine to become chef-owner of one of the most celebrated restaurants in Paris in the 1950s: La Boule d'Or. Chambrette came of age under the influence of another celebrated twentieth-century chef, Fernand Point. When asked the secret of great cuisine, the latter famously replied: *Du beurre, du beurre, et encore du beurre* ("Butter, butter, and more butter"). Chambrette used butter, cream, and egg yolks with a profligacy that would shock today. The result was food so delicious I can still remember the taste decades later. Consider his *petits pots de crème*, insanely rich vanilla cream custards served in tiny ceramic pots. Yes, they contain dizzying doses of heavy cream and egg yolks. Yes, you'll love every bite. The recipe will leave you with a lot of egg whites. Use them to make meringue—or low-fat omelets to counterbalance the richness of the dessert.

Makes 6 pots de crème

2 cups heavy cream

½ cup whole milk

1 vanilla bean, split

6 to 7 tablespoons granulated sugar, divided, or to taste

A pinch of salt

6 large egg yolks

You'll also need:

six 6-ounce ramekins, plus a baking dish large enough to hold them

1. Preheat the oven to 300°F. Bring a saucepan or kettle of water to a boil.
2. Scald the cream, milk, vanilla bean, 3 tablespoons sugar, and salt in a

heavy saucepan—that is, gently heat it to a bare simmer. Remove the pan from the heat and set aside to let the mixture infuse for 15 minutes.

3. Set 6 ramekins in a large baking dish.
4. In a heatproof mixing bowl, place the remaining 3 to 4 tablespoons sugar and the egg yolks and whisk to mix, but not so much that the yolks become foamy.
5. Gently and gradually whisk ½ cup of the hot cream mixture into the yolk mixture. Gradually whisk this mixture back into the remaining cream in the saucepan.
6. Cook the yolk-enriched cream mixture over medium-low heat, stirring constantly with a wooden spoon, until it thickens slightly, about 2 minutes. When it's the proper consistency, it will thickly coat the back of the spoon. Under no circumstances let the mixture simmer or boil or you'll curdle the egg yolks.
7. Immediately, pour the custard mixture through a fine-mesh strainer into the ramekins. (Or strain it into a large measuring cup with a spout, then pour it into the ramekins.) Carefully add the hot water to the baking dish to come halfway up the sides of the ramekins, taking care not to drip any into the custards.
8. Place the baking dish with the ramekins in the oven and bake until the custards are just set, 20 to 30 minutes. To test for doneness, gently shake one of the ramekins; the custard should quiver, not ripple.
9. Remove the baking dish from the oven and transfer the ramekins to a wire rack to cool to room temperature. Refrigerate for at least 4 hours or as long as overnight. Serve with espresso spoons for eating, and think of Chef Chambrette and young Steven Raichlen when you take a bite.

Note: Chef Chambrette also made chocolate pots de crème. To do that, whisk 3½ ounces chopped bittersweet chocolate into the cream mixture while scalding it. Use only half a vanilla bean.

Chapter Seven

HUNGRY IN THE HUB

1977–1990

A restaurant critic maintains his anonymity.

In December 1977, thieves broke into my apartment in Cambridge. As they did the previous month. And three months before that.

At the time, I lived in a rent-controlled three-decker (make that tenement) in the pre-gentrified neighborhood of Central Square. The robbers didn't rifle my drawers for money. They didn't steal my camera, like they did on the last visit. They took what Karl Marx would have called my means of production: my IBM Selectric typewriter.

Fortunately, these thieves had a conscience of sorts, because they removed the page I was working on from my typewriter and left it on my desk. That page turned out to be the most lucrative piece of writing of my fledgling journalism career to date. It was a translation from the original French of a Marquis de Sade short story called "There's Room for Two." *Playboy* magazine paid me the then-astronomical sum of $400 for the work. To put that in perspective, the check would cover four months' rent. The story came out—much to the benefit of my bank account, and the disapprobation of my family. I then embarked on an exhaustive study of erotic French literature, looking for other ribald classics to translate. It was a curious way to make my French literature degree pay off.

I had moved to Cambridge to be with my girlfriend at the time, Susan, who was attending Harvard Law School. We lived in a group house (group meals, group chores) on Harvard Street. By then, I had decided what I wanted to do for a living: I wanted to be a food writer. So, I wrote three stories on spec (without a guaranteed purchaser) and mailed them off to potential publishers.

The first story profiled one of the chefs I trained with in Paris, Fernand Chambrette. I sent it to *The Washington Post*, where Susan's mother had a connection. Much to my delight, they published it. The second story chronicled my year studying medieval cooking on the Watson Fellowship. I sent it to *The Oregonian*—the daily newspaper of Portland, Oregon, where I went to college. They published it too.

The third story focused on chowder and its French antecedents. (Our word *chowder* comes from the French *chaudière*—the cauldron where fish stews were simmered.) I sent that one to *The Real Paper*, an alternative weekly

In my office—sans typewriter.

based in Cambridge. A week passed, then two, then four. No response. Finally, I screwed up my courage (I wasn't very assertive back then) and went to the editorial offices.

"It's not very considerate, not to mention very alternative, to ignore a struggling freelancer's query," I told the lifestyle-section editor.

Like my typewriter thief, she had a conscience too. She apologized and accepted my story. She took other stories I proposed, and pretty soon, I was writing food stories for *The Real Paper* on a regular basis. The pay, however, was something like $30 per story, which didn't go far toward paying the rent.

A few months earlier, I had applied to the Columbia University Graduate School of Journalism in New York City. But by the time I received my acceptance letter, I was making a living of sorts as a freelance writer. I turned Columbia down—much to the chagrin of my father. In retrospect, Columbia would have taught me a lot about journalism that I had to figure out the hard way. It probably would have paved the way to a staff position, instead of a life of freelancing. Which might have made my life more secure, but a lot less interesting.

Fortunately, the last month I was in Paris, I had secured a writing project that did provide some security. Claude Terrail, the owner of the celebrated La Tour d'Argent restaurant, had just published a memoir called *Ma Tour d'Argent*. I proposed translating it into English. I talked my way into an appointment with Monsieur Terrail, donning my best clothes (a ratty sports coat and worn khakis) for the meeting.

In 1976, La Tour d'Argent ("Silver Tower," literally) was arguably the most famous restaurant in Paris, possibly in the world. It had three Michelin stars and a sixth-floor dining room with a glass wall overlooking Notre Dame. The flying buttresses of the medieval cathedral loomed close enough almost to touch.

The original Tour d'Argent was a swanky inn built on the banks of the Seine in the late 1500s. It quickly became *the* place to see and be seen for Paris aristocrats during the reign of King Henri III. Legend has it that the fork first made its appearance in France at the Tour d'Argent at a dinner hosted by Henri's son. The history books recount extravagant banquets (one with forty separate courses) at the Tour throughout the seventeenth and eighteenth centuries. After the French Revolution, La Tour d'Argent became a restaurant, eventually purchased by one André Terrail in 1911. André's son, Claude, took over in 1947 and ran the restaurant until his death in 2006.

Claude Terrail was a tall man, regal in bearing, impeccably dressed, with a cornflower in his lapel. I could never imagine him in shorts or a T-shirt. He looked me up and down for what seemed like forever before deigning to shake my hand. I'm not sure what intimidated me more: his arrogant self-confidence or the opulent surroundings of his restaurant.

I enumerated my meager qualifications. Monsieur Terrail nodded distractedly.

I cited several passages from his book. Monsieur Terrail's interest perked up.

I told him what a brilliant writer he was and what a fascinating life he had led. For the first time in our interview, the restaurateur smiled.

Then he asked me a question that should have been obvious, but that, in my enthusiasm, I hadn't prepared for: "How much would my translation cost?"

I threw out a wild figure: 5,000 francs (about $1,200). Terrail agreed without hesitation (no doubt amused by how little I had asked for). The meeting lasted all of a half hour. I left with 2,500 francs and the promise of 2,500 more when I turned in the manuscript.

Back in Cambridge, I began my translation, scribbling a rough draft on a yellow legal pad. As the text unfolded, I learned how young Claude intended to pursue a career in acting but, at his father's urging, returned to the restaurant. At the outset of World War II he served in the French second armored division under General Leclerc. After France's surrender, he came back to Paris, where his first initiative was to wall off a large portion of La Tour d'Argent's wine cellar, keeping twenty thousand bottles of rare French wines out of the hands of the larcenous Nazis. After the war he was appointed a Commander of the Légion d'Honneur.

Of course, the irony of translating a memoir about a restaurant serving such exquisite food to such a big-spender crowd was not lost on me. At the time, I was earning $4,000 a year, and I could no more afford a meal at the Tour d'Argent than I could walk on the moon. (Curiously, that was the last year of my life I truly felt I possessed everything I wanted.)

Happily, my contract included a meal for two at the restaurant once I turned in the translation. The following June, true to his word, Terrail paid me the remaining 2,500 francs and invited me for lunch.

The view was every bit as spectacular as described in Terrail's memoir and the dining room lived up to the hype. The silverware was just that—solid sterling—and should a guest be tempted to purloin a knife or fork as a souvenir, the waiters discreetly added its cost to the bill. The phone booth was cleverly concealed in an eighteenth-century sedan chair—the sort nobles used to be carried around in before the French revolutionaries marched them to the guillotine.

The meal both impressed and disappointed. Ironically, the disappointment turned out to be the house specialty—*caneton Tour d'Argent*—a roasted Châlons duckling, its meat ceremoniously carved at tableside, its carcass pressed with equal ceremony in a monumental silver duck press to extract the juices and blood, which were then simmered into a sauce. In those days, *la nouvelle cuisine* was all the rage, and the duck sauce seemed as dated as the sedan chair and as leaden as medieval gravy. But the towering Grand Marnier soufflé for dessert, served with a seemingly endless succession of *mignardises,* candies, and petit fours, dazzled as much as the soaring view of Notre Dame.

When I turned in my translation—neatly typed and bound—Monsieur Terrail opened a drawer in his office. In it he showed me the half dozen other translations of his memoir that he had commissioned. My six months of hard work turned out to be a vanity project for a man who had a lot to be vain about.

Armed with "clips" (writing samples) from *The Real Paper* and a letter of recommendation from Monsieur Terrail, I approached larger publications. *Bon Appétit* magazine took my story on *nouvelle patisserie,* the pastry equivalent to the nouvelle cuisine that was revolutionizing France pastry shops. *Esquire* ran my story on escargots, then on steak tartare, then on islands off the west coast of Florida. (By then I had strayed into travel writing.) The

Los Angeles Times brought me on as a food columnist, reaching newspapers across the US. (That led to a Best Newspaper Column Award from the Association of Food Journalists.) Along the way, I started writing for *The New York Times.*

A new magazine with the obnoxious name of *Millionaire* sent me to Paris to write about a dream big-spender vacation. That story gained me rare access to Coco Chanel's private apartment. (On learning of her affair with a Nazi officer during the war, I lost interest.) It also got me into the hot new restaurant Robuchon, where Joël Robuchon, then a thirty-nine-year-old culinary wunderkind, had just achieved his third Michelin star. "My spoon—Christofle silver—glides through an ethereal layer of cauliflower cream to a cache of caviar encased in shimmering aspic," I wrote. "This must be what the angels eat." It also taught me to exercise caution about writing for new magazines. The extravagantly named *Millionaire* went bankrupt before I got paid.

Then, in March 1984, I received a call from an editor at *GQ* magazine. He had read my work in various magazines and wanted to talk. At the time, *GQ* wasn't really my sort of publication. I didn't even know it belonged to Si Newhouse, which made it one of the most prestigious and well-funded magazines in the world. The editor took me to lunch at Boston's power restaurant, Grill 23. He ordered martinis for us, then a second for himself, then a third. My head spun after a few sips.

"Would you be interested in writing a wine and spirits column for *GQ*?" the editor asked. "Does one thousand dollars per story sound okay?"

At the time, that was more than twice the going rate for my articles. Wine and spirits? *GQ*? Martini lunches? Heck, yeah!

Over the next two years, I wrote about vodka (which means "little water" in Russian). David Letterman was on the cover of that issue. Kurt Russell headlined the issue with my story on aperitifs (from the Latin *aprire*, "to open," as in a drink to open a meal with). Ted Danson companioned my

Reporting on wine from Beaune (Burgundy), France.

dessert wine story; Harrison Ford, my piece on eaux de vie (fruit brandies); Michael Douglas, looking like the thirtysomething he was back in 1984, highlighted the issue with my story on gifts for wine lovers.

I enjoyed every minute of those writing assignments. It didn't hurt that my subject matter contained alcohol.

I'VE ALWAYS LOVED RESTAURANTS for the obvious reasons: stimulating food, solicitous service, seductive surroundings. The way a good restaurant takes you out of the mainstream of your life for a few hours, creating a convivial space to share with family, friends, a business associate, a lover (or potential lover)—or all of the above. But even more than that, I love restaurants for what they can teach me: a new way to think about ingredients, flavors, and how to put them together. When someone tells me about a recent restaurant meal, I'm less interested in how they liked it. What I really want to know is what they learned.

"So what?" you're thinking. "Doesn't everyone love restaurants? Especially everyone in the food business?"

They don't. My wife, Barbara, for example, dislikes restaurants, even though she was a restaurant publicist for several decades. (Or perhaps *because* she was a restaurant publicist for several decades.) Give Barbara the choice between dining out or dining in and she'll almost always choose a meal at home.

I remember restaurant meals much better than I remember names, faces, and to-do lists. My first significant meal out took place at a long-gone restaurant in Baltimore, the 3900, where my family would go for Sunday-night suppers. A few years later, I took my first serious date not to the movies or a party, but to a restaurant. I saved my lawn-mowing money, and when I had enough, I invited her to a quirky Baltimore restaurant called Martick's. We feasted on sweet potato soup and lobster à la Martick (a riff on French lobster thermidor). We were too young to order wine, but we polished off the peach bread pudding with élan.

As for my first Michelin three-star in Paris, it wasn't La Tour d'Argent, but a restaurant named for a famous medieval chef. Taillevent occupied an elegant nineteenth-century townhouse in the tony sixteenth arrondissement. I tried to order the crayfish bisque followed by a langoustine gratin. The maître d' sternly observed that both dishes featured crustaceans.

"I don't mind," I said.

"But Monsieur," the maître d' objected.

"Really, it's okay. That's what I want."

We went back and forth a few times. Eventually, I let him talk me into sweetbreads for my main course instead. You could say I lost the battle, but I definitely won the war. I had never experienced a meal of such finesse.

So when at long last I got the call from *Boston* magazine, it was the opportunity I had dreamed of for a decade. "This is senior editor

Curtis Hartman," the voice said. "We need a new restaurant critic. Are you interested?"

I tried to sound noncommittal—a negotiating strategy that lasted for about sixty seconds. "When do I start?" I said. We met later that week.

Boston wasn't Paris, but then, as now, it was an interesting place to be a restaurant critic. Some of the oldest restaurants in America were still operating—landmarks like Durgin-Park (founded in 1827, at a time when patrons could order possum and bear); the men's club–like Locke-Ober (founded in 1875—women were banned from the dining room until 1970); and the Parker House, birthplace of the eponymous rolls and Boston cream pie. Incidentally, the Parker House is where a young chef named Emeril Lagasse from Fall River, Massachusetts, got his start.

Boston boasted distinctive local specialties, like fried clams (invented by "Chubby" Woodman on July 3, 1916), scrod (cod or haddock broiled with breadcrumbs and butter), brown bread, and Indian pudding. It gave birth to many other dishes that today are American icons, from seafood chowder to baked beans. It was home to distinguished cooking authorities, from Fanny Farmer to Julia Child. The first cookbook in colonial America was printed in Boston (Paul Revere engraved the plates). Boston also had thriving international communities: a historic Little Italy (the North End), a vibrant Chinatown, the world's third-largest Armenian population, and a sizable Portuguese community in Cambridge, not to mention a wealth of restaurants ranging from Ethiopian to Burmese.

All that I would learn, and a lot more, when I accepted Curtis's offer.

Curtis has a tactful way of saying a story needed rewriting. "Why don't you put it through your typewriter again," he would say.

My first column went back through the typewriter. I had reviewed an Armenian restaurant in Watertown. For a perverse reason I still can't explain, I wrote a poem to open the review, the refrain of which ran "Let's

Eat Armenian Tonight." (The lead was so childish, I still shudder to think of it forty-five years later.) I wondered if Curtis had hirer's remorse.

Then, there was the time I criticized a dish of beer-battered shrimp served with apricot-horseradish sauce. "So many competing flavors left the palate perplexed," I wrote. The owner of the restaurant, the Harvest in Cambridge, took me to task on that one, but Curtis stood by my silly remark.

One time Curtis and I attended a caviar tasting. I suspect neither one of us had ever sampled the good stuff.

"Imagine you were telling a reader who had never before eaten caviar," Curtis said. "How should he do it?" I surveyed the platter with beluga, blinis (miniature buckwheat pancakes), sour cream, sieved hard-boiled eggs, minced onion, and parsley. How complicated could it be?

"Spread a blini with sour cream, then spoon the caviar on top. Sprinkle with egg, onion, and parsley," I told him with as much conviction as I could muster.

I now know there's only *one* proper way to eat beluga: directly out of the tin with an ivory spoon, leaving the garnishes for everyone else.

Gradually, I found my groove with restaurant reviewing—inspired by an exciting new generation of chefs hell-bent on pushing Boston into modern times.

There was Jasper White, another former Parker House chef, whose eponymous restaurant in a former molasses factory reimagined chowders, cobblers, and Portuguese stews to create a sort of nouvelle New England cuisine. (His building had survived the Great Molasses Flood of 1919, which sent a tidal wave of two million gallons of molasses through Boston's streets, killing twenty-one people and injuring hundreds.)

There was Lydia Shire, who rose from salad girl at the hallowed Maison Robert to open such cutting-edge restaurants as Biba (short for "Back In Boston Again"), Pignoli, and Scampo. There weren't many American chefs who, like Lydia, installed tandoors (Indian barbecue pits) in their restaurants back then, and even fewer who, in their late seventies, still take on new projects today.

There was Todd English, whose Olives restaurant in the shadow of Bunker Hill revolutionized the local Italian food scene. Todd went on to open other branches of Olives in New York, Las Vegas, Mexico City, and beyond.

And Gordon Hamersley, of course, whose garlic- and lemon-roasted chicken raised French bistro dining to the level of art. We ate at Hamersley's Bistro in the South End every time we came to Boston until it closed—sadly—in 2014.

And who could forget a shy young Frenchman from Alsace who moved to Boston to helm the Julien restaurant at the then newly opened Meridien Hotel. "Chef Vongerichten serves some of the best food in Boston," I wrote in my review, praising his *oeuf au caviar*, "a meticulously hollowed-out eggshell stuffed with scrambled eggs, vodka cream, and beluga." His *ravioli de clams* "channeled traditional New England chowder in a pasta casing." Today he is better known by his first two names—Jean-Georges—and his restaurant empire now spans the planet.

But the restaurant that would have the most impact on me was the boisterous East Coast Grill in Inman Square in Cambridge. Chef-owner Chris Schlesinger built his menu around a wood-burning grill set smack-dab in the middle of the dining room. "The food at a Barbados beach shack excited me more than any French sauce I learned at the CIA [Culinary Institute of America]," Chris would say. Prophetically, his groundbreaking cookbook, *The Thrill of The Grill*, paved the way for future books like *The Barbecue! Bible.*

EVERY RESTAURANT CRITIC DEVELOPS his own code of ethics. Mine ran as follows:

1. When possible, dine anonymously.
2. Visit a restaurant at least two times; three times for a bad review.
3. Bring multiple guests, and make sure everyone orders something different.
4. Always pay for your food—even if you're recognized and the restaurant tries to comp you.
5. If a new restaurant is really awful, and you suspect the owner mortgaged his home to open it, just don't write about it rather than put the poor guy or gal out of business with a bad review.

I'm not sure that last one served my readers, but it left me with a clean conscience. Today, of course, thanks to Yelp and TikTok, everyone has become a restaurant critic. Not everyone should be. The average American eats fast food one hundred times a year. I don't mean to sound like a snob (actually, I do), but that's not someone I want telling me where to eat.

I took my restaurant critic job seriously and had the credentials to back it up. I trained with some of the finest chefs in Paris. I spent a summer working in the kitchen of a Michelin-starred restaurant, L'Auberge de la Porte, in Lannion, Brittany. I had a wall full of cookbooks in my library and traveled several months a year to educate my palate. People may not have agreed with my reviews, but I tried to make them consistent.

I wound up reviewing restaurants for *Boston* magazine for eight years. The first three years were a privilege; the next three were a job; the last two years bordered on penitence. But as a freelancer (a medieval military term, incidentally, referring to a soldier who hires himself out for pay), I was loath to surrender a steady paycheck.

In the end, it was a new editor at the magazine who made the decision for me. His name was Don Forst—a martinet who once left an expletive-filled message on my answering machine. (My parents happened to be at my apartment when I played it back—they were aghast.) One day, Forst called to give me a last-minute assignment. I was leaving for France the next day and told him I couldn't do it.

"You're fired," he said on the spot. Eight years of loyal service and, just like that, an upstart from New York at the magazine only for a few months fired me. He wouldn't even let me write a farewell column. In the ego-bruising shock that followed, I had lost my identity. For weeks I felt invalidated and crushed.

I didn't realize it at the time, but the man did me a favor. I came to understand that restaurant reviewing was a poor business model. I'd write a story that ran in one issue, then disappeared (except for out-of-date issues in doctors' office waiting rooms). I got paid once for work that ultimately wound up in the trash. In Marxian terms, I was a worker, but the means of production—much less the rewards—were beyond my reach.

No, if I was really going to make money in the writing game, it had to be for something I owned and could keep selling. Not a one-shot article for a newspaper or magazine. Or to put it in Marxist terms, I needed to own both what I produced and the means of producing it.

I remembered the words of my mentor, Anne Willan. "You know, Steven, you'll never earn a living writing cookbooks." But what if I could prove Anne wrong?

SMOKED FISH CHOWDER

Forget about baked beans and Boston cream pie. Forget about brown bread and Indian pudding. If there's one dish that epitomizes Boston cuisine, it's chowder. Chowder became a Bay State staple. It was made with ingredients fishermen readily had on hand: salt pork for richness; ship's biscuits for thickening; and fish, of course, as the primary protein. A "chouder" (chowder) recipe appeared in *The Boston Evening Post* as early as 1751—in rhyming couplets, no less! Herman Melville captured chowder's ubiquity in *Moby-Dick*: "I felt as if I had been stuffed with fishbones till they were coming out through my clothes." When I moved to Boston, chowder quickly became part of my culinary repertory, and in a gesture that would presage my *Project Smoke* TV show, I took to making it with smoked fish. I also replaced the traditional salt pork with bacon (it's more flavorful). Smoky, satisfying, and mercifully free of the usual starchy thickeners, this is chowder at its best.

Serves 4

1 tablespoon unsalted butter

2 strips smoky bacon, cut crosswise into ¼-inch slivers

2 leeks, trimmed, washed, and thinly sliced (about ¾ cup), or 2 shallots, peeled and minced, or 1 medium onion, finely chopped

2 Yukon Gold potatoes, peeled and cut into ½-inch dice (about 1 cup)

1 bay leaf

1 ½ cups bottled clam broth or chicken stock

1 ½ cups water or more chicken stock

1 cup half-and-half or heavy cream

1 pound kippered (hot-smoked) salmon, finnan haddie (smoked haddock), smoked trout, or other smoked fish, broken into 1-inch flakes

Sea salt and freshly ground black pepper to taste

2 tablespoons minced fresh chives or scallion greens

1. Melt the butter in a large heavy saucepan over medium-high heat. Add the bacon and cook until lightly browned, 3 to 4 minutes. Halfway through, add the leeks and cook until lightly browned as well, another 2 minutes. Stir in the potatoes and bay leaf and cook for 1 minute.
2. Stir in the clam broth, water, and half-and-half and gently simmer the

chowder over medium heat until the potatoes are almost tender, 6 to 10 minutes.

3. Stir in the smoked fish and gently simmer for 5 minutes more, or until the potatoes are cooked. Add salt (just a little—the clam broth and fish are already quite salty) and pepper to taste; the chowder should be highly seasoned.
4. Sprinkle the chowder with chives and serve at once.

Chapter Eight

"YOU'LL NEVER MAKE A LIVING WRITING COOKBOOKS"

1980–1990

My first office in Cambridge—surrounded, as always, by books.

Our word *book* comes from the proto-Germanic *bōk*, meaning "beech tree"—a reference to the beechwood tablets on which the early Germanic tribes carved runes (their mystical alphabet).

Our word *library* comes from the Latin *librarium*, "a place for books," which in turn comes from *liber*, thin sheets of tree bark on which the ancients wrote before the advent of wax tablets and scrolls.

Our word *bibliophile* (book lover) comes from Byblos, a Phoenician port city (today in Lebanon) famed for its papyrus—a river plant whose stalks provided writing material for the ancient Egyptians. (*Papyrus*, logically, gave us our word *paper*.) *Philos* was the ancient Greek word for "loving" or "friend"—an expression that survives today in Philadelphia, literally "City of Brotherly Love."

You've probably noticed by now that I'm an incorrigible logophile (lover of words).

By the time I had my Marxist epiphany—to make serious money I needed to own my writing, not just sell it outright month by month—I had already written two booklets and three books. The booklets were glossaries of French cooking terms and French garnishes that I wrote for La Varenne cooking school in Paris. The former covered 248 terms likely to be heard in a French kitchen (excluding French profanities, which were the likeliest to be heard of all). The latter focused not on tomato roses or decorative sprinkles of chopped parsley in the sense that we use the word *garnish* in English, but on a codified collection of auxiliary ingredients that define and complete a traditional French dish.

Huh? Let me explain.

In French cooking, garnishes aren't mere decorations; they govern a dish's flavor and identity. *A la Talleyrand*, for example, refers to France's

The first publications—admittedly modest—to bear my byline.

most famous diplomat, Charles-Maurice de Talleyrand-Périgord, who managed to remain a power broker throughout the most turbulent half century in French history. His gastronomic predilections ran to foie gras and black truffles, thus a dish with his name would contain these ingredients. The great chef Auguste Escoffier listed more than two hundred garnishes in his 1903 *Guide Culinaire,* and they contain powerful cultural messages about the places, people, and social structures that have shaped French cuisine.

The booklets were modest—thirty-some pages—but they bore my name as author and signature. I cannot tell you the pride I felt seeing my name in print. It was intoxicating. If seeing your byline is a drug, I was addicted.

My first full-length book was *Dining in Boston,* featuring menus and recipes from twenty-one top Boston restaurants. Much to my surprise, it made the local bestseller list. It did well enough to warrant a second edition, which came back from the printer missing two signatures—that's sixty-four pages. (A signature is a jumbo printed sheet folded and cut to make the smaller individual pages of a book.) Despite my protests, the publisher sold the book anyway, and I had to field irate letters from readers demanding a refund. The publisher was always late on payments—until he stopped making them altogether. Welcome to the world of publishing.

More books on Boston restaurants followed, including one published by *Yankee* magazine. The cover had a striking image of a lobster claw reaching for a lemon and an author photo of me in a tuxedo wearing a mask to preserve my anonymity. The advances and sales were modest, but at least these books had all their pages.

A quick side note on the economics of publishing you'll need to understand the rest of this book: Normally, the author earns a royalty—a percentage of the price for which each book is sold. That royalty can run as low as 4 percent for a softcover with full-color photos throughout (color photographs make a book more expensive to produce) and as high as 15 percent for a photo-less hardcover. Of course, if you're Stephen King, those numbers might stretch higher. Many contracts—including the one for this book—have an escalation clause: The royalty rate increases as certain sales thresholds are passed.

The publisher pays some of the royalty money in a lump sum up front to help the author cover research and living expenses. This is called the advance. The author seeks as large an advance as possible. That puts the onus on the publisher to sell enough books to recoup its investment. The publisher, on the other hand, tries to pay the smallest advance possible, leaving the author dependent on eventual royalties—which may or may not accrue.

The year after I moved to Boston, I decided to teach cooking classes in my rent-controlled apartment in Cambridge to augment my meager income from writing. (Meager? At one point I had $36 in my bank account.)

A journalist friend, Ken Winokur, wrote about my classes for an alternatively weekly newspaper, *The Boston Phoenix*:

> *Dinner tonight? How about a thick slice of veal pâté, a delicate cream of watercress soup, crab soufflé, a sauté of wild boar (always in season),*

> *dandelion salad, and a rich and luscious puff pastry with strawberries? Sound incredible? Actually, the wild boar is a humble pork shoulder in disguise, but everything else at Steven Raichlen's cooking classes is authentic, just as you would find in Paris—or, better yet, in that little out-of-the-way inn in the French provinces.*

My phone started ringing, and I quickly had eight students lined up for my first class.

I was too naive to ask for deposits, so only two students showed up. The three of us filed into my kitchen, where we cooked *cotriade Breton* (Brittany fish chowder), *navarin de mouton* (spring lamb stew), and a buttery *tarte aux poires normande* (Normandy pear pie) for dessert. I lost money on that class, but the wine flowed, so at least we had a great time.

My first cooking school: classes in my rent-controlled apartment in Cambridge.

Over the following weeks, more students trickled in, including two ladies from the posh suburb of Newton, who braved my dodgy neighborhood and draped their mink coats (really) on the secondhand couch in my living room. Another student, the maître d' of a prominent local restaurant, signed on, bringing serious wines to the class. The great time got even better.

Inspired by Julia Child and fueled by an insatiable hunger at the time for all things French (in the beginning, my menus were strictly French), my little cooking school did well enough to warrant a second weekly session, then a move out of my apartment. I started making guest appearances at cooking schools outside Boston. Before long I was teaching in Connecticut, Ohio, and California.

Around this time, I met an entrepreneur who had recently purchased the Bernerhof Inn in Glen, New Hampshire. Ted wanted to publicize the inn. Would I be interested in starting a cooking school there? We brought on a third partner, Cronan, and A Taste of the Mountains Cooking School was born.

The school came to the attention of *Bon Appétit* writer Zack Hanle, who wrote us up in the magazine. Soon, students flocked to our school from all over the country to learn French cuisine from an American cooking teacher in a Swiss-style inn in New Hampshire's White Mountains.

Hanle called A Taste of the Mountains "a perfect little school in a perfect setting." (Under her breath she muttered that it was barely organized chaos.) A few years later, *Bon Appétit* named me "Cooking Teacher of the Year."

Which brings me to my first serious cookbook.

In the mid-1980s, I connected with a New York book agent named Meg Ruley. Meg thought she could sell *A Taste of the Mountains Cooking School Cookbook*. Sure enough, a month later I had a contract from Poseidon Press, a division of Simon & Schuster. The advance was $30,000—substantially more money than I made in a year. (Fun fact: Julia Child received an advance of $1,500 for *Mastering the Art of French Cooking.*)

I decided this would be a teaching cookbook. Each of the fifty-three lessons would explore an essential technique or iconic dish—explained in a master recipe. Two or three variation recipes would follow, showing the versatility of the technique.

I began with soups, such as *potage garbure*—a wine-enriched vegetable soup from the southwest of France. (In the movie *Jean de Florette,* Ugolin Soubeyran adds wine to his soup in just this manner.) That lesson focused on the proper way to slice and dice vegetables and how to sharpen and care for knives. As the book unfolded, I explained how to make mayonnaise from scratch, how to "purge eggplants" (by sprinkling them with salt to draw out bitter juices), and how to steam duck before roasting to reduce the fat and crisp the skin.

To illustrate the book, I enlisted my artist friend Susan Mattman. We decided that my pedagogical approach would be best served by Susan's charming pen-and-ink drawings.

But my real goal was to teach process, not recipes.

A Taste of the Mountains Cooking School Cookbook came out in spring 1986. *Publishers Weekly* called the book "affable, nondogmatic, venturesome . . . an impressive cookbook."

Publishers play a long game—or at least they used to. Sometimes they have to invest in multiple books before a relationship with an author pays off. That was the logic Meg used to sell my second book to Poseidon, wisely completing the transaction before the publisher saw the first book's final sales numbers.

Enter my treatise on seasonal cooking: *A Celebration of the Seasons.*

"For all human history," I wrote in the introduction, "save the last hundred years, people have feasted on seasonal produce." Thus, the book would unfold month by month, exploring the season's best foods and how to cook them. I explained the origins of the month names (did you know that July was named for Julius Caesar?); I evoked my adventures foraging for fiddlehead ferns in Vermont and clamming on Cape Cod. I ended the book with a fundamental truth: "No amount of culinary artifice can rival a fresh ingredient that is simply cooked and served at its seasonal best."

A Celebration of the Seasons*: my love song to seasonal cooking.*

Up to this point, I thought the author's task was simple: Write the book and trust the publisher to do the promotion and sales.

Man, was I wrong. I delivered the manuscript, sat back in my office, and waited for the royalties to roll in. I couldn't understand why they didn't. I now owned my work, no longer doing it for just hire (thanks, Karl Marx). But ownership didn't translate into revenue.

To make that happen, I would need to take three steps:

- Move to Miami.
- Marry a publicist.
- Switch to a publishing house called Workman.

A TASTE OF THE MOUNTAINS CHEESE FONDUE

We served cheese fondue at the welcome dinner at A Taste of the Mountains Cooking School. I know—no one gives fondue sets as wedding presents anymore. But cheese fondue is anything but dated. I found it everywhere on a recent trip to Switzerland, and it's a welcome après ski classic the world over. To up the ante, I call for dipping broccoli, mushrooms, cherry tomatoes, and kielbasa in the fondue in addition to the traditional bread.

Serves 4

For dipping:

1 crusty baguette, cut into 1-inch chunks

1 bunch broccoli, cut into 1-inch pieces, parboiled in lightly salted water for 3 minutes, then drained, rinsed under cold water, and drained again

6 ounces small fresh button mushrooms, trimmed and wiped clean with a damp cloth

1 crisp apple, cored and cut into bite-size chunks

8 ounces kielbasa or other cooked sausage, sliced ½ inch thick

For the fondue:

4 ounces Gruyère cheese (preferably cave-aged), coarsely grated

4 ounces Emmenthaler cheese, coarsely grated

1 tablespoon all-purpose flour

¼ teaspoon cayenne pepper

¼ teaspoon grated nutmeg

1 teaspoon extra-virgin olive oil

1 clove garlic, peeled and cut in half

1 cup dry white wine

1 tablespoon kirsch (cherry brandy) or cognac

Salt and freshly ground black pepper to taste

You'll also need:

a fondue pot with long-handled forks

1. Arrange the dipping ingredients on a platter.
2. Place the grated cheeses, flour, cayenne, and nutmeg in a mixing bowl and mix well with your fingers. Lightly oil the inside of a fondue pot or saucepan and rub it with the cut garlic. Add the wine and bring to a boil. Gradually stir in the cheese mixture with a wooden spoon. Bring the fondue to a boil to melt the cheese, then turn the heat down and simmer until thick and bubbling, 2 to 3 minutes. Stir in the kirsch and season with salt and pepper to taste.
3. Have each guest skewer bread pieces, vegetables, and kielbasa and dip them into the fondue. The cheese that burns onto the bottom of the pan is considered the best part of the fondue—scrape it out with your fondue fork.

Note: To give the fondue a bit of Raichlen smoke and fire, substitute smoked provolone or cheddar for the Emmenthaler cheese, and grill the bread and vegetables.

Chapter Nine

A TASTE OF THE TROPICS

1990–1998

Barbara in her white angora sweater meets a young food writer at La Varenne.

Miami is different. Miami is weird. And never did it feel weirder than during my first Thanksgiving as a full-time Floridian. I had moved here from New England, where T-day meant frosty windows (and sometimes snow) and mountains of traditional foods enjoyed by the warmth of a blazing fireplace. Traditional meant roast turkey with stuffing, cranberry sauce, mashed potatoes, sweet potato casserole, and pumpkin pie.

Here I was surrounded by palm trees, with a temperature in the mid-eighties. Our housekeeper, Elida Proenza, cooked our turkey Cuban-style, which meant stuffed under the skin with *adobo* (cumin–sour orange marinade) and sauced with *mojo* (Cuba's ubiquitous fried garlic citrus sauce). Black beans and rice replaced the mashed potatoes, and an odd root vegetable called boniato stood in for the sweet potatoes. (Boniato has a pleasing chestnut flavor I quickly grew to like.) For dessert we feasted on another Florida specialty: key lime pie.

Like I said, it was weird.

People move to Miami for different reasons. For some, it's the weather. (I must admit—after fifteen years in Boston, it's nice to be able to wear shorts and a T-shirt in January.) For others, it's the beaches and water. (As a boat guy, I certainly appreciate being able to sail year-round.) For yet others, it's the absence of state income tax. (A welcome benefit after the hefty vig I paid in Massachusetts.) But my reason was infinitely more complicated: I moved there for love.

When I was at La Varenne, I met a stunning brunette with bright red lipstick and nail polish. Barbara Seldin was smart. She was sexy. She was self-confident and stylishly dressed—which left me wondering what she could possibly see in me.

We made eye contact during one of the classes I was translating. I watched her turn to whisper to the friend sitting next to her. Had I been able to eavesdrop, I would have heard her say, "Wow, he's cute and he speaks French."

Then the chef encountered a difficulty—seized chocolate or a curdled crème anglaise—I don't remember. I liberally translated his explicative as "Oy."

"My God," Barbara said to her friend. "He's Jewish. That's the man I'm going to marry."

I never had a prayer.

After our ten-year courtship (it takes some guys a while to recognize a good thing—even when it hits them over the head), Barbara and I finally tied the knot.

They say opposites attract. We couldn't have been more different. Barbara lived with her two kids in a townhouse in the Miami suburbs. (She had been married previously.) I had two cats in a rent-controlled apartment in Cambridge's funky Central Square. Barbara had four TV sets. I didn't own one. Barbara drove a silver Peugeot. I got around in a vintage Volkswagen.

Barbara was a restaurant publicist. I was a restaurant critic who avoided publicists like the plague. Barbara dressed up in white angora sweaters and heels. I dressed down in my habitual flannel shirt and desert boots. Barbara's favorite song at the time was "Cracklin' Rosie" by Neil Diamond. I was deep into Dylan. (One listen to *Highway 61 Revisited* turned Barbara into a bigger Dylan fan than I am.) Barbara is hyper-organized. I was and am chaotic—tendencies that characterize us to this day.

But we did have a few things in common. We both loved food and cooking. We both loved France and French cuisine. We were both Jewish, which was a sine qua non for dating Barbara. As for me, Barbara was one of the rare Jewish women I had dated, my preference up to that point tending toward Catholics. (Catholics, like Jews, I would joke, share a finely tuned sense of guilt.)

Once a month, I would fly to Miami or Barbara to Boston. Nightly we would speak on the phone. We spent summers together in France and winter breaks traveling the Caribbean, Florida Keys, or wherever my writing assignments took us.

On my first trip to Miami, I met Barbara's kids. Betsy (age eight at the time) produced a pink boom box and demonstrated her latest gymnastics routine. Jake (age ten) promptly carried my suitcase from Barbara's room to the guest room. (I get it, kid: no premarital fraternizing.) As an avowed bachelor, my experience with kids was limited. What was I getting myself into?

Long-distance relationships have advantages. Every time you meet, it's a honeymoon. On the downside, it takes time to get reacquainted—it's sort of like a first date all over again. You don't get an accurate sense of what living with the other person is really like. Suffice it to say that, for both of us, cohabitation required major adjustment.

Barbara was born and raised on Miami Beach, making her a rarity in this city of transients and immigrants: a native. Her father owned the legendary Raphil's deli. Frank Sinatra, Dean Martin, and Sammy Davis Jr. lunched here often when they were in town; crime boss Meyer Lansky had his corner stool on Fridays. Barbara's roots in Miami run deep, and even now, her Beach High friends play a big part in our life.

Sometimes, Barbara's larger-than-life personality drove me crazy. Other times, I couldn't imagine living without her. So, seven years into our courtship, I did something that surprised both of us. I proposed.

At the time, I was still restaurant critic for *Boston* magazine. Once a year, we did an issue on the country inns of New England. I knew the owner of the Four Columns Inn in Newfane, Vermont, from a previous story, so I called ahead with a few special requests. The first was to have flowers and champagne waiting for us at our table. The second was to ask the chef to insert two carrots upright in a French bread and deliver it at my signal. We took our seats, and the waiter poured the champagne. I dropped on bended knee and took Barbara's hand.

"These flights and phone calls to Miami are bankrupting me," I said. "Will you marry me?"

Barbara turned the color of our soon-to-be-served beet salad and said, "Yes." Affection played a part in her response, but so did embarrassment. "Everyone in the dining room is looking at us!" she said. She just wanted me to get up.

As for the French bread with carrots, it was an IOU of sorts. Barbara had confided she wanted a two-carat diamond engagement ring with step-down baguettes. (Carat—carrot. French bread—baguette. Get it?) We called our respective parents: mine surprised; her mother skeptical. But nowhere as skeptical as Barbara's friends. "You're giving up your alimony for a starving writer from Cambridge?" they asked incredulously.

Ten years to the day since I met her, I married Barbara Seldin in Miami.

It shows the faith Barbara had in me to become a decent breadwinner—faith I'm not sure I had in myself.

The next question was where to live. Barbara had a thriving public relations business. As a writer, I could work anywhere. We decided I would move to Miami. Twenty-seven cartons of my books arrived at Barbara's townhouse before I did. The next time the UPS delivery truck pulled up, Barbara hid.

Our wedding invitation pictured a pair of flamingos: a pink one with a thought bubble over its head reading: "This is the man I'm going to marry." The thought bubble over the blue flamingo said: "Cute, but not to be taken seriously." The inscription on the inside of the invitation read: "Barbara and Steven invite you to their wedding on October 20, 1990." Ten years to the day had passed since I first spotted that cute brunette in cooking class, and Barbara whispered to her friend: "That's the man I'm going to marry."

IF I HAD MADE A LIST of the one hundred cities in the world where I would want to live, Miami would not have been among of them. I always thought of America's southernmost metropolis as a cultural wasteland. I was giving up Cambridge with its multitudinous museums and bookstores for a hedonistic city where every third shop seemed to sell bathing suits.

But Miami did have one thing going for it: It was in the midst of a culinary revolution. A new generation of chefs was pioneering a new regional American cuisine. They called themselves the "Mango Mafia" and they wove tropical ingredients, Caribbean and Latin American cooking techniques, and an estival dining style into a cuisine we could truly call our own.

They sure had a lot to work with. Exotic fruits such as mangoes, lychees, mameys, sapotes, and starfruit from the Redlands, an agricultural district south of Miami. Caribbean tubers, like yuca, boniato, and malanga. Oysters from Apalachicola and stone crabs from the Florida Keys. More than five hundred kinds of fin fish, including snapper, pompano, and mullet. (Mullet, I would learn, is popular as a smoked fish dip on Florida's west coast.)

But even more influential was Miami's incredible cultural diversity. Even back then, 50 percent of our population spoke Spanish as a first language (today, that figure is closer to 80 percent). Our utility bills and voter ballots come in three languages: English, Spanish, and Creole. Miami boasts the largest Haitian population outside of Haiti and the largest Venezuelan community outside of Caracas. As for Cubans, we often joke that Miami is Cuba's sixth province. Miami may be the southernmost city in the United States, but its heart beats to the pulse of Latin America.

Miami diets reflect that melting pot culture too. For many Miamians, breakfast means *croquetas* (ham croquettes) and *cortadito* (murderously strong Cuban coffee with sugar and hot milk). At lunch, we eat *medianoches* (ham-, pork-, pickle-, and cheese-stuffed "midnighter" sandwiches) or *arepas* (Colombian cheese-filled corn cakes). Miami's culinary lexicon is filled with unfamiliar food terms, like *maduros* (candy-like fried sweet plantains), *griots* (fiery Haitian fried pork bites), *pastelitos* (sugared meat pies), and *tres leches* (Nicaraguan "three milks" cake). In case you're wondering, the three milks are cow milk, evaporated milk, and sweetened condensed milk.

When the Mango Mafia considered the rising popularity of such regional American cuisines as Cajun, Southwestern, and Californian, they saw no need to imitate Paul Prudhomme, Mark Miller, or Alice Waters. Florida was like a blank canvas waiting for culinary innovations of its own. And my wife, Barbara, publicist to these rising culinary stars, was right in the thick of it.

Barbara represented three of Miami's most talented chefs. First came Mark Militello of Mark's Place in North Miami. His daily-changing menu included the likes of Key West pink shrimp brûlée (topped with a giant potato crisp crust) and icky-sticky coconut pudding with toffee rum sauce for dessert. Allen Susser—better known by the name of his restaurant, Chef Allen—applied classical cooking techniques to edgy Florida ingredients. Creations such as stone crab cobbler and mango tarte tatin with foie gras earned him the title of "The Ponce de Leon of New Floridian Cooking."

A third client, Efrain Veiga, owned the popular YUCA—a Hispanic root vegetable and a playful acronym for Young Urban Cuban American. YUCA chef Douglas Rodriguez turned traditional Cuban cooking on its head, serving dishes like guava-glazed baby back ribs with yuca fries, and a chocolate "cigar" that paid homage to Cuba's coveted *cohibas*.

Collectively, they created what journalists hailed as the "New Floridian cuisine." Their restaurants received rave write-ups in all the major food magazines. Barbara made sure of that.

We had the chefs and restaurants, a multilingual food culture, and a cornucopia of unique ingredients. The only thing we lacked to make it official? A cookbook.

IT'S ONE THING TO CONCEPTUALIZE a book. It's quite another to sell it. My previous two cookbooks—*A Taste of the Mountains Cookbook* and *A Celebration of the Seasons*—came out with a major New York publisher. The critics were more enthusiastic than the book-buying public. I was not well known outside of Boston at the time, and I didn't realize that an author's job was not just to write the book but to promote it.

So when it came time to find a publisher for *Hot Food* (my awful working title for the book that would become *Miami Spice*), I basically started from scratch. I sent pitch letters to twenty publishers; six agreed to meet me in person. Barbara and I flew to New York for a week. I learned the meaning of pounding the pavement. I introduced myself to editors at Simon & Schuster, Harper & Row, William Morrow, Random House, Penguin, and Workman. The first five were conventional publishers with spacious conference rooms and orderly cubicles with tidy desks. I was politely received and told my proposal sounded "interesting." I quickly learned that "interesting" is publishing shorthand for "not interested."

Workman Publishing was my last stop. I rode a rickety elevator to the sixth floor of 708 Broadway in Greenwich Village. I walked into utter chaos. Books stood in towering piles everywhere; papers cascaded off worktables, and people sat cross-legged in the aisles collating manuscripts. From the relaxed dress code, it was hard to tell the interns from the bosses. A petite slender woman introduced herself as Suzanne Rafer and led me to an office where more books stood in more perilous stacks and unruly piles of papers carpeted her desk. Every two minutes, someone would rush in with layouts to approve or galleys for Suzanne to review. It was pure pandemonium and, for the first time in a week, I felt at home. I returned to our hotel ecstatic. "I found my publisher!" I told Barbara. "I was born to be a Workman author."

Suzanne Rafer was a legend in the editorial world. She had recently turned *The Silver Palate Cookbook* by Sheila Lukins and Julee Rosso into a multimillion-copy bestseller. (Chicken Marbella, anyone?) When it came to dotting i's and crossing t's, no one was more conscientious, but she also saw the big picture. It was Suzanne who would turn my bland *Hot Food* title into the sizzling *Miami Spice*.

At the end of our meeting, Suzanne introduced me to a tall man with a shock of brown hair, shirtsleeves rolled up, and a paisley tie dangling from his collar. His desk was less messy than Suzanne's, but only slightly. He stood up, shook my hand, and introduced himself as Peter Workman. He was so unassuming, it took me a moment to realize that this was *the* Peter Workman—one of whose first books, *The Official Preppy Handbook,* became a million-copy bestseller. (I remember when the book came out—my Aunt Linda bought me a copy.) Peter's publishing successes included the *Brain Quest* series (more than fifty million units sold) and the internationally bestselling *1,000 Places to See Before You Die*.

Over the years, Peter would become a mentor and friend, and I would go on to publish fifteen books and counting with Workman. I didn't know that then. What I did know was that my Florida cookbook proposal disappeared in the mounds of manuscripts on Suzanne Rafer's desk and it would take nine months for her to decide to publish it. During those months, I came close to telling her where she could shove my manuscript several times. But the ever-wise Barbara reminded me that silence did not mean outright rejection. I had plenty of that from the other publishers I met with in New York. No one else wanted my Florida cookbook.

Finally, Suzanne came to Miami. Barbara arranged a spectacular dinner for us at Mark's Place. Suzanne told me that Workman would, indeed, publish the book and offered me a respectable advance. Patience, I learned, pays off.

THE RESEARCH FOR *MIAMI SPICE* began, as with most of my books, with a road trip. Over the next year, Barbara and I crisscrossed the state, ferreting out restaurants, chefs, dishes, and recipes that tell the story of Floridian cuisine.

In Key West (known locally as the "Conch Republic") we feasted on conch fritters, conch salad, and "cracked conch" (breaded fried conch steaks)—a legacy of the once-thriving conch fishery here. Today, conch is a protected species, so restaurants use shellfish imported from the Bahamas.

In Christmas, Florida (located halfway between Orlando and Cape Canaveral; population 1665), I visited an alligator farm. Yes, we eat fried alligator here in Florida—it tastes like a cross between pork and perch. Barbara said no thanks.

In Okeechobee we drove past the vast fields of sugarcane that make Florida the number one sugar producer in the US. Visit a *loncheria* (Cuban lunch counter) in Miami and you can try *guarapo,* freshly squeezed sugar-cane juice, which has a surprising acidic edge that balances the sweetness.

Much of my research was participatory.

In the Everglades, I rode on an airboat one night, "jigging" for frogs, whose sweet meaty legs have been a delicacy in Miami since the days of the Tequesta Indians. You do this on a dark night so you can spot the green glow of the amphibians' eyes.

In Biscayne Bay, I boarded a crab boat to learn the renewable art of harvesting stone crabs: Snap off the claws and return the live crabs to the water. In a year or so, they grow new claws, known as "retreads." I wrote about that adventure for *The New York Times.*

In the Redlands agricultural district, I learned how to "hedgehog" a mango (slice and cut it in a crisscross pattern and turn it inside out so that the fruit sticks out in easy-to-eat diamonds). Farmers Kiki and Mark Ellenby introduced me to jackfruit, a huge armadillo-shaped fruit that tastes like a cross between melon, honey, and apricot. (Today vegetarian pitmasters use jackfruit to make vegan barbecue.) I also sampled monstera deliciosa, a weird phallic-shaped fruit covered with green scales and a soft musky flesh that tastes like a cross between banana and lychee.

In Islamorada in the Florida Keys, we sipped rum runners—the signature drink at the Holiday Isle Tiki Bar, where bartenders (they weren't called mixologists back then) blend banana and blackberry liqueurs, orange and pineapple juices, grenadine, and two kinds of rum into a cocktail that goes down as easily as it packs a wallop.

Closer to home, Barbara took me to Joe's Stone Crab, founded in 1913 by New York waiter Joe Weiss, who retired to Florida to open a tiny eatery at the southern tip of Miami Beach. Today, the restaurant seats 450 and serves up to 1,800 people a day. Miami Beach boasts hundreds of new restaurants, but my family still celebrates birthdays, anniversaries, and graduations at Joe's, much as Barbara and her parents did when she was growing up.

Publisher Peter Workman and editor Suzanne Rafer at the launch of Miami Spice.

To test my recipes, I hired a young woman named Michelle Bernstein—a dancer who thought she might like a career in cooking. We tested each of the two hundred recipes at our home in Coconut Grove—another reason why Barbara deserves sainthood.

Miami Spice came out in 1993 and became my first 100,000-plus-copy bestseller. A year later, it won an IACP–Julia Child Cookbook Award for Best Regional American Cookbook. I had a new publishing partner—Workman Publishing—a relationship that still thrives after three decades.

AND THE LEGACY OF *MIAMI SPICE*? My recipe tester, Michelle, went on to train with French superstar chef Jean-Louis Palladin and became a TV chef and serial restaurateur. Her latest ventures at this writing are Sra. Martinez in Coral Gables and La Cañita in Kendall—both high-style restaurants specializing in modern Hispano-Miami cuisine. I have no doubt she'll open more in the years to come.

Speaking of restaurants, my book even had a brief reincarnation as a restaurant in Hong Kong. A restaurateur there had acquired a copy of my book. He asked to license the *Miami Spice* concept for Asia. The menu would be based on the recipes in the book. We helped him source Haitian art and Fiestaware crockery in Miami to decorate the restaurant. One warm spring day, we arrived in Hong Kong and watched a human chain ferry the artwork, plates, cookware, and ingredients to a second-floor dining room at 12–16 Humphries Avenue in the trans Hong Kong Harbor neighborhood of Tsim Sha Shui. Barbara's son, Jake, served as chef. The restaurant opened to critical acclaim and was successful—until it wasn't. Two years later, like most restaurants that open anywhere, it closed.

In the decades that followed the publication of *Miami Spice,* our local restaurant scene came to be dominated by New Yorkers. Happily, the pendulum has swung back, and today many of Miami's popular chefs are homegrown.

Meanwhile, I was about to meet my real destiny, and yes, it involved a grill.

MANGO-SPACHO

Mango-spacho is the perfect embodiment of the new Floridian cuisine. It starts with the best of our abundant tropical fruits: fresh Florida mango. You serve it cold, which brings welcome relief in our steamy summers. It takes its inspiration from Spain—a nod to our Spanish-speaking community (which makes up about 80 percent of Miami's population). And it takes all of ten minutes to make, which leaves you plenty of time to go to the beach.

Serves 4

3 to 5 cold, ripe mangoes (my preference goes to the Tommy Atkins variety)—enough to make 6 cups diced

¾ cup very finely diced red onion

1 cucumber, peeled, seeded, and very finely diced (about 1 cup)

¼ cup extra-virgin olive oil

2 to 3 tablespoons rice vinegar

½ cup water

½ cup finely chopped fresh cilantro or ¼ cup chopped fresh mint leaves

1 to 2 tablespoons sugar (white, light brown, or dark brown—your choice), or to taste

1. Peel the mangoes and cut into ¼-inch dice, discarding the pits. Place the diced onion in a strainer and rinse under cold running water for 1 minute.
2. Combine 4 cups of diced mango, half each of the onion and cucumber, the olive oil, vinegar, water, and half the cilantro in a blender; and blend to form a smooth, pourable puree. If the mixture is too tart, add a bit of sugar to taste for sweetness.
3. Pour the mango mixture into 4 soup bowls. Spoon in the remaining diced mango, onion, and cucumber. Sprinkle with the remaining cilantro and serve at once.

Chapter Ten

FOLLOW THE FIRE: THE BIRTH OF *THE BARBECUE! BIBLE*

1998–2002

The Barbecue! Bible*: my 556-page homage to the art of global grilling.*

Half a million years ago, the world witnessed a revolution. An ape-like creature destined to become man became the first animal to cook its dinner. The mastery of fire by Homo erectus *. . . ultimately led to language, art, religion, and complex social organization. In other words, you could truly say that barbecue begat civilization.*

I wrote these lines at the start of a book that changed my life forever. That book was *The Barbecue! Bible* (I'll explain the exclamation mark in a minute), and I like to think it launched the modern barbecue revolution.

The Barbecue! Bible went on to sell more than a million copies, with translations in a dozen languages. That it's still in print more than a quarter century later speaks to our enduring passion for live-fire cooking and the foresight of my publisher (more on that in a minute too).

Some book ideas are the result of months or years of reflection. *The Barbecue! Bible* came to me like a thunderbolt. The year was 1994, the second week of November; the place, my home in Coconut Grove, Florida. I remember the weather (a clear, sunny day without an ounce of humidity), where I was sitting (on an Adirondack chair on whose arm I would balance my laptop), and even what I was wearing (a white polo shirt and blue shorts).

Time slowed down, as it does at life-changing moments. It was as though I heard a voice from on high ordering me to "follow the fire."

Well, maybe it was a little less biblical than that. What the voice really said was:

"Grilling is the world's oldest and most universal cooking method, but every culture does it differently. Wouldn't it be cool to travel around the world and document how grilling varies from country to country?" If I planned it right, I could make it my midlife Watson Fellowship. Normally, book proposals take weeks to write. I dashed this one off the next morning. Normally proposals take weeks or months to be accepted or rejected. Two weeks later I had a contract. Workman offered me a six-figure advance, which was more money than I had ever seen in my lifetime.

It was only after I signed the contract that I realized what a colossal—make that foolhardy—project I had undertaken. I had pledged to travel around the world documenting grilling on every continent except Antarctica. When I started to investigate airfares and hotel prices, that generous advance would prove woefully inadequate.

I figured *The Barbecue! Bible* would take me a year to write. I'd visit a dozen countries. Draft a hundred recipes. Well, *The Barbecue! Bible* grew to more than five hundred recipes and it took me four years to write. I spent that generous advance the first year.

It turned out that the subject required an encyclopedia, not just a cookbook. That's what it would take to describe the many hundreds of different dishes and grilling techniques found along the world's barbecue trail. Fortunately, I had two things working in my favor: a boundless curiosity about live-fire cooking, and complete ignorance about just how huge a task I had undertaken and how I would possibly pull it off.

Hard as it is to conceive, back then we had no internet, email, Google, or Claude. So I reached out to food writers, chefs, academics, tourism boards, and hotel concierges. When multiple sources suggested a place to visit, I added it to my destination list. Taxi drivers (we didn't have Ubers back then either) provided some of the best information. I'd ask them to take me not to the tourist places, but to the grill joints where they themselves ate. That's how I discovered the restaurant Mitla in Juarez, Mexico, home of one of my favorite beef recipes: Steak from Hell.

For my first research trip, I picked Jamaica. Its live-fire specialty—jerk—was the closest modern descendant to the dish (or more accurately, the grill) that inspired our word *barbecue*. That word is *barbacoa*, and to understand it we need to travel back in time to sixteenth-century Hispaniola (today Haiti and the Dominican Republic).

Among the colorful characters who people the history of barbecue was a Spanish adventurer named Gonzalo Fernández de Oviedo y Valdés. In 1512, he joined an armada of galleons headed for the newly "discovered" New World, where he had landed the plum assignment of setting up a gold mine in Colombia. His ship pulled into Santo Domingo to take on supplies. Unlike his more rapacious compatriots, Gonzalo was curious about the local culture. He came across a group of Taíno Indians cooking on a device made up of four upright wooden posts with small saplings stretched across them to form a grate. On this rustic grill, they roasted fish, game, and—to Oviedo's horror—iguana. He asked the name of this singular setup. They replied: *barbacoa*.

This answers the age-old question: What is barbecue? Is it a device (the so-called barbecue grill), a cooking technique (to barbecue), a specific food (such as in brisket or ribs), a meal cooked and eaten outdoors, or a civic feast? In some sense, today *barbecue* means all those things, but it originally meant a grill.

This point was driven home to me when I landed at Kingston Airport and took a cab to Boston Beach on the northeastern coast of Jamaica. Jamaica's national barbecue—indeed, its national dish—is jerk: pork, chicken, or other meat marinated in a fiery paste of Scotch bonnet chilies, alliums, ginger, rum, and numerous spices, chief among them, pimento (allspice). As a seasoning, it strikes just about every note on the palate: sweet, salty, spicy, aromatic, herbaceous, and tart with lime and vinegar. The chilies jolt the tongue like a bite of a high-voltage cable.

A Taíno Indian "barbacoa" in the 1500s—origin of our word barbecue.

Boston Beach is a small fishing village that once supplied the Boston Fruit Company with Jamaican bananas. Jerk is served across Jamaica, but Boston Beach allegedly serves the best—as I was told by my guide into all things jerk, one Prince Duncan Sufferer, proprietor of Sufferer's Jerk Pork Front Line No. 1—a bamboo shack with a dirt floor and four rickety tables. "Suffer" seems to have been the operative word here, especially for the cook charged with reducing twenty-four pounds of Scotch bonnet chilies (fifty times hotter than a jalapeño) to a puree in a hand-cranked meat grinder to make the base of the jerk seasoning. Equally remarkable was the butchery of the pig—butterflied open, boned from snout to tail, and accordion-cut so that no section of meat was thicker than a fist.

Mr. Sufferer and crew slow-roasted the pork over a smoky allspice wood fire for five hours. What blew my mind was the grill grate—formed from allspice wood sticks, which slowly charred during the cooking process, to be replenished as needed with fresh sticks. Here I was, 482 years after Gonzalo set foot on Santo Domingo, eating pork blasted with island spices and cooked on a wooden grate directly descended from the Taíno Indian *barbacoa*. It would turn out to be some of the best barbecue I have eaten in my life.

TO TELL YOU ABOUT ALL my adventures would fill a five-hundred-plus-page book. (It did.) But I would like to highlight three of the most memorable experiences because they demonstrate how obsessive I became in my efforts to get the global barbecue story.

The first was in France, where Barbara and I were taking a weekend off after a month of hard traveling and research in the town of Arles in Provence. I made the mistake of calling fellow Workman author Patricia Wells, who at the time was the restaurant critic for the *International Herald Tribune*. Pat told me about a restaurant she had discovered in the Languedoc. "Steven, you must go there," she said. "They serve escargots grilled over grapevines."

I immediately called the L'Hostal in the village of Castellon near Perpignan. Yes, they served grilled snails. Sorry, they were closed the following two nights. They would reopen on Wednesday—the day Barbara and I were scheduled to return to the United States. I asked the ever-patient Barbara if she minded leaving our beautiful Relais & Châteaux hotel so I could experience grilled escargots. (Note: Barbara doesn't eat escargots.) I did some quick calculations: If we left immediately and drove for four hours at one hundred miles an hour (you could do that in France back then), we could make it to the restaurant before closing time.

We arrived in a handsomely restored medieval citadel and took our seats on a cliffside terrace with spectacular views of the Roussillon Valley. The snails—*petits-gris* ("little grays")—had, indeed, been grilled over grapevine trimmings; their texture was soft, moist, even drooly (the French would say *baveuse*), their flavor pungent, tangy, and aromatic. I could taste in them the wild thyme that carpeted the nearby hillsides.

When factoring in the gas, tolls, and hotel where we stayed after dinner, the twelve snails cost somewhere around $400, making them the most expensive escargots—or barbecue, for that matter—I have ever eaten. The secret to their extraordinary succulence was an ingredient few people in the US use anymore: lard.

The second experience took place in Bali, Indonesia. We were staying at Amandari, an ultra-posh property in the artsy town of Ubud. Bali's contribution to the pantheon of world barbecue is a spice- and herb-blasted spit-roasted pig called *babi guling*. I arranged to meet a local pitmaster to see how the pig was prepared.

At 4:30 the next morning, a slight, wiry man named Iingah Kepidana picked me up in a white pickup truck. Our destination: a farm fifteen kilometers outside Ubud. He selected a lively young pig and led it out of the pen. He laid his hands on the animal and calmed it into a somnolent state with a gesture I could only describe as spiritual. I've never witnessed anything like it. He handed me a long, slender knife and gave me the honor of dispatching the pig. It was almost as if the animal understood that its sacrifice was part of the Balinese natural order.

Mr. Kepidana then slit the pig's throat and collected the warm blood in a bowl. He grated a fresh coconut into the bowl and gestured for me to taste it. Apparently, coconut blood soup for breakfast was part of the *babi guling* ritual. After I got over my initial repugnance, I found it quite tasty—the blood salty and sweet, the coconut sweet and crunchy—an experience to be savored once and, hopefully, never again.

Our next stop was an open-air market, where Kepidana purchased the ingredients for the *bumbu*, spice paste. Many of the ingredients I recognized:

fresh ginger, turmeric, bird peppers, and lemongrass. Others, such as candlenuts, galangal, and makrut lime leaves, were new to me. We drove to his kitchen, where Kepidana pounded these flavorings and a dozen more in a mortar the size of a washtub with a pestle the size of a baseball bat. He stuffed the incredibly aromatic paste into the now-gutted pig, which would marinate for eight hours.

When I returned to his kitchen late that afternoon, he had skewered the pig on a sapling spit and set it over a coconut shell fire. He spit-roasted it for several hours, basting it with coconut oil. When the pig was the color of topaz, he carved it with a giant meat cleaver. The crisp, buttery skin made a sound like broken glass when I bit into it, giving way to steamy, tender meat scented with the explosively flavorful seasonings. No wonder Indonesia was formerly known as the Spice Islands. My plate was a banana leaf; my utensils my fingers, and I don't believe I've ever enjoyed roast pork more in my life.

The third experience took place in Bangkok. I asked local food experts who did the best grilling in Thailand, and the word *Isaan* kept coming up. The Isaan are a people of Laotian descent living in a province in northeast Thailand. According to my guide, the Isaan became master grillers by necessity: Coconut charcoal was cheap and ubiquitous. The Isaan are famous throughout Thailand for their *gai yang* (grilled chicken) and *pla yang* (grilled fish).

Which brought me to my next destination, an Isaan "restaurant"—a squalid hole-in-the-wall in the Dusit district in Bangkok. The houses opened to the sidewalks, where women squatted on the sidewalks washing dishes, clothes, and children. The restaurant had plastic chairs, rickety tables, and kittens scrounging for food scraps on the floor. They even had air conditioning, but a customer had to pay a few *bahts* to get it turned on.

Even more primitive was the kitchen, with an open window overlooking a stagnant *klong* (canal). A dead dog and garbage moldered in the stagnant water. Flies buzzed in and out of the screenless window and swarmed the food.

But I was the guest of honor, and as the proprietor, a Mr. Noi, brought out course after course, common courtesy demanded I sample every dish. We started with *som tom*, Thailand's green papaya salad so laced with chilies it damn near melted my fillings. Then came a gullet-scorching oxtail soup followed by the star attraction, *gai yang*—a spatchcocked grilled chicken, all smoky and crisp, pungent with garlic and cilantro root. As with most Isaan grilled meats, a vegetable platter accompanied the chicken: sliced cabbage and celery leaves, long beans, and basil—all alarmingly raw. As for the sticky rice—steamed in a length of bamboo—I ate it Isaan-style, with my fingers.

I thanked Mr. Noi with much bowing and *sabadi kaaps.* Once back at my hotel, I waited for the inevitable gastric distress requiring Lomotil,

Learning to "bake" naan in a tandoor (charcoal-fired barbecue pit) in New Delhi.

Pepto-Bismol, and the other abdominal soothers I carried in my travel medical kit. Quite miraculously, no illness followed, and the next day I turned my attention to another Thai barbecue specialty: satay. I thanked the benevolence of the god of barbecue—and the sterilizing effects of hot fire.

My travels on the world's barbecue trail continued for three years, and, yes, I did get sick on occasion. Usually, this resulted from letting my reportorial enthusiasm outweigh my common sense, like when I ate grilled cheese kebabs from a street stall of dubious cleanliness in Delhi. But by and large, I emerged from my barbecue research unscathed.

Wondering how I communicated with the hundreds of sidewalk grill jockeys I interviewed on my travels? I speak French, rudimentary Italian and Spanish, with a smattering of German (which helped in Poland and Turkey). I hired interpreters when I could; otherwise, I relied on pointing and gesturing.

Grill masters have a reputation for being secretive about their recipes, but most of the people I met generously shared their knowledge. Some scrawled recipes in their native tongues, which I had translated back at the hotel. Others drew pictures or showed me ingredient bottles. A few even thrust tongs into my hands and bade me take a turn at the grill.

My fourth year writing *The Barbecue! Bible* was devoted to recipe development and testing. I used a three-step process. First, I'd write the recipe, based on what I saw and tasted. Then I'd grill it myself, making corrections as needed. Finally, I brought in a team of recipe testers to prepare the dish one final time. We checked for the obvious taste, appearance, and authenticity. We also checked more mundane issues—are the ingredient measurements correct and listed in their order of use? Are the cooking temperatures and times accurate? How about the yields?

Unlike my previous books, the global scope of *The Barbecue! Bible* presented another set of challenges. Back in the 1990s, most Americans weren't familiar with fish sauce, lemongrass, coconut milk, and other Southeast Asian flavorings. It was hard to find Peruvian *aji amarillo* (yellow chili paste), or Indonesian candlenuts, or even strained yogurt—the cornerstone of Indian, Afghan, and Persian marinades.

To make my recipes accessible, I had to suggest workarounds: soy sauce plus anchovy paste to replicate fish sauce, for example, or grated lemon zest plus ginger for lemongrass. I instructed readers how to make coconut milk from scratch. Combining yellow bell peppers, jalapeños, and ground turmeric made a reasonable substitute for *aji amarillo*. As for candlenuts, well, macadamias don't have the same flavor, but they get you in the ballpark.

Today, my local supermarket stocks these ingredients and dozens more, and I like to think that books like *The Barbecue! Bible* and *Planet Barbecue* have helped make our larders more cosmopolitan. Thanks to the ubiquity of thick Greek-style yogurt, we no longer need to strain yogurt. The proliferation of international restaurants has brought many of the dishes I traveled so far to discover to cities large and small across the US.

It turned out that there was so much to say about barbecue (it's kept me busy and fascinated for the last thirty years). I'd probably still be writing *The Barbecue! Bible* today, if, at one point, my editor, Suzanne Rafer, hadn't ordered me to stop writing. "Not a single paragraph or recipe more," she said. "Take the page out of the printer. Send in what you've written so far, or we'll never have a book we can publish."

Originally, I proposed calling the book *Barbacoa*. That title would work today, as most grill enthusiasts have some knowledge of the history of barbecue. But back in 1998, we probably would have sold two hundred copies. (As it turns out, a book entitled *Barbacoa* did come out recently—a treatise on Tex-Mex grilling written by Brandon Hurtado.)

We went back and forth on dozens of titles. Finally, someone at

Workman said: "Hey, the thing is as thick as the Bible." My gospel of grilling became *The Barbecue! Bible,* and so it has been ever since.

Peter Workman took a schizophrenic approach to publishing. He loved big, thick, exhaustively comprehensive books, which he called "category killers." He also loved funny, quirky little books like *Dinosnores* by Sandra Boynton. Which brings me to the exclamation mark. If I had to sum up the key to Peter's phenomenal success in a single word, it would be whimsy. Even his serious books had a whimsical element—hence the ! in *The Barbecue! Bible.* For the record, I hated the exclamation mark—I still do. I always felt it took away from the seriousness of the book. But after a million-plus copies sold, I've learned to live with it.

As for the author photo, I was flown to New York, where the art director dressed me in a turquoise shirt with a red undershirt and had me take off my glasses. It was, perhaps, the worst photo ever taken of me. I didn't even look like me! (I've worn glasses since the second grade.) If you have a first edition of the book with this photo, burn it! I'll send you a fresh copy.

In spring 1999, *The Barbecue! Bible* won an IACP–Julia Child Award. When I went up onstage, Julia gave me the award personally, with a hug and kiss to go with it. In my acceptance speech, I thanked three major female figures in my life: Julia, Barbara, and Suzanne. I dedicated the award, as I did the book, to my grandfather Samuel "Dear" Raichlen. I don't remember much about what I said that night, but I do remember the last words of my speech: "I miss my grandfather a lot."

A few years later, *The Barbecue! Bible* joined a kettle grill, James Beard's *Complete Book of Barbecue and Rotisserie Cooking* (1954), and the *Sunset Barbecue Cookbook* (1958) in an exhibit on American barbecue at the Smithsonian Institution. It landed me an interview on NPR's *Fresh Air* with Terry Gross. It even made a cameo appearance in the 2000 movie *Bait,* starring Jamie Foxx.

Since then, *The Barbecue! Bible* has been through two major revisions and five different covers, and has gone from a black-and-white book with woodcuts (most cookbooks did not have color photographs at the time of its publication) to full color throughout. The food on the cover went from grilled shrimp (two iterations) to baby backs (two iterations) to the monster beef ribs on the current edition. But most of the content has remained the same—and much to my astonishment, most of it has remained relevant. It remains one of my most translated books, with versions in French, German, Finnish, Russian, Chinese, Japanese, and more. *La Bibbia di Barbecue* was reissued in Italian a few years ago—it became a bestseller. In an age of disposable content and dwindling attention spans, I'm amazed that people still want to buy a 556-page door stopper.

VIETNAMESE GRILLED BASIL PORK ROLLS

I'm often asked what my favorite country for grilling is. I can't say and won't, but my tastes naturally gravitate to the vibrant flavors of Southeast Asia. Consider these simple and explosively flavorful basil pork rolls, which represent Vietnamese grilling at its best. You start with ground pork, which you flavor with garlic, black pepper, and fish sauce, with a whisper of sugar for sweetness. You grill the mixture wrapped in fresh basil leaves for even more flavor, threading the rolls onto bamboo skewers to form tiny kebabs.

Note: Fish sauce is a malodorous but delicious and umami-rich condiment made from pickled anchovies. My favorite brand is Red Boat. If unavailable, substitute soy sauce.

Makes around 70 rolls, which will serve 4 as a light first course

1 pound ground pork

2 cloves garlic, minced

2 ½ tablespoons fish sauce, or to taste

1 ½ tablespoons sugar, or to taste

2 teaspoons freshly ground black pepper

2 bunches of basil (enough to provide 70 large leaves)

½ cup finely chopped roasted peanuts

Dipping Sauce (recipe follows)

You'll also need:

slender bamboo skewers; a 12- by 18-inch sheet of aluminum foil folded in thirds like a business letter (to serve as a grill shield)

1. Combine the pork, garlic, fish sauce, sugar, and pepper in a mixing bowl and stir to mix. Correct the seasoning, adding fish sauce or sugar to taste: The mixture should be both salty and sweet. (To avoid tasting raw pork, grill a tiny patty or cook in a frying pan.)
2. Mound 2 teaspoons or so of the pork mixture on a basil leaf (shiny side down) and roll lengthwise into a compact cylinder. Repeat until all the pork mixture and basil leaves are used up.
3. Skewer the rolls widthwise on bamboo skewers, 4 or 5 rolls to a skewer. The recipe can be prepared ahead up to this stage.
4. Set up your grill for direct grilling and heat to high. Brush or scrape the grill grate clean and oil it well.
5. Arrange the pork roll kebabs on the grate, sliding the foil under the exposed part of the skewers to keep them from burning. Grill the pork rolls until cooked through—the basil will become lightly browned and the rolls will be sizzling and hot to the touch, 2 minutes per side or so. Transfer to a platter and sprinkle with the roasted peanuts. Serve with the dipping sauce (recipe follows).

VIETNAMESE DIPPING SAUCE

This delicate, topaz-colored condiment is Vietnam's national dipping sauce. Sugar makes it sweet; lime juice and vinegar make it sour; fish sauce provides the salt and characteristic umami flavor. Two fine brands of fish sauce (which is made with pickled anchovies) are Red Boat and Three Crabs. The trick to julienning the carrots is to slice them with a vegetable peeler.

Makes 1 cup (enough to serve 4)

A 2-inch section of carrot (peeled)
1 clove garlic
3 tablespoons granulated sugar
⅓ cup Asian fish sauce
⅓ cup fresh lime juice
1 small hot red chile, thinly sliced crosswise

1. Slice the carrot lengthwise with a vegetable peeler and pile the slices on top of one another. Then, using a sharp knife, slice the carrot lengthwise into the thinnest imaginable strands. Place the carrots in a mixing bowl.
2. Using a microplane, grate the garlic into the bowl. Stir in the sugar and let stand for 5 minutes to soften the carrots.
3. Add the fish sauce, lime juice, and ½ cup warm water. Stir until the sugar is dissolved. Taste for seasoning, adding more fish sauce, lime juice, or sugar as needed: The sauce should strike a delicate balance between salty, tart, and sweet.
4. Just before serving, divide the sauce between 4 small bowls. Float a few chili slices in each and serve with the rolls for dipping.

Chapter Eleven

A MAN MAKES A PLAN

1999

My barbecue career takes off with a book, TV series, and Barbecue University.

Some people are planners—you know the type (maybe *you* are the type)—with five-year, ten-year, and lifetime plans.

For the first half of my adult life, I drifted like smoke rising from a campfire. In college I majored in perhaps the least practical subject in the curriculum: French literature. I followed opportunities as they came along, cooking for a psychodrama retreat group, freelancing for an alternative weekly newspaper, reviewing restaurants, writing books about everything from French cuisine to seasonal cooking to low-fat food to Caribbean cuisine. I would probably be jumping from subject to subject still, if it weren't for *The Barbecue! Bible.*

You could call me an aspirational pothead. Pothead, because I love getting stoned—how it slows time, intensifies the senses, and unspools my creativity. Aspirational, because I'm a workaholic, and pot impedes my ability to think clearly and work the next morning. Consequently, I smoke only when I have nothing major pending the next day, which, given my typical seven-day workweek, very rarely happens.

But one evening, I did get stoned—rip-roaring stoned—and the idea of a barbecue empire came to me. I grabbed a notepad and made a list of all the things I could do with barbecue. There would be other books—many books—covering the various aspects of live-fire cooking. One would be a how-to book, focusing on grilling and smoking techniques. Another would explore the sauces, spice rubs, and condiments that accompany barbecue around the world. A third book would do a deep dive into regional American barbecue.

There would be a TV show, because no one had ever done a how-to TV show on the techniques of live-fire cooking. To delve into those techniques further, I'd start a cooking school—let's call it Barbecue University. (I trademarked the name a few years later.) Hmm, *Barbecue University* would make a cool name for the TV show . . .

I fired up another joint and the ideas came fast and furious.

How about a line of products? I'd already written about the world's best barbecue sauces and seasonings; why not turn my prose into condiments?

Speaking of products, there ought to be a line of tools, fuels, and grilling accessories designed by someone who actually grills (most existing tools being dreamed up by industrial designers).

To promote all these books and products, I'd launch a website. That would involve weekly (and eventually biweekly) blog postings and a newsletter inspired by my still-smoldering joint: *Up in Smoke.*

And to spread the gospel of grilling worldwide, I would develop foreign markets—for my books, products, and dreamed-of TV show.

Finally, wouldn't it be cool to have a barbecue restaurant—make that a chain—where the public could come to sample Raichlen recipes?

When I looked at the list the next morning—nursing a dope-over with a triple espresso—I realized I had a plan. But how on earth would I make it happen?

TWO YEARS EARLIER, I HAD picked up a book called *Think and Grow Rich* by Napoleon Hill (I'm something of a sucker for self-help books). Hill's book analyzed the success of such early-twentieth-century tycoons as Andrew Carnegie and John D. Rockefeller. I've summarized his recommendations below, and they're as timely today as they were when *Think and Grow Rich* was first published in 1937:

1. Start with a strong desire for success.
2. Visualize that success and have faith in yourself and your vision.
3. Reprogram your subconscious through affirmations and positive thinking.

4. Acquire the specialized knowledge you'll need to make your plan work.
5. Imagine creative ways to reach your goals.
6. Make a concrete, actionable plan to achieve your goals.
7. Make decisions quickly and change them slowly, if at all.
8. Be persistent. I repeat, be persistent.
9. Surround yourself with positive, successful people.
10. Trust your intuition and feed your brain with positive thoughts.

One of Mr. Hill's techniques as a writer is to imply that some people "get it" and others don't. By the time you finish his book, you definitely want to be one of the in-crowd.

He also advocates making lists and reviewing them daily. So I copied out that list of what I wanted to accomplish with barbecue and reviewed it every morning. This lasted about a week; then I put it in my wallet and forgot about it.

I dismissed *Think and Grow Rich* as just more wishful thinking and continued slogging my way through *The Barbecue! Bible.*

THEN SOME STRANGE THINGS HAPPENED. I was having dinner with Peter Workman and Suzanne Rafer at one of Peter's favorite restaurants, Beppe, in New York's Flatiron District. I casually mentioned my dream of creating a barbecue TV show. "I'll put up $100,000 for it," Peter said without missing a beat. (Suzanne all but choked on her wine.)

A few weeks later, I was at the Food & Wine Classic in Aspen. At the festival, I met Michael Mondavi and told him about my crazy TV-show idea. "Come see me the next time you're in the Napa Valley," he said. A month later, I met Michael at the winery and by the end of lunch, I had

A TV show at long last: another item checked off on my to-do list.

our second sponsor. Weber Grills came on board a few weeks later, followed by Royal Oak Charcoal. The *Barbecue University* TV show launched on PBS the following spring, and I checked off the first item on my barbecue to-do list.

Around this time, the Greenbrier Resort in White Sulphur Springs, West Virginia, hosted one of the most respected cooking schools in the country. The school's director was none other than my mentor and La Varenne founder, Anne Willan. Anne brought me to the school as a guest instructor, first to teach healthy cooking, then to focus on my emerging specialty: global grilling.

At one session, I mentioned my crazy idea for a Barbecue University to the Greenbrier Food and Beverage Director.

"We just renovated a hillside lodge called Kate's Mountain," he said. "Barbecue University could be a great way to steer business to our new venue."

I started collecting grills, planning menus, and drafting recipes. In May

2000, we held our first class, and Barbecue University was born. Check off to-do list item 2.

A few months after that, I was at a trade show and met Chuck Adams, founder and CEO of a leading barbecue accessory manufacturer, The Companion Group. Chuck got his start in the barbecue business by manufacturing chimney starters. He soon branched out to grill brushes, tongs, and other grill accessories sold under a brand called Charcoal Companion.

I explained my idea for a line of premium barbecue tools designed by someone who grills for a living—the sort of accessories I wish I had but didn't yet exist.

"We've always wanted to work with a brand," said Chuck. (I guess I had become a brand.) "Tell me some of your ideas."

I showed Chuck a prototype of my "luma-tongs"—barbecue tongs with a flashlight built into one arm. "People are always cooking in the shadow cast by the griller between the patio light and the grill grate," I explained. "Now you can see what you're grilling." Chuck also liked my idea for a square chimney starter (which holds 30 percent more charcoal than a round chimney), and my smoking puck—a grate-top smoking device for a gas grill.

A few weeks later, we signed a contract, and the Best of Barbecue grilling accessory line—complete with tools, fuels, barbecue sauces, and rubs—was born.

Check off items 3 and 4 on the list.

And so it continued. Peter Workman agreed to partner with me on a website. We would call it BarbecueBible.com, with a newsletter called *Up in Smoke*. Our foreign initiatives began with the French, then German, then Dutch and Finnish translations of *The Barbecue! Bible.*

And, damn if, by the end of a year, I hadn't accomplished almost every item on that to-do list. I never did open a barbecue restaurant of my own—a

Spice rubs in my newly launched Best of Barbecue line.

definite red line for Barbara, whose father was in the restaurant business and worked the bone-crushing hours it required. I have, however, consulted on several restaurant projects, so people have had a chance to taste my recipes firsthand. Besides, never say never.

I read Napoleon Hill with skepticism. I became a believer. Ever since, on my birthday and on New Year's Eve, I make lists of what I want to achieve in the coming year. Whenever I start a new project, I make a list of the steps I need to accomplish it. I keep these lists in my wallet and even if I don't look at them for months, I know they're always with me. And somehow, mysteriously, they guide me.

That's not to say I don't still make mistakes and miss opportunities. But I've hit the ball more than I've struck out, and what's important is to keep on swinging for the fences.

The last thing I did to finalize my plan was not in *Think and Grow Rich*. I read it in another self-help book. I wrote a mission statement.

Steven Raichlen Mission Statement (dated 9/23/00)

My mission is to know more about barbecuing and grilling than anyone else on the planet and to share that knowledge with my readers, viewers, followers, and fans.

During those *Barbecue Bible!* years, I was a regular at the Food & Wine Classic in Aspen. I remember one year being invited to a radio interview roundtable there. Seated around the table were some of the biggest names in food, including Wolfgang Puck, Danny Meyer, and Todd English. They all stood up to congratulate me. Talk about recognition by your peers!

Which brings me back to Mr. Hill, and I'm paraphrasing here:

"If you can conceive it, and believe it, you can achieve it."

Amen!

BARBECUE UNIVERSITY

You've probably gathered by now that I'm a wannabe academic. So when I decided to launch a cooking school, what better name to call it than Barbecue University? Like a college class, it would have a curriculum—in this case, covering the history and geography of barbecue and the five methods of live-fire cooking. (Can you name them? Direct grilling. Indirect grilling. Smoking. Spit-roasting. And grilling on the embers.) As at a university, there would be a final exam and a diploma upon graduation.

I chose for my "campus" the luxurious Greenbrier Resort in White Sulphur Springs, West Virginia. I equipped our classroom with more than three dozen grills and smokers, plus mountains of charcoal and wood to fuel them. We supplied our students with state-of-the-art grilling accessories and cutting-edge ingredients. Our textbook comprised recipes from my cookbooks, which in turn derived from my travels around the world's barbecue trail.

We ran our first class in spring 2000. *Travel & Leisure*, *Esquire*, and The Food Network reported on the school (the latter calling it the "#1 barbecue experience in the US"). Soon we were running five sessions a summer. Our students come from virtually every state in the US; and from as far away as Sydney, Hong Kong, and Dubai. Some of our students are professionals; a few have never fired up a grill. Most are people who love barbecuing and grilling and want to do it better.

I've always believed that people learn best not just from watching, but by doing. Each class begins with a lecture in which I explain the day's techniques—how to spatchcock a chicken, for example, or reverse-sear a beef tomahawk. The real fun begins when I divide the class into teams, each responsible for executing the day's menus. Invariably, the scene devolves into chaos, but damn if by noon, a splendid meal isn't ready—presented with pride, and dare I say, artistry—the prelude to a belt-loosening lunch.

I organize each day's lesson by theme: "Planet Barbecue," for example, or "Regional American Barbecue," or a "Global Tailgate Party." The students have three hours to prepare eight dishes. A recent menu at the school featured:

Thai-style wings with sriracha mayonnaise

Grilled oysters with charred corn salsa

Island spice lobster tails

Balkan smash burgers
Chicken yassa
Huli huli ribs
Grilled corn with barbecue butter
Bacon bourbon apple crisp

The students panic initially when they see the workload, but by the next day, they're cranking out dishes like a seasoned kitchen brigade. Some even contrive new dishes for extra credit. In the process, they have the opportunity to test-drive new grills, like our $25,000 Kalamazoo Hybrid Fire Grill and a Kamodo Kamado from Indonesia.

As for the dreaded "final exam" (I really give one), it's designed to remind students of the techniques they learned during class: the difference between barbecuing and grilling, for example, or how to tell a wet rub from a brine or marinade. If someone gets stumped on an answer, I invite their classmates to help them. It's not about getting the right answer. It's about remembering what we've learned. Of the thousands of students we've graduated, I'm pleased to say that no one has had to repeat the class. Unless they want to. Some of our students have attended a dozen sessions of Barbecue University or more.

Over the years, I've moved Barbecue University from West Virgina to the foothills of the Rockies at the Broadmoor in Colorado Springs. For three years, we grilled at Montage Palmetto Bluffs in the South Carolina Lowcountry. Our current home is the majestic Alisal Ranch in Solvang, California (convenient to 150-plus wineries in the surrounding Santa Ynez Valley).

It may not be an academic setting, but each session of Barbecue University is one of the high points of my year.

EPIPHANY BARBECUE RUB

This spice rub—my all-purpose barbecue rub—has literary roots. It was inspired by the novel *Cold Mountain* by Charles Frazier. Ruby (one of the more colorful characters in the story) swaps coffee beans for a brisket, which she seasons with salt, pepper, paprika, and brown sugar (one teacup of each). I can't give you the exact formula (I now sell it under my Planet Barbecue brand). Here is the broad outline—customize the optional flavors to suit your taste.

Makes 1 cup

¼ cup salt (kosher, sea, or smoked)

¼ cup freshly ground pepper (black or white)

¼ cup paprika (sweet, hot, or smoked)

¼ cup sugar (white, light brown, or dark brown)

Optional flavorings:

2 teaspoons granulated garlic

2 teaspoons granulated onion

1 teaspoon celery seed

1 teaspoon cayenne pepper

1. Combine the ingredients in a bowl and mix with your fingers, breaking up any lumps in the sugar. Use 1 tablespoon for each pound of meat. Store in a sealed jar away from heat and light—it will keep for several months.

Chapter Twelve

TEACHING THE WORLD HOW TO GRILL

1999–2001

A private grilling class for Howard Stern.

It isn't often that Oprah Winfrey and Howard Stern wax rhapsodic about the same book. But that's exactly what happened when my next barbecue book came out in spring 2002. There was even a bit of competition—at least from Mr. Stern's side.

How to Grill became a multimillion-copy international bestseller, not to mention the book that put me on the world stage as a global grilling authority. I mean that quite literally: To date, *How to Grill* has appeared in seventeen languages—from Swedish to Croatian to Mandarin Chinese—and is a bestseller in many of those countries as well.

I like to think that it was the author's singular brilliance that accounted for these remarkable sales, but I'm the first to acknowledge that it was the right book at the right time. The *Barbecue! Bible* opened people's minds to the wonders of global grilling. *How to Grill* taught them how to do it.

It almost didn't happen. When I brought the idea to Peter Workman, the publishing visionary didn't get it. I proposed a four-book deal (authors love multibook deals—as a freelancer, it means steady work for years). He initially signed off on three titles: *Barbecue Sauces, Rubs, and Marinades*; *BBQ USA*; and *Beer Can Chicken*. As for a fourth book on how to grill, he didn't think people would buy it. Fortunately, my editor, Suzanne Rafer, saw the promise of the idea and badgered Peter until he gave in.

The idea for *How to Grill* began a year earlier, at one of my numerous book signings—this one under a giant sycamore tree in Pittsboro, North Carolina. I concluded my talk with a Q&A session, which invariably unfolded the same way.

The women in the audience asked smart questions; the men remained stubbornly silent. But as I prepared to leave, guys stopped me in the parking lot. "Why are my steaks always tough?" "Why does my chicken catch fire?" "Why does my fish stick to the grill grate?"

Up to this point, grilling and barbecue were practiced more by

How to Grill: *My first million-copy bestseller and the book that put me on the world barbecue stage.*

superstition than science. People grilled the way their fathers did. And if they possessed Y-chromosomes, they thought they knew everything there was to know about grilling by birthright. They (or maybe I should say we, as I plead guilty to this too) repeated the same mistakes over and over, like building too hot a fire or overcrowding the grill grate. Each time, we expect the results to be different, which I believe is what Albert Einstein called the definition of insanity.

I started compiling their questions and catastrophes in a notebook. Someone needed to bring order to the chaotic world of live-fire cooking.

That someone would be me. I've always thought of cooking in terms of language. The ingredients are the vocabulary. The techniques are the grammar. I resolved to become the linguist of the grill.

The premise of the book was simple: Pick the essential dishes in barbecuing and grilling—dishes everyone should know how to grill. Explain the following:

- Why the dish belongs in your repertory
- What you need to know when you shop for the ingredients
- How to prepare/butcher/stuff/truss the primary protein or vegetable
- How to set up your grill or smoker
- How to grill or smoke the dish
- What your masterpiece should look like when it's finished

To do this, I would prepare each dish in front of a photographer, ingredient by ingredient, step by step, and walk the reader through its execution. I'd conclude with a mouthwatering beauty shot to inspire readers to fire up the grill and try it.

That may sound easy, but it wasn't. The first challenge was picking the dishes—which eventually I narrowed down to ninety-three—plus eighteen sauces and barbecue rubs that everyone should master. Some were obvious: steak, chicken, brisket, ribs, pork shoulder, hamburgers, shrimp, fish steaks, corn on the cob, etc. Make that many steaks (porterhouse, T-bone, strip steak, filet mignon, flank steak, and London broil), and many chickens (whole birds, half birds, spatchcocked birds, wings, breasts, and kebabs). Any self-respecting griller should know how to cook these items.

Next came dishes of a more whimsical or esoteric nature, such as grilled oysters, grilled pizza, and barbecued cabbage. The sort of dishes you don't necessarily think of grilling right off the bat, but that once you see them, you want to try them.

The final category was dishes that are clearly aspirational: Most people will not attempt to grill a whole hog, lamb, or salmon. But I'm nothing if not obsessive, so I decided they, too, belonged in the book. And once again, in typical Raichlen fashion, a simple idea grew into a 498-page monster.

How to Grill required less travel and writing than *The Barbecue! Bible.* In fact, the only travel needed was daily trips to the grocery store and from my house to the photographer's studio. On the other hand, the book required a *lot* in the way of photography. Like one thousand color photographs. *How to Grill*, I'm proud to say, was Workman Publishing's first book with color photographs.

I joined forces with a seasoned food photographer, Greg Schneider. At his studio, we fired up the grills and started to cook our way through the manuscript. Today, thanks to digital cameras, photography is instantaneous. Back in those days, it took forever to set up the lighting and take the Polaroids needed to verify the framing and exposure. Each Polaroid took five minutes to develop, and sometimes we'd shoot a half dozen to verify the lighting.

When *How to Grill* came out, many Americans didn't understand the difference between direct grilling and indirect grilling. So, at the head of each recipe, we showed how to configure the charcoal: spread in an even layer for direct grilling; raked (or, more accurately, hoed) into mounds at opposite sides of the grill with an empty foil pan in the center for indirect grilling. The camera didn't really capture the fiery glow of the charcoal, so the art department Photoshopped in additional orange fire. I hate to admit it, but today, those fires look pretty lame.

Miami lies midway between the rest of the United States and Latin

America. Thus, many of the dishes in *How to Grill*—such as Nicaraguan churrasco (thin, flat beef tenderloin steaks cut with the grain, not against it, with chimichurri as the sauce accompaniment) and vegetable- and cheese-studded Brazilian rib roast—reflected our Latino surroundings. Others—like Thai grilled beef salad and Persian kubideh (saffron-scented minced lamb kebabs)—derived from my travels on the world's barbecue trail. Of course we included such solid American classics as barbecued chicken, spareribs, brisket, and pork shoulder. We also included some mind-benders, like chipotle crème brûlée.

How to Grill launched in May 2001 at Harpo Studios in Chicago, Illinois. Yes, my brilliant publicist at the time, Andrea Glickson, had arranged as my out-of-the-gate media appearance an interview with Oprah.

A COOKING APPEARANCE ON A SHOW like *Oprah* requires a lot more than the five minutes you see onstage. First, you select a demonstration dish, which Oprah must approve. A demo dish for television needs to be simple enough to execute in five minutes (while still leaving time for conversation). It should be sufficiently straightforward so that anyone in the audience can make it, using affordable and readily available ingredients. And it ought to have one memorable twist or detail that sticks with viewers long after the show—enough to inspire them to purchase the book.

I had the perfect candidate: a riff on Italian *pollo al mattone* (chicken under a brick). In this case, it was America's easiest protein—boneless, skinless chicken breast—marinated with fresh lemon juice, herbs, and olive oil, and grilled under a foil-wrapped brick. The heavy weight keeps the bird moist and helps it crisp. (It also looks cool as all get-out.) I'd top it with a Mediterranean salsa spiked with kalamata olives and capers.

Oprah approved my choice with one addition: hot sauce—lots of hot sauce. The lady has an asbestos gullet. My wardrobe had to complement hers, with a shirt any color but white. (White makes the image on television look "hot.") We went with blue denim. My publisher would supply a free book for each of the two-hundred-plus people in the audience. I went over the cooking sequence with the stage manager: what would be where on the demo table and how I would sequence the cooking. I paced back and forth in the green room, trying not to look any more nervous than I was.

Then, after what seemed like an interminable wait, they rushed me to the stage. I stood at my demo table and Oprah walked up beside me. People talk of star power, and I felt it more than with any of the many other TV hosts I've appeared with. The moment she started talking, it was like standing next to a ten-thousand-watt light bulb.

She promptly christened me the "Gladiator of the Grill," making my previous sobriquet the "Grilling Guru" seem trite. She guided me through the segment like a conductor leading an orchestra (or perhaps a circus trainer cowing his lions). It was over before it started (five-minute TV segments are like that), and I have no memory of what I said. I believe I cut her a piece of the chicken; I believe she tasted it and liked it. I was ushered off the stage, my five minutes of fame with Oprah over.

Well, not completely over, because the next day *How to Grill* climbed to number seven on the Amazon bestseller list. Not number seven in cookbooks—number seven in all books sold. But I was too busy to notice. I was on my way to the next stop in a twenty-four-city book tour.

THE CALL CAME AT 7 AM. That morning, I was in Los Angeles. "Howard Stern is talking about you," said my young friend. "He's been talking about you all morning."

Apparently, Howard had acquired a copy of *How to Grill*. He had recently purchased a stainless-steel super-grill and *How to Grill* had blown his mind.

Over the next few days, Howard continued to talk about *How to Grill*, and our book sales skyrocketed. I wanted to thank him in the sincerest way I could. I had my publicist reach out to his people to offer him a private grilling class.

Much to my surprise, Howard accepted. We agreed on a menu:

Grilled garlic bread
Buffa-que wings
Honey-sesame shrimp on the barbie
Beer can chicken with cola barbecue sauce
Cedar-planked salmon
Rosemary grilled scallops
Grilled tomatoes and zucchini
Cinnamon grilled peaches for dessert

We worked with a local caterer, Art of Eating, to do all the shopping and prep work. So far, so good.

Well, not really. The minute Jake and Betsy heard I was going to grill with Howard Stern, they wanted in. "No way you're going there without us." So, with no small embarrassment, I had to call Howard back to ask if I could bring my twentysomething stepson and stepdaughter with me. He graciously agreed. "I'll invite some staff and we'll make it a party!"

The other challenge was getting there. We live on Chappaquiddick, an island at the eastern end of Martha's Vineyard (more on that later). The trip to Howard's home on the Hamptons requires five ferries—a two-minute ferry on the "On Time" across Edgartown Harbor, a forty-five-minute Steamship Authority ferry from Vineyard Haven to Cape Cod, then an hour-long trip on the Cross Sound Ferry from New London, Connecticut, to Orient Point on Long Island. From there, a short ferry brought us from Greenport to Shelter Island, followed by a final ferry to Sag Harbor.

Don't get me wrong: I'm a water guy, and the only thing better than five ferries in one day would be six. It's often said that the best part of travel is the journey, not the destination. That was true that day, but the destination wasn't bad either.

Howard and his wife, Beth, lived in an ultra-modern house nestled among the Hamptons sand dunes. Howard himself opened the door to greet us. For a guy who trafficked in bad taste on the airwaves, his house was a paragon of Zen understatement and *Architectural Digest* high style. For a guy who virtually invented the genre of shock-jock radio, Howard was a true gentleman—hospitable, courteous, and warm.

Over the next three hours, we skewered honey-sesame shrimp, grilled herb- and butter-slathered garlic bread, stood chickens on cans of Coca-Cola (my teetotal version of beer can chicken), roasted mustard-glazed salmon on cedar planks, and grilled peach quarters on cinnamon sticks. It was a splendid meal, and Howard invited some of his neighbors to join in.

At various points during the class, we added wood chips to his grill's smoker box. Howard asked, with great concern—his new grill being his pride and joy—"Could you really taste the wood smoke?" A moral dilemma faced me: Should I say yes and make Howard happy? Should I be honest and say no? (You can't really smoke effectively on a gas grill—there, I said it.) I opted for honesty. I hope Howard wasn't too disappointed.

When I went to check out of my hotel the next morning, the desk clerk informed me that Mr. Stern had paid the bill. A class act from a classy guy for whom shock jock seemed just a persona.

By the way, Howard's on-air enthusiasm for *How to Grill* put us at

From Reed College to How to Grill*—an improbable journey that somehow made sense.*

number six on Amazon's bestseller list (again, for all books, not just cookbooks). That was one point better than Oprah. Howard took great pleasure in that!

HOW TO GRILL HAS SOLD NEARLY two million copies to date, with translations around the world. The French edition alone sold more than one hundred thousand copies. Thanks to the book's popularity, I did book tours in Italy, Germany, and France. At one event in Copenhagen, people drove as long as eight hours to meet the author. Chefs loved the book. Tom Colicchio called it "the definitive how-to guide." In 2021, *How to Grill* got a new, more modern cover. Two decades later, it's still in print.

And yet . . . when I look at *How to Grill* today, I feel a twinge of embarrassment. The photos feel dated. I've always described grilling as a dance on a razor's edge between cooked and burnt. A lot of the food in *How to Grill* looks as though it was baked in the oven. (It wasn't, but it doesn't look like the food I grill today.) At that time, I didn't fully appreciate the chiaroscuro beauty of fire-scorching and char marks. I didn't realize that a butterflied pork loin spread with black spirals of olive tapenade would look like bad nouvelle cuisine.

Withal, *How to Grill* changed my life and opened up opportunities for me worldwide I never would have dreamed possible. I like to believe that the book—even more than *The Barbecue! Bible*—brought barbecue into the twenty-first century. When I started in barbecue, people grilled mostly on special occasions. The fare was limited to protein (usually burgers, hot dogs, or steaks). Today we grill literally 24/7, and our repertory includes appetizers, bread, pizza, salads, vegetables, and yes, even dessert. Eight in ten Americans own grills; one in three of them own more than one.

And that's what I call a barbecue revolution!

CHICKEN FOR OPRAH

(Breast Under a Brick)

In selecting a dish to grill for Oprah, I chose a grilling technique that would make people sit up and take notice. You can't get more dramatic than Italian *pollo al mattone*, chicken grilled under a brick. The brick compacts the meat, making it crisp and producing killer grill marks. Of course, Italians wouldn't use jalapeño peppers and Tabasco sauce, but Oprah's producer told me the lady likes her food hot.

Serves 2

- 2 (6- to 8-ounce) boneless, skinless chicken breasts, trimmed
- Coarse sea salt and cracked black peppercorns
- ½ to 1 tablespoon hot pepper flakes
- 2 cloves garlic, minced
- 1 jalapeño chili, minced (for milder chicken, discard the seeds)
- 2 tablespoons chopped fresh rosemary
- 2 tablespoons chopped fresh sage, plus 4 to 6 whole leaves
- Grated zest and juice of 1 lemon, plus lemon wedges for serving
- Tabasco sauce to taste
- 3 tablespoons extra-virgin olive oil, plus more for the grill and for drizzling

You'll also need:

- 2 bricks, wrapped in aluminum foil (shiny side out) or a 10-inch cast-iron skillet

1. Arrange the chicken breasts in a baking dish just large enough to hold them. Season generously on both sides with salt, black pepper, and hot pepper flakes. Sprinkle the chicken breasts on both sides with the garlic, jalapeño, rosemary, chopped sage, and grated lemon zest. Squeeze the lemon juice over the chicken, turning to coat both sides. Squirt hot sauce over the chicken breasts on both sides. Drizzle with the olive oil, turning to coat both sides. Press the whole sage leaves onto each breast. Let the chicken marinate while you light the grill.
2. Set up your grill for direct grilling and heat to high. Brush or scrape the grill grate clean and oil it well. Arrange the chicken breasts on the grate running diagonal to the bars of the grate. Place a brick atop each. Grill for 1½ minutes, then give each breast a quarter turn and grill for another 1½ minutes, or until the bottom is nicely browned.
3. Remove the bricks, flip the chicken breasts, and replace the bricks. Continue grilling, giving each breast a quarter turn after 1½ minutes

or so. The total cooking time will be 6 to 8 minutes; the internal temperature of the breast in the thickest part should be 165°F. If you use an instant-read thermometer—and you should—insert the probe through the thicker end of the chicken, not from top to bottom.

4. Transfer the chicken breasts to a platter, sage leaf side up. Drizzle with olive oil and serve with lemon wedges for squeezing.

Chapter Thirteen

LIGHTS. CAMERA. PANIC.

2002–2006

Bringing the gospel of grilling to TV—it wasn't easy!

Some people are naturals on television. Jacques Pépin is a natural. Julia Child was a super-natural. Stanley Tucci inhabits a TV screen with perfect grace—although he rarely speaks directly to camera. (Perhaps that's one of his secrets.)

I am not a natural. In fact, mastering television (to the extent I have succeeded) has been the hardest thing I've done in my professional life. So, when a producer from *Good Morning America* called to invite me on the show—not just for a single appearance, but for a three-day booking—I rejoiced. Then panicked. They'd fly me to New York and put me up at the *GMA* apartment, the producer explained. (TV networks had guest apartments back then—a perk that has mostly disappeared with corporate cost-cutting.) All I had to do was deliver three consecutive six-minute segments.

Back in the early 2000s, I was so ignorant, I asked how much *GMA* would pay for my appearance. The producer sounded taken aback, then offered $1,000. "Per day?" I asked, revealing more ignorance. The producer sounded even more taken aback—then reluctantly agreed.

I didn't realize at the time that almost no one receives a fee for appearing on a morning TV show. On the contrary, many people pay publicists large sums to land bookings on shows like *GMA*. To this day, I can't believe I actually got paid.

Only after I agreed to the booking did terror set in. What did I know about television? The few times I practiced in front of a friend's video camera, my performance was painful to watch. I didn't even own a TV set until I was thirty-seven years old, and that one I acquired by marriage.

My publisher suggested media training with a public relations firm run by Lisa Ekus. Off I went to her office in Hatfield, Massachusetts, where Lisa's husband at the time, Lou, put me on a mock TV set with a kitchen counter and a video camera.

Lou told me we had five minutes for our segment, then proceeded to pepper me with questions. "Where were you born?" he asked. "Japan? I've always wanted to visit Japan. Where do you live now?" he continued. "How long have you been a writer? How do you like New York?"

I dutifully answered each question until Lou interrupted and said: "Well, thanks for being on the show. Maybe next time we'll get to talk about your book." Five minutes had elapsed, and I hadn't once mentioned the book or touched the food I had planned to demonstrate.

Lesson #1: Five minutes on television goes by in an eyeblink. It's up to you to steer the conversation—ideally to your book.

At our next practice session, I managed to reference the book and start my food prep. Meanwhile, a delivery person walked in behind us—previously and secretly arranged by Lou—delivering a huge box, a refrigerator or washing machine. The man made a lot of noise and asked me to sign for the delivery. I explained to him I was in the middle of a TV taping.

"Time's up," said Lou.

Getting comfortable in front of the camera. It helped that the videographer was a junior high school classmate.

Lesson #2: Distractions occur on a TV set. It's your job to ignore them.

At our third practice session, Lou played the querulous host. I was preparing a salmon fillet. Lou said he hated salmon. "Why aren't you cooking chicken?" he asked. "I love chicken." Lou also loved butter and heavy cream. "Would your *High-Flavor, Low-Fat* cookbook force me to eliminate those?" he asked, openly hostile. His questions put me on the defensive, and the interview ended on a sour note.

Then Lou explained the technique of bridging: that a television interview isn't really a conversation. It's an opportunity for both parties to deliver their respective messages—with a veneer of amiability to smooth the exchange.

The better response to the host's first comment, suggested Lou, would have been something like: "It's true a lot of people like chicken, and you'll find lots of chicken recipes in my book. But salmon is popular, too, and the beauty of this recipe is that the same seasonings work with both."

"As for butter and cream, of course they're delicious, but an equally tasty, heart-healthy alternative would be extra-virgin olive oil and vegetable stock."

Lou's point: It's your job to turn the conversation to your benefit, and it's the host's job to make both of you (but especially the host) look good.

I can't say I felt prepared when my first *Good Morning America* appearance arrived. Time slowed down, as it does when you're in the green room waiting to go on—then accelerated when they hurried me to the set. It was over almost before it began, and I didn't remember to look at the host, stand up straight, smile, reference the book, relax, or apply any of the lessons I'd learned during media training. I don't even remember what I cooked.

The second morning went a little better. I managed to prepare my dish (the erstwhile spurned salmon), while still having time for a little banter with Joan Lunden.

That night, Barbara gave me a pep talk. "Don't get bogged down with the recipe. People want to watch you connect with the host. Share a laugh and have fun."

Well, the third morning I gave Joan a warm tap on the shoulder and mostly ignored the food; we had a beauty shot (finished dish) on the set for the camera anyway. We talked about my personal story (the health issue—high cholesterol levels—that drove me to high-flavor, low-fat cooking) and shared a few laughs.

The producer—who up to this point regretted his $3,000—said, "Nice segment," and that he looked forward to having me back.

Over the years, I've appeared on *Good Morning America*, the *Today* show, and *CBS This Morning* dozens of times and done hundreds of local morning TV shows. I always try to balance earnestness with congeniality—to give viewers actionable tips while sharing a laugh with the host. I haven't always succeeded, but I've definitely improved. Barbara was right (as she usually is) that it's not just the food. It's the connection.

IT'S ONE THING TO APPEAR as a guest on an established TV show. It's another to create and host a show of your own. I did just that in 2001 with *Barbecue University.*

To make the show happen, I needed:

- a location
- an outlet
- a producer
- a crew
- financing

Curiously, the last item came the easiest. As mentioned earlier, Peter

Workman stepped up as my first sponsor, quickly followed by Weber Grills, Royal Oak Charcoal, and Robert Mondavi. I fell over myself with gratitude—until Barbara reminded me how much each sponsor had to gain from the show:

"Workman will sell more books," Barbara said. "Weber will move more grills; Royal Oak, more charcoal; and Mondavi will be able to persuade the public to drink wine with barbecue, not just beer." As usual, Barbara was right.

The location came easily too. My Barbecue University classes at the Greenbrier Resort were going gangbusters. The Greenbrier had recently renovated a streamside lodge called Howard's Creek, which would make a perfect backdrop for the show.

I saw—and still see—myself more as an educator than an entertainer, which made PBS my dream network. After all, Julia Child virtually invented the cooking show on public television. I could only hope to do for barbecue what Julia did for French cuisine. In a curious side note, the *Los Angeles Times* called me the "Julia Child of Barbecue." I was flattered by the comparison.

The animating force of my TV shows—and my life.

Which left finding a producer. Several people mentioned a New York director/producer named Charlie Pinsky. Charlie had made shows with many of the culinary stars I admired: chefs like Jacques Pépin and Pierre Franey (not that I'm a chef—I'm not); pastry masters like Jacques Torres; and specialty cooking shows like *Jewish Cooking in America* with Joan Nathan. He had a seasoned crew in place and a long track record with public television. He loved barbecue. What could possibly go wrong?

I planned the show roster, drafted the recipes, and ordered the grills and accessories. For wardrobe, I would wear a button-down denim shirt with a red embroidered BBQ U logo, neatly tucked into my jeans. I thought I looked professional. Barbara hated it.

We converged on the Greenbrier in September 2000, and after two days of setup, we were ready to begin taping. What the viewer sees on *Barbecue University* is a guy behind a worktable flanked by grills, with a stream and rustic cabin in the background. What I saw as I looked out were three cameramen, a sound person, a gaffer, and best boy (handling electricity and lighting), two field cooks to help with food prep, a stage manager, a couple of PAs (production assistants), plus Charlie and his engineers in the control tent. They all looked competent and prepared. I was terrified.

And then began the countdown. "Three. Two. One. Action!"

I opened my mouth. Only nothing came out. We were about to tape the first episode of a show I had dreamed of making for a decade. Here I was on the set, with fifteen crewmembers looking at me expectantly—and I couldn't think of a single word to say.

The problem was twofold. First, I'm a writer. I tend to think in phrases, sentences, and paragraphs. I edit my words as I write, and nothing leaves my desk until I'm satisfied with how it sounds. I'd start to say something to the camera, then stop abruptly, rewording what I had just said in my head. With luck, I could finish one sentence, but if the next word sounded wrong, I froze.

"Just keep going," Charlie said. "We can edit out your mistakes."

Only, in my head, I couldn't edit out my mistakes. I couldn't finish a take unless I felt the wording was perfect.

TV requires a completely different mindset. You're supposed to speak like you're talking to a friend. Which brings me to the second problem: the camera. When we talk to a person, we get constant feedback: a smile, a nod, a cocked head. That feedback boosts our energy and enthusiasm. Multiply that by twenty or fifty or two hundred people, and the energy is off the charts.

I do a lot of public speaking, and whether I'm addressing an audience of fifteen or fifteen hundred, I'm comfortable and relaxed. I can speak without notes, smiling and happy, for as long as the engagement requires.

A camera, on the other hand, is an inanimate object composed of gears, dials, and buttons with, at its center, a sterile glass lens. That lens stopped me cold, recording every verbal miscue and mistake.

Charlie wanted me to speak extemporaneously. "Imagine the camera lens is me or Barbara. Pretend you're talking to us." That was probably good advice for most people—and probably what most TV personalities do on television. It didn't work for me.

I wanted the comfort of cue cards or a teleprompter. Or at the very least, to write out my intros ahead of time and rehearse them before taping. Charlie wouldn't hear of it. He wanted me to relax, let my teaching personality come out on camera. A power struggle emerged.

Compounding the problem, Charlie had set up elaborate show openers with the jib camera. (A jib camera sits at the end of a long boom attached to a trolley on rails, grabbing shots from high overhead and in sweeping arcs. It's the camera used to create energy in rock-concert videos.) It probably would have lent energy to *Barbecue University*. But instead, in addition to thinking out loud and improvising my intros, I had to make eye contact with a camera that was literally over my head and constantly moving as I walked toward it.

That made performing even harder, and sometimes it took thirty or forty minutes just to complete a four-line opener. I was frustrated. The crew was frustrated. And we lost a lot of time shooting. It wasn't until I started talking about gear (for instance, "This is a kettle grill, that's a water smoker") that I felt comfortable enough to string sentences together. Grills I knew backward and forward. (I certainly had enough of them in my backyard.) As for the recipes, I knew their step-by-step preparation cold.

But making a recipe on camera is a lot different from cooking it for family or friends. You need to see the ingredients from the camera's point of view, moving in a slow, steady, logical sequence so the camera can follow. Consider a dish from the *Barbecue University* show: a seemingly simple beef kebab from the island of Madeira called *espetada.* (As I would explain on camera, *espetada* means "skewered," from the Portuguese word *espeta*, "sword.")

The beef arrives on set in a glass baking dish over a pan of ice. (On rare occasions when we'd forget to ice the meat, we'd get a flood of mail about food safety.) The diced onion, garlic, bay leaves, wine, and olive oil come in small glass bowls, which the close-up camera videos one by one to create a sort of visual ingredient list. When I go to make the marinade, I need to remember to dump the ingredients into a mixing bowl away from me and toward the camera—an awkward gesture that runs counter to the way you really cook.

I stir them together, again toward the camera, taking care not to block the shot with my arm. The beef is supposed to marinate for four hours, so we have a marinated version to swap out to keep the show moving. Threading marinated meat onto a metal skewer is messy to begin with, but it's even more challenging when trying to do so neatly—and away from you and toward the camera. Especially when inserting a bay leaf between each chunk of beef, which is part of what makes these kebabs so distinctive. (So does grilling it on laurel branches, as they do in Madeira, but we couldn't find those in West Virginia.)

Next comes the grill, which I show how to set up for direct grilling: lighting the charcoal in a chimney starter, raking the embers out in an even layer with a garden hoe. I'm careful to leave a quarter of the grill ember-free to create a "safety zone," where I can move the kebabs if they start to burn.

At this point, I utter my now-infamous grill mantra: "Keep it hot. Keep it clean. Keep it lubricated." (That is, start with a hot grill, clean the grate with a scraper or wire brush, and oil it well with a tightly folded paper towel dipped in vegetable oil and drawn across the grate at the end of tongs.) "The advice works in the bedroom too," I quip with a wink. Charlie says he'll edit that comment out.

I show how to gauge the grill temperature by holding my hand three inches above the grate and counting. "One, two, three Mississippi—ouch!" for a hot fire. "Five or six Mississippi—ouch!" for a moderate fire. "Eight to ten Mississippi" for a cool fire. You get the idea.

I arrange the kebabs on the grate, where they start sizzling amid leaping flames. Enter one of Charlie's coolest innovations: Grill Cam. Charlie had holes cut in the grill fireboxes and fitted each with fireproof glass and a miniature "lipstick" camera. This allowed us to show the barbecue from the ember point of view. It was as surprising as it was effective.

Once grilled, I arrange the kebabs on a platter (neatly and lovingly, please), then transfer one to a plate for tasting. The "taste" would seem like the easiest part of the segment, but it, too, is surprisingly challenging. The bite needs to be big enough to be convincing, but not so large that you talk with your mouth full. Then you describe what you're tasting—meaty, smoky, crisp, tender, salty, spicy, herbal, aromatic—in terms vivid and appetizing enough to make your viewers hungry and, more important, to keep them watching the show.

In one episode, I would prepare three to five recipes, which translates to fifty-some dishes in a thirteen-week series. Try coming up with fifty different ways to describe a fairly confined range of textures and flavors. It isn't easy, believe me. And that's for a guy who writes about food for a living.

The kebabs are, indeed, delicious (a word I normally avoid, because it doesn't really tell you about the specific textures and flavors). The beef has a smoky char flavor, scented with the aroma of fire-singed bay leaves. The onions and garlic add bass notes, while the wine lends a high-pitched touch of acidity. Not bad for a six-ingredient recipe! Here I crack a smile. And speaking of wine, how about a nice earthy red to accompany the *espetada*? I raise a wineglass. Only I'm not allowed to say the name of the winery, because PBS rules prohibit mentioning a sponsor by name.

Back to our kebabs, which the crew dive-bombs and devours the minute the stage manager shouts "Cut." If preparing the recipe at home, it might take thirty minutes of prep and grilling time. This particular segment took us five hours to tape. That's not including the several days in the studio needed to edit those five hours of tape on three different cameras down to an eight-minute segment. Which is why it takes so long—and costs so much—to make a cooking show. And that was only one of fifty segments ahead of us.

Long before streaming, there were DVDs—here featuring the greatest hits of Barbecue University.

As time passed, I got more comfortable in front of the camera. We worked our way through

Louisville wings and cedar-planked salmon; through lemongrass-scented pork satays and fresh ripe plum quarters grilled on giant cinnamon sticks for dessert. (I've always been a sucker for grilled desserts.) I named our shows with shameful puns: "A Little Lamb" (a show on America's underappreciated red meat) and "Grateful Bread" (focusing on bruschetta and grilled pizza).

I took to writing out my intros and practicing them surreptitiously off set. Meanwhile, Charlie and I argued about openers, sponsors, presentation platters, and more. Charlie was used to calling the shots, and my diffidence and lack of experience didn't help. The tension was heightened by the weather; our shoot dates fell between the arrival of Tropical Storm Hanna and Tropical Storm Kyle, which dumped oceans of rain on the Greenbrier. I soldiered on, and we finished the shoot within hours of a torrential downpour.

Charlie and I went on to make three more seasons of *Barbecue University*. The shoots weren't always fun (that's an understatement), but they taught me a lot about television. I like to think they benefited our viewers and helped raise the general level of grilling too.

Never having done television before, I just assumed that it was supposed to be tense and painful. That would change with my next series and a new producer—but I wouldn't know that for a couple more years.

Charlie did leave me with one parting gift: the perfect slogan for my cooking school:

"Barbecue University, where the only marks you get are grill marks."

ɔu happened to be strolling swanky Rodeo Drive in Beverly
ls on a sunny June day in 2003, you might have seen a strange sight:
ıt yellow school bus emblazoned with oversize barbecue book covers
ɪrtraits of its author, yours truly.

was the Barbecue Bus—brainchild of Peter Workman and an inge-
tool for marketing my newest book, *BBQ USA*. The challenge, Peter
reasoned, was giving the media a reason to promote yet another
ɪen book after the huge coverage of *The Barbecue! Bible* and *How*
ll. The Barbecue Bus worked like magic. Part of its success lay in its
ʒy (a barbecue bus is certainly whimsical). Part of it stemmed from
s philosophy as a publisher: Books should inform, but above all, they
l make people happy.

ad our Rodeo Drive shopper set down her Prada and Gucci shopping
ong enough to board the Barbecue Bus—and was not worried about
ıg her Chanel pumps—she would have found there three Weber
(a kettle, a Summit gas grill, and a huge Ranch grill), plus crammed
to-ceiling charcoal, hardwood, chimney starters, tongs, a folding table,
ll the other essentials for staging an impromptu barbecue. But she
bly wouldn't have been able to board, because there wasn't a square
o spare.

he Barbecue Bus was designed to serve as a one-stop entertainment
r, enabling me to do grilling demonstrations at TV stations, fund-
s, and crowd feedings at book signings, and to serve as eye candy at
cue festivals and parades. There was nothing supernatural about the
ecue Bus, but the sight of it inspired an emotion that marketers every-
e strive to capture: delight.

he Barbecue Bus had covered a lot of miles since it left its outfitter
nnecticut to arrive on Rodeo Drive. It parked in Rockefeller Plaza in
York City for an appearance on the *Today* show. It rode in the place

THE RAICHLEN BUTTER BURGER

When I was young, my mom and I loved to eat hamburger meat raw. (I got an early start on steak tartare.) This was back in the days before we Americans worried about salmonella and E. coli. Today, you'd have to be crazy to eat raw ground beef. Which brings me to a dilemma that faces anyone who grills or eats a hamburger. To keep it safe, you need to cook it—make that overcook it—to an internal temperature of 160°F. Safety doesn't necessarily translate to succulence, but I've come up with a workaround: I fold frozen butter into the ground beef; it melts as you grill it, keeping your hamburger succulent even when you cook it all the way through. Here I give you the Raichlen butter burger.

Makes 4 burgers

2 pounds well-chilled ground beef (18 to 20 percent fat)

½ stick (4 tablespoons) cold unsalted butter, cut crosswise into 4 slices, plus 2 tablespoons melted for the buns

Coarse sea salt and freshly ground black pepper

4 brioche hamburger buns or kaiser rolls

4 (1-ounce) slices cheddar or provolone cheese (optional)

To serve the burgers:

4 Boston or bibb lettuce leaves

1 luscious red ripe tomato (preferably heirloom), thinly sliced

Paper-thin slices of sweet onion (optional)

Pickle slices (optional)

Ketchup, Dijon-style mustard, and/or mayonnaise (or mix all three to make your "special sauce")

1. Wet your hands with cold water. Working as quickly and gently as possible, divide the ground beef into 4 balls. Fold a cold slice of butter into the center of each. Flatten each ball into a patty 1 inch thick,

making a dimple in the center. Arrange the burgers on a plate lined with plastic wrap, and cover with more plastic wrap. Refrigerate for at least 30 minutes or for as long as 6 hours while you prepare the garnishes and light your grill.

2. Set up your grill for direct grilling and heat to high. Ideally, you'll grill over a wood fire or over charcoal or gas (adding 1 cup hardwood chips or chunks to the fire to generate wood smoke). Brush or scrape the grill grate clean and oil it well.
3. Just before cooking, generously season the burgers on both sides with salt and pepper, turning gently. Brush the cut sides of the brioche rolls with melted butter.
4. Arrange the burgers on the grate. Grill until the bottoms are browned, 3 to 4 minutes. Gently invert the burgers, using a spatula. (However, never press the burgers with the spatula—you'll force out the succulent juices.). If adding cheese, lay a slice on top of each burger and lower the grill lid. Continue grilling until the cheese is melted and the burgers are cooked to taste, 6 to 8 minutes in all for medium. Use an instant-read thermometer inserted through the side of the burger to check the internal temperature; it should be at least 160°F.
5. Meanwhile, toast the buttered buns, cut side down, on the grill, 1 to 2 minutes.
6. To assemble the burgers, place a lettuce leaf on the bottom bun. (This keeps the meat juices from making the bun soggy.) Place the burger on the lettuce and top with tomato, onion, pickles, and condiments or special sauce.

Chapter Fourteen

HONK IF YOU LOVE BARBECUE

2003

The Barbecue Bus on Rodeo Drive.

of honor in a Brat Days parade in Sheboygan, Wisconsin. It broke down in Death Valley, where a barbecue-obsessed mechanic towed it to his garage to make the repairs necessary to get it back on the road.

And everywhere we went, people honked. This was disconcerting at first, until I remembered the slogan painted on the back of the bus: "Honk if you love barbecue!" And honk people did: from St. Louis to San Antonio, from Baltimore to Birmingham, from Houston to Seattle. During its two years in service, the Barbecue Bus crisscrossed the country three times.

My goal with *BBQ USA* had been to conduct the same sort of exhaustive exploration of American barbecue that I did for global grilling in *The Barbecue! Bible.* I traveled the country from East Coast to West, North to South, visiting all fifty states and southern Canada. I dined at the landmark barbecue restaurants and grill joints. I sampled the iconic dishes and interviewed grill masters and pit bosses, from the established legends to the up-and-comers. Unlike for *The Barbecue! Bible,* I gave myself plenty of time to write *BBQ USA*. Of course, the two years I allotted proved woefully inadequate. I barely finished the book in four.

As a reminder, barbecue refers to large cuts of meat that are cooked "low and slow" with lots of wood smoke; grilling is a fast, high-heat method done directly over the fire. Of course, in barbecue, as in life, there are exceptions to every category, and my travels on the American barbecue trail would reveal them. Would you really call a Connecticut shad "bake" (fish nailed to boards and roasted upright in front of a campfire) grilling? Would you really call El Paso's *barbacoa* (steer head roasted in a fire-heated but smokeless underground pit) barbecue? But rather than quibble over these exceptions, I would celebrate them, because at this point in my journey to live-fire enlightenment, the more exotic the method, the better I liked it.

I wrote *BBQ USA* at an interesting time in American food history. The barbecue titans of the early twentieth century—Sonny Bryans of Dallas and Arthur Bryant and George Gates of Kansas City—had recently passed away. But their influence still loomed large over their successors. Today's new guard of barbecue greats—like Aaron Franklin of Austin, Billy Durney of Brooklyn, and John Lewis of Charleston—were barely out of high school. Some weren't even born yet. Even so, there was plenty to write about when I started *BBQ USA*. There is plenty to write about now, and God willing, there will be plenty to write about a century from now.

The roots of American barbecue go deep. A 1591 engraving by the Belgian engraver Theodor de Bry (I own one of the prints!) depicted a *barbacoa* in central Florida—a raised wooden grate loaded with venison, alligator, and even snake over a blazing fire. One of the first laws promulgated in the Colony of Virginia forbade the discharge of firearms at a barbecue (even back in 1774, we Americans were obsessed with guns and meat). George Washington wrote in his journal about memorable barbecues he attended. (One in Alexandria, Virginia, went on for three days.) When the Hannibal Bridge—the first to span the Mississippi—opened in Kansas City in 1896, the celebratory feast was, you guessed it, a barbecue.

Any book about barbecue had to start with the big four—that is, the barbecue of Texas, North Carolina, Memphis, and Kansas City. I visited all of these places multiple times, dining at such landmark restaurants as Goode Co. in Houston; Wilber's in Goldsboro, North Carolina; Little Jake's Eat It and Beat It in Kansas City (colorfully named and now sadly closed); and the Rendezvous in Memphis.

I ate a lot of remarkable barbecue during my research trips, but what I remember most now are the backstories. How a family feud forced Rick Schmidt to construct a new building to house the venerable Kreuz Market in Lockhart, Texas. (Rick inherited the business, but his sister was bequeathed

A sixteenth-century mixed grill in what would become my home state, Florida.

the original building—today called Smitty's.) Rick paraded embers from the original pit through the streets of Lockhart to light the fires at the new restaurant.

Or how the historic Snow's BBQ in Lexington, Texas, opens at 8 AM (and opens only on Saturday) because it's not uncommon for Texans to eat barbecue for breakfast. Incidentally, Snow's pitmaster, Tootsie Tomanetz, recently celebrated her ninetieth birthday and is still going strong.

Or how Greek immigrant Charlie Vergos opened a sandwich shop—today the Rendezvous—in a Memphis basement in the 1940s, smoking his chickens and hams in a repurposed coal chute. One day, his meat salesman gave him a case of baby back ribs—back then considered a trash cut. Charlie seasoned them with a Peloponnese-inspired spice blend of oregano, garlic salt, and pepper, then grilled them over charcoal. But they didn't become famous until Charlie added paprika to his spice rub, because in Memphis, it isn't barbecue unless it's red. (These rank among my favorite ribs—precisely because they're free of sugary barbecue sauce.)

I first visited Memphis to write about one of the three big American barbecue festivals, the Memphis in May World Championship Barbecue Cooking Contest. I wasn't alone. Even back then, the festival attracted ninety thousand people. Over the years, I've attended Memphis in May; the American Royal in Kansas City; the Jack Daniels Invitational in Lynchburg, Tennessee; and many other barbecue festivals as a journalist, judge, and even honorary team member. My team didn't win, but I did get to sample some singular Memphis specialties, such as barbecued bologna (at Cozy Corner) and barbecued pizza (at Coletta's, a restaurant once patronized by Elvis).

The big four barbecue styles are well documented by many people (including yours truly). What fascinated me more were the micro-regions of American barbecue. One day, after a book signing in Louisville, Kentucky, I drove to Owensboro to experience a style of barbecue found within a thirty-mile radius of this Ohio River town and nowhere else on the planet: barbecued mutton with black dip. Mutton is a lot gamier and stronger-tasting than commonplace lamb, but a half day in a wood-burning pit at restaurants like Old Hickory Bar-B-Q (with roots dating back to 1918) and the Moonlite Bar-B-Q Inn (founded in 1950) transforms it into something not only palatable, but crave-worthy. Black dip is an amalgam of Worcestershire sauce, lemon juice, and melted butter—a mixture that most Americans wouldn't recognize as barbecue sauce, but one that makes the perfect counterpoint for sheep.

In Decatur, Alabama, I learned how a portly railroad man—the appropriately named Big Bob Gibson—developed an odd white barbecue sauce made of mayonnaise, vinegar, and black pepper, lots of black pepper. According to the restaurant's fourth-generation co-owner, Chris Lilly,

Big Bob created the sauce for a customer with an aversion to tomatoes. I watched Chris dip the smoke-bronzed chicken in the sauce twice—first during the cooking, then just prior to serving. Yet another dish that defies the common conception that barbecue should be sweet and red.

Some of the most interesting barbecue I experienced wasn't at restaurants at all. A drive out to the Olympic Peninsula in Washington State brought me to a Makah Indian village, where the locals were celebrating a historic event—a whale hunt in hand-paddled canoes, using spears with inflated seal bladders attached to keep the leviathan from diving to escape. (Whale hunting had been outlawed for decades, but after a long legal battle, the Makah won the right to stage their heritage hunt.) They celebrated with another Makah specialty—a salmon "bake." A great bonfire had been lit and around it stood butterflied king salmon pinioned to upright cedar stakes with crossbars. The seasonings were limited to fresh air and wood smoke. The romantic in me rhapsodized about the experience. The food writer craved a sauce.

We almost missed my cousin Martha's wedding in Salinas, California, on account of a sign I saw on the drive up from San Francisco. "Barbecue today," the sign read, so of course, I made a detour. In those parts, "barbecue" means oysters—grilled in the half shell with garlic butter, grated Parmesan cheese, and a vivifying splash of tequila.

Everywhere I went, people generously shared their time and expertise. Robb Walsh, a respected journalist and barbecue expert in his own right, took me on a tour of Texas Hill Country barbecue. In the space of a day, we ate ourselves silly at the Kreuz Market in Lockhart, Louie Mueller's in Taylor, and the City Market in Luling—the last one famed for its "hot guts," barbecued beef sausage.

A student at my Barbecue University flew me in his Cherokee Six from Wilber's Barbecue in Goldsboro, North Carolina, to Lexington Barbecue two hundred miles to the west. My quest: to settle the debate between eastern and western North Carolina as to whose pulled pork is better. Wilber's cooks whole hog over hickory embers, dousing them with vinegar sauce piqued with red pepper. Lexington Barbecue starts with pork shoulder, adding a vinegar sauce enhanced with a whisper of ketchup. In both cases, the pork is chopped to a fine hash, to be piled on a burger bun, which renders the original cut of hog almost pointless. I'll let Carolinians keep debating. Both are shamelessly good.

A subject as sprawling as American barbecue warranted an equally sprawling book. *BBQ USA* gave it 774 pages. I'd probably still be writing had my editor not reminded me of the deadline clause in my contract. *BBQ USA* came out in spring 2003, shortly followed by the Barbecue Bus.

My wife, who is my biggest supporter and fan, wasn't crazy about *BBQ USA*. She disapproved of its sprawl and lack of focus. "What is superstar chef Thomas Keller doing in a book about American barbecue?" she asked. (He was sharing his recipe for his mother's mayonnaise-slathered roast turkey breast, but I see Barbara's point: You'd hardly call Keller a grill guy.) "Why is Charlie Trotter in the book?" At least the late chef-owner of the acclaimed restaurant that bore his name in Chicago had a wood-burning grill in his Michelin-starred restaurant. He earned his place in *BBQ USA* with a grilled beef and Roquefort salad.

Then there was the artwork—much of it documentary and on point—but some of it decidedly silly. Did I really need to show the New York foie gras mogul, Michael Ginor, with baby ducklings on his head? For that matter, did grilled foie gras really belong in a barbecue book? As I thumb through *BBQ USA* now (careful not to drop it, lest the four-pound monster break my foot), I have to agree with Barbara—the book contains too many recipes and too much material that is not directly connected to barbecue. But at that stage of life, I was still in overcompensation mode: I subconsciously believed a big book would help make up my self-imagined shortcomings. I could probably have cut the book by a third and still produced an authoritative treatise.

James Beard Award—my fifth—for BBQ USA.

Whatever the book's flaws, it was nominated for a James Beard Award—my fifth. Barbara had a prior engagement and was unable to attend the ceremony. When it came time to announce the winner of the Best Single-Subject Cookbook category, much to my surprise, they called my name. I called Barbara and set my cell phone on speaker so she could hear the presentation of the award and my acceptance speech. I relished the "I told you so" moment, even if I realized, deep down inside, that *BBQ USA* would have been a much better book had I followed Barbara's advice.

BBQ USA went on to sell more than four hundred thousand copies—fewer than *Barbecue! Bible* or *How to Grill,* but quite respectable in the publishing world. As the years passed, restaurants closed and pitmasters moved on. The book finally went out of print in 2024. So if you still have a copy, hold on to it. Not that it will become a collector's item. But it does offer a snapshot—and a damn comprehensive one, if I may say—of the state of American barbecue in the early twenty-first century.

FIRE-DIPPED PORK STEAKS

BBQ USA was my love song to regional American barbecue. The book focuses on America's major barbecue regions, such as Memphis, Texas, Kansas City, and the Carolinas. I also covered what I call micro-barbecue regions, like Upstate New York, with its Cornell chicken; and Santa Maria, California, with its oak-grilled tri-tip. But one region escaped me, even after four years of traveling the barbecue trail and 774 pages. Monroe County, Kentucky, specializes in pork shoulder steaks—grilled over blazing hickory and double dipped in a fiery sauce made from cayenne pepper, black pepper, hot sauce, and melted lard. Can't find pork shoulder steaks? Substitute pork chops. And to be a touch more modern, I call for melted butter instead of lard.

Serves 4

For the dip:

¾ cup distilled white vinegar

¾ cup (12 tablespoons) unsalted butter

2 tablespoons Crystal Hot Sauce or other favorite hot sauce

1 tablespoon Dijon mustard (optional)

1 to 2 teaspoons cayenne pepper (or as much as you can bear)

1 to 2 teaspoons freshly ground black pepper (or as much as you can bear)

2 teaspoons salt

2 pounds (¼ to ½ inch thick) pork shoulder steaks or pork rib chops

You'll also need:

hickory or other hardwood chips or chunks

1. Place the ingredients for the dip in a deep pot and simmer over medium heat until the butter melts, whisking to dissolve the sauce.

Simmer the dip until richly flavored, 5 minutes. Pour half of the dip into a baking dish or foil pan the size and shape of the pork steaks.

2. Meanwhile, set up your grill for direct grilling and heat to high. In the best of worlds, you'd grill over hickory. If using a charcoal grill, toss hickory chips or chunks on the coals. If using a gas grill, place a few hickory chunks under the grate over the burners. Brush or scrape the grill grate clean and oil it well.
3. Dip the pork steaks in the dip in the baking dish, turning with tongs to coat both sides. Arrange the pork steaks on the grate. Grill until browned on both sides and cooked to taste, 3 to 5 minutes per side for medium.
4. Dip the cooked pork steaks into the pot of remaining dip before serving. For extra punishment, ladle this second batch of dip into small bowls or cups for serving on the side by way of a sauce.

Chapter Fifteen

PRIMAL GRILL

2008–2010

The "Cactus" poster launched my second TV series: Primal Grill.

We wrapped *Barbecue University*.

I had a new look: black jeans and untucked Oxford shirts in place of the tucked-in logoed denim. I had a new location: southern Arizona, where we wouldn't have to worry about hurricanes. Above all, I had a new attitude toward television, which had gone from being an ordeal to an activity I actually enjoyed.

This was largely thanks to my new producer, Matt Cohen of Resolution Pictures. (I love the play on words.) Matt had won Emmys for two of his shows, but he didn't boast or grandstand. He was thoughtful and soft-spoken. In the fifteen years we've worked together, I've never heard him raise his voice on the set. Matt produces by building consensus and directs as much by question as by dictate. "Maybe we should try this," he says when faced with a decision, or "What if we do that?" His crew loves him—many have worked with him for decades. Matt is also my build and height: We used to joke that if he grew a beard, he could be my stand-in.

At the time, I was deep into my research for my next book, *Planet Barbecue.* I had just written the book's opener—a history of barbecue chronicling the birth of live-fire cooking 1.8 million years ago and how it shaped human evolution and civilization. Mindful of barbecue's prehistoric roots, we decided to call the series *Primal Grill.*

The book also inspired our content. *Primal Grill* would take the international message of *Barbecue University* even further. Over the next three seasons, I would grill *sosaties* (beef kebabs) from South Africa, *picanha* (spit-roasted fat-cap sirloin) from Brazil, *barbacoa* (pit-roasted pork shoulder) from Mexico, and vertically skewered swordfish in a genuine Indian tandoor.

Befitting the show's name, we did more extreme grilling in *Primal Grill.* In one show, I impaled king salmon fillets onto cedar stakes to be roasted in front of a campfire. I grilled T-bones "caveman" style—directly on the embers—and served them under a sizzling pan-fry of jalapeños, cilantro, and garlic. (I called it "hellfire hot sauce.") I roasted artichokes in a clay beehive oven and topped wood-fired pizzas with potatoes and bacon, in the style of French *tartiflette.* I spit-roasted chickens and rib roasts, to be sure, but also spun foods not normally associated with the rotisserie, like pineapple.

But the biggest difference between *Barbecue University* and *Primal Grill* was our relationship with the audience. In most cooking shows, viewers watch a host behind a counter, unaware of the twenty crewmembers behind the scenes. Matt and I agreed we wanted our viewers to see not just me, but the team that makes a TV show happen. We broke down the fourth wall as it were, showing how we build the set, sync the cameras, and fly the "silk" (a huge square of fabric positioned overhead to compensate for the light changes caused by clouds and sunlight). We joined the fire wranglers as they assembled the grills and hauled them on and off the set.

We followed our field chef, Chris Lynch, as he cooked the half dozen packer (whole) briskets needed to tape an eight-minute segment: a raw brisket for me to trim and season; a partially cooked brisket to show what the meat should look like halfway through the cook; a third brisket wrapped in butcher paper; a fourth brisket resting in an insulated cooler; a fifth brisket for me to slice and taste. Plus, an extra brisket for backup, in case our beauty burned, fell, or otherwise became unpresentable.

Matt also came up with the idea of filling the background with flaming grills and smokers. Our goal was educational as well as aspirational—we wanted our viewers to learn how to use as many different grills as possible. We also wanted people to dream of a backyard that looked like ours.

This gave rise to two frequently asked questions from our viewers:

"Do you actually cook food in all those grills and smokers or are they just for show?"

"Who gets to eat all the food?"

My director/producer, Matt Cohen, of Resolution Pictures.

Yes, indeed, we used all the grills and smokers in the background. That's where we smoked those six briskets, for example, and where we prepared the backups for all the dishes I demonstrated on the set. As for the second question: Everyone eats the food. The host. The crew. The hotel staff. As you can imagine, the leftovers made us very popular at the resort where we shot the series.

Also new for this show: We brought in a professional food stylist. Her job was to create the mouthwatering food shots seen when the show opens. Our DP (director of photography) mounted a camera on a trolley on rails so he could take slow-moving videos of the finished dishes. These graceful beauty sequences became one of the trademarks of our show—and they'd get more mouthwatering with each successive season.

Primal Grill gave me the opportunity to cook on some cool new grills. A Grillworks wood-burner joined the collection: an Argentinean asado-style grill with V-shaped grate bars (to channel off the fat) and a grate that raised and lowered with a crank and a ratchet. We fired up a wood-burning brick pizza oven. Weber was back with its mammoth Ranch grill (it looks like a kettle grill on steroids) and a host of impressive new gas grills. If you geek out on grills like I do, it was paradise.

We shot the first season of *Primal Grill* at the Tubac Golf Resort and Spa in an artist town in southern Arizona. Our set was a pasture, which Matt dressed up with a wooden fence and an antique hay wagon. Cows would wander in and out of the background, and it amazed me how attuned they were to the moods of the humans on the set. They became downright restive the final day of the shoot, as if sensing our imminent departure. For my part, I sure felt guilty whenever I grilled a steak.

The next season, we moved to the Esplendor Resort in Rio Rico, Arizona. Our backdrop was the Arizona desert with the Tumacácori Highlands in the distance. Matt found a vintage pickup truck, which we parked on the set to add local color. We also installed a corral with a couple horses.

Group meeting on the set of Primal Grill. *My longtime assistant, Nancy Loseke, is second from the left.*

Our days were long; it typically took four to five hours to shoot a single dish from start to finish. Often, we ran behind, which prompted another cool visual in *Primal Grill*: the night shoot. Come sunset, our gaffers would set up huge projection lights to illuminate the set and the background. The temperature dropped forty degrees from the height of the day. I took to wearing fleece vests in a vain attempt to stay warm.

I loved the look of our night shoots, but they made my life more difficult. At night I didn't have some of the visual cues I had during the daytime. Once, doing a segment on tandoori fish and flatbread, I grabbed a screaming-hot metal skewer with my bare hand. My flesh hissed like meat on the grill. Happily, the ensuing blister was on my palm, so I could hide it during the rest of the shoot.

Some of my all-time favorite recipes came out of that shoot:

- The Tubac T-bone (topped with sizzling jalapeños)
- Huli huli ribs from Hawaii, cooked on the rotisserie with a sweet-salty pineapple-soy glaze
- Buffa-que shrimp—a grilled seafood version of the fiery wing made famous by the Anchor Bar in Buffalo, New York
- Drunken sailors—oysters grilled in the shells with tequila, cilantro, and Asiago cheese

Our grand finale in season three was a magisterial whole hog cooked by the resort's food and beverage manager. It was hard work, with backbreaking hours and extreme weather conditions. I loved every minute.

Primal Grill continued for three seasons, and it represented a breakthrough in my television career. I went from dreading a TV shoot to counting the days until the next one.

GREEN LIGHTNING SHRIMP TACOS

Grilled shrimp turn up all along the world's barbecue trail. This version takes its inspiration from coastal Mexico—hence the chilies, cilantro, scallion, garlic, and lime marinade. For the best results, use shrimp local to your area: Key West pinks in my neck of the woods (Florida), Gulf shrimp in Louisiana, Carolina shrimp in the Southeast, spot prawns on the West Coast—you get the idea. Mezcal is the smoky cousin of tequila, but the latter works in a pinch. I like to grill the shrimp kebab-style and serve them on tacos. The sour cream tames some of the chili heat.

Serves 4

2 pounds extra-large shrimp, peeled and deveined

For the marinade:

4 jalapeño peppers, seeded and coarsely chopped (for hotter shrimp, leave some or all of the seeds in)

3 scallions, trimmed and rough chopped

2 cloves garlic, rough chopped

1 bunch cilantro, rinsed, shaken dry, stemmed, and chopped

1 or 2 canned chipotle chilies, stemmed and rough chopped

1 teaspoon ground cumin

1 teaspoon dried oregano

½ cup extra-virgin olive oil

¼ cup fresh lime juice

2 tablespoons mezcal or tequila

Coarse salt and freshly ground black pepper to taste

For serving:

1 ½ cups finely shredded green cabbage or iceberg lettuce

1 large ripe red tomato, diced

Sour cream or Mexican crema

Lime wedges, for squeezing

8 corn or small flour tortillas, warmed

You'll also need:

bamboo or metal skewers

1. Thread the shrimp onto skewers. The skewer should pass through the head and tail ends, so the shrimp lie flat. Arrange the kebabs in a baking dish just large enough to hold them.
2. Make the marinade: Place the jalapeños, scallions, garlic, cilantro, chipotles, cumin, and oregano in a food processor and puree to a smooth paste. Work in the olive oil, lime juice, mezcal, and salt and pepper to taste—the marinade should be highly seasoned.
3. Pour the marinade over the kebabs, turning to coat both sides. Cover and marinate the shrimp in the refrigerator for 30 to 60 minutes, turning the kebabs once or twice.
4. Set up your grill for direct grilling and heat to high. Brush or scrape the grill grate clean and oil it well.
5. Arrange the cabbage, tomato, sour cream, and lime wedges in bowls or on a platter.
6. Remove the shrimp kebabs from the marinade, discarding the marinade. Arrange the kebabs on the grate and grill until the shrimp are sizzling, browned, and cooked through, 1 to 2 minutes per side. While you're at it, warm the tortillas on the grill and wrap in a cloth napkin.
7. To serve, unskewer the shrimp and place several on a warmed tortilla. Top with cabbage, tomato, sour cream, and a squeeze of lime juice. Repeat until all the shrimp and tortillas are used up. Dig in!

Chapter Sixteen

TRAVELS ON THE WORLD'S BARBECUE TRAIL

2006–2010

Sampling barbecued eel with Barbara at a Tokyo grill parlor.

Long before my *Planet Barbecue* TV show, there was a book—and a very odd reason for writing it. Not for money, although the money was good. Not to fill an editorial niche, although there had never been a book quite like it. Not even because I always welcome the chance to pack my suitcase and hit the world's barbecue trail. No, *Planet Barbecue* came into being for the oddest reason of all: It was supposed to be the title of another book.

Flash back to spring 1998. My first grill book, *The Barbecue! Bible,* was at the printer. The editorial department had signed off on the bluelines—the final page proofs—and bound copies would arrive in two weeks.

Around this time, I was telling the editor of a travel magazine I wrote for about the new book.

"You should call it *Planet Barbecue,*" he said.

Eureka! After months of struggling to come up with the right title, I found it. But the book was literally on press, and no matter how much I begged or pleaded, it was too late to change the title. *The Barbecue! Bible* it would be.

I loved the name *Planet Barbecue.* In two words, it summed up my approach to live-fire cooking and my life's work. If I couldn't use the title for the existing book, I decided, I'd just have to write a new one.

Ten years later, I pitched the idea to Workman. My editor, Suzanne Rafer, asked the obvious question: "How would *Planet Barbecue* differ from *The Barbecue! Bible*?"

"In three fundamental narratives," I said, improvising on the spot. "Places. People. Photos. And all new recipes, of course, which are the soul of any cookbook." I rattled off some of the new places I would visit: Australia and South Africa, Central Asia and Eastern Europe.

"I'll point readers to the must-try grill specialties in all the world's barbecue cultures," I told Suzanne. "I'll name the single best grill restaurant in each country and the must-try dish to order there. I'll open the book with a two-million-year history of barbecue and close it with a crash course on fuels, tools, grills, and grilling techniques. Along the way, I'll pack the book with practical tips and behind-the-scenes insights, turning *Planet Barbecue* into a must-have not just for cooks, but also for food lovers and travelers of every stripe."

"The second differentiator is people," I told Suzanne, improvising further. (I was definitely getting better at improvising.) "I'll include titans of global grilling, like South America's Francis Mallmann" (who had recently published his visionary book, *Seven Fires*, with Workman's sister publisher, Artisan) "and live-fire legends like Toshihiro Wada of Tokyo's Bird Land" (a robatayaki bar frequented by such culinary luminaries as Jamie Oliver and Joël Robuchon). "Throughout the book I'll profile 'Fire Starters'—the world's foremost grill masters, complete with their secrets," I said.

Finally, there would be photographs. *The Barbecue! Bible* came out in black and white, illustrated with woodcuts. (Workman wouldn't add photographs until a later anniversary edition.) "We'll fill *Planet Barbecue* with gorgeous images," I told Suzanne. "Evocative travel scenes. Thrilling shots of blazing grills and smoke-shrouded grill masters. Drop-dead-gorgeous food photos. A book so hunger-inducing, readers will want to lick the pages."

Then I brought out my strongest argument: *The Barbecue! Bible* and *How to Grill* had become million-copy bestsellers. *Planet Barbecue* would be the sequel—a *Barbecue! Bible* on steroids.

Suzanne suggested I negotiate directly with Peter Workman. Peter offered a generous advance. I had the chutzpah to ask for double. I must have caught him in a weak moment, because the normally cautious publisher agreed. We shook hands, and *Planet Barbecue* was born.

AND THEN CAME THE HARD PART: the research. I organized my travels across four broad regions.

The Asia trip took me from India to Australia, with stops in Singapore, Malaysia, Indonesia, Thailand, Cambodia, Vietnam, Laos, Japan, Korea, and perhaps the best-kept barbecue secret in the Far East: the Philippines. More accurately, I should say "our" trip, because Barbara gamely agreed to join me. Provided I lodge her in five-star hotels, I was free to prowl funky grill joints and barbecue back alleys to my heart's content.

The Latin American journey covered Argentina, Uruguay, Brazil, Peru, and Mexico. It confirmed a theory I'd long held: The older a civilization, the more sophisticated its cuisine and its grilling. Consider Mexico and Peru. Long before the Spanish arrived, the Maya developed such icons of Mexican barbecue as *tikin xik* and *cochinita pibil.* (The former is sour-orange-and-cumin-marinated grilled snapper; the latter, banana-leaf-wrapped, pit-roasted pulled pork.) Peru's beloved *cuy* (rotisserie guinea pig) and *anticuchos* (beef heart kebabs) originated with the Inca centuries before Pizarro set sail from Spain.

On the European trip, I revisited grill cultures I already knew well—France, Italy, Greece, Spain, and Turkey—ferreting out new dishes from each. I also explored countries with highly evolved barbecue traditions I'd never realized existed. For example, who knew about Germany's *Spiessbraten*—pork roast stuffed with sliced onions and cooked on a hand-cranked rotisserie over a beechwood fire in Saarbrücken? Or *Schweinhaxe,* spit-roasted ham hocks seasoned with an herb popular in the Middle Ages, mugwort?

EVERYWHERE, I MARVELED AT the ingenuity of the world's grill masters. Cowboys in the Australian outback grilled lamb chops on a shovel blade over a campfire. In Bogotá, artist-turned-restaurateur Andrés Jaramillo packed a beef tenderloin with salt, bundled it in a cotton cloth, and charred it directly in the embers to make Colombia's beloved *lomo al trapo* ("tenderloin in cloth"). Normally, tenderloin is the least flavorful cut of steer. This version came as a revelation.

I certainly learned some interesting new grilling techniques:

- A Belgian grill master who tosses "fire spice" (bay leaves, juniper berries, coriander seeds, rosemary, and oregano) onto the fire to pump up the fragrance of the wood smoke.
- An Afghan griller turned me on to onion water—an incredibly flavorful marinade made by grating and straining an onion.
- An Israeli grill master showed me how to dip a half onion at the end of a barbecue fork in vegetable oil and use it to grease the grill grate—a technique I still use today.
- A Japanese yakitori master introduced me to *tare,* a grilling sauce that had been two decades in the making. Each time he dipped a grilled chicken skewer into the sauce, he increased its flavor—a tradition he started twenty years earlier. (He replenishes the ingredients and re-boils the sauce to sterilize it each day.)
- A Laotian grill mistress had a simple trick for handling charcoal: Put plastic bags over your hands to keep them clean.

Grilled eggs became an unexpected leitmotif on my travels. In Hanoi, I watched a street vendor roast eggs in the shell on a grill fashioned from a tire rim. (She served them wrapped in lettuce leaves with sliced chilies, fresh basil, and mint, alongside Vietnam's ubiquitous sweet-salty-sour *nuoc cham* dipping sauce.) At the Auberge Shulamit in Rosh Pina, Israel, eggs came smoked in a silky pâté—the world's most interesting egg salad. In Cambodia, grill mistresses emptied fresh eggs through tiny holes in the shells, scrambling them with pepper, sugar, and fish sauce. They refilled the eggs through a funnel and grilled them kebab-style on bamboo skewers.

The world's weirdest barbecue? Kokoretzi in Greece. Think of it as haggis on a spit.

Determined to leave no barbecue uneaten, I sampled my share of oddities. In Uruguay, I feasted on *choto,* lamb intestines rolled into neat coils and grilled over charcoal until crusty. In Bogotá, I tasted capybara—a giant rodent with sweet, pork-like flesh. In Australia, I sampled kangaroo (it was surprisingly beefy). In Kyoto I tried a springtime delicacy—*ayu* ("sweetfish"), a finger-length grilled fish you eat head, gills, guts, bones, and all.

The single strangest dish I sampled on *Planet Barbecue*? That would be *kokoretsi*—a Greek mixed grill of sorts featuring lamb brains, liver, lungs, spleen, and other organs threaded onto long skewers, wrapped in small intestines, then spit-roasted over charcoal. I like to think of it as haggis on a spit and, amazingly, I liked it enough to clean my plate.

One of the great rewards of researching *Planet Barbecue* was meeting the world's master grillers. I spent time with hundreds—many legends in their countries, some internationally acclaimed.

There was Haji Samuri, who began his career as an itinerant satay vendor in Java, carrying his "kitchen" on a shoulder yoke—brazier on one side, tiny table and stools on the other. Over the decades, he built a restaurant empire that now serves five thousand people a day. A barbecue success story in the best rags-to-riches tradition.

There was Hassan Bin Brik, the then-octogenarian owner of Marrakech's legendary Haj Brik restaurant, who single-handedly launched the local barbecue scene from a grill mounted on a pushcart. I wondered if I would still burn with passion for barbecue when I was in my eighties.

There was Milica Perunović in Belgrade, Serbia; and Azlinah Kudari in Melaka, Malaysia—two grill mistresses from opposite ends of the planet, whose standing-room-only restaurants proved barbecue isn't just a guy thing.

But the master who impressed me most was Victor Arguinzoniz, the autodidact chef-owner of Asador Etxebarri in Spain's Basque Country. Etxebarri was the world's first grill restaurant to earn a Michelin star, and today, it ranks number two on the *World's 50 Best Restaurants* list. I don't believe I've ever met someone as obsessed by live-fire cooking as Victor—and that includes me. Victor designed a custom grill with a series of grates that raise and lower with the turn of a crank. He burns oak logs to embers, which he transfers to the grill with a shovel, building a separate fire for each dish he cooks. You read that right: each. From Victor, I learned a trick I use to this day: spritzing grilled seafood with dry white wine from a spray bottle.

The logistics of researching *Planet Barbecue* were daunting and expensive (by the time I turned in the *Planet Barbecue* manuscript, I had visited seventy-three countries on six continents, including such unexpected barbecue destinations as Mauritius and Laos.) But even canceled flights had benefits. If our flight from Luang Prabang, Laos, to Bangkok had departed on time, I never would have wandered the night market, where freshwater fish from the Mekong River come grilled Popsicle-style on sticks, served with fire-seared rice cakes for snacking.

Some trips were spur of the moment. I was so impressed by the Azeri barbecue I experienced in Moscow, I hopped a last-minute flight to Baku, Azerbaijan. There, grill master Mehman Huseynov (I called him the "Emeril of Azerbaijan") wowed me with *lula* (cumin-scented minced lamb kebabs), *govurmasi* (turmeric-rubbed lamb roasted in a *tanir*, Azerbaijan's version of an Indian tandoor), and *kartof kebab* (mashed potatoes grilled on a skewer).

Mehman even indulged in some culinary showboating, dipping vanilla ice cream balls in beaten egg, rolling them in shredded coconut, then threading them onto skewers. He grilled them over a screaming-hot fire on a *mangal* (open metal box grill) just long enough to toast the coconut and set the egg—without melting the center. Grilled ice cream. What will they think of next?

As for the single most memorable day of my *Planet Barbecue* adventures? It began in Argentina with a wee-hours breakfast of "Buenos Aires heart-stopper"—charcoal-grilled strip steak topped with fried eggs and bacon. From there, I flew to Montevideo, Uruguay, for a full-bore *parrillada* (mixed grill) lunch served by a local barbecue club. Later that afternoon, I boarded another plane for Porto Alegre, Brazil, where I had dinner at the Galpão Crioulo (Creole Ranch). The meat-centric meal included *picanha* (fat-cap sirloin), *fraldinha* (flank steak), *maminha* (tri-tip), and *alcatra* (top sirloin). The grand finale? A spit-roasted pineapple carved shawarma-style onto my plate. Three different styles of barbecue. And three amazing meals in three different countries in twenty-four hours. It was quite a day.

THE PHOTOGRAPHY FOR THE BOOK posed a whole other set of challenges. Initially, we hired a professional photographer, Penny De Los Santos, who accompanied me on a barbecue crawl in Moscow. (Moscow, I reasoned, provided the best opportunity to experience the barbecue of the former republics of the Soviet Union without logging weeks of travel.) Penny shot some amazing scenes, which can be admired in the Russian and Uzbek sections of the book. But we quickly realized that it made more sense for me to complete my research before bringing a photographer on board. However, by the time that photographer arrived, I would have moved on to the next country.

So, I took photos with my Canon ELPH camera (cell-phone photography was just coming into its own). They weren't of Penny's quality, not by a long shot, but Workman photo director Anne Kerman came up with an ingenious way to make them work. She reframed my photos as Polaroids—grabbed on the fly while doing my research. That gave the book an immediacy and energy despite my lack of professional skills. We wound up with six hundred photos in the book.

Planet Barbecue took four years to write. It damn near killed me. I woke at four every morning to get a jump on the workday. Recipe testing alone took months, taxing Barbara's patience as a small army of testers invaded our kitchen.

Planet Barbecue launched on May 1, 2010 (appropriately, International Workers Day and spring festival day in much of Europe). The dedication page featured a photo of who at the time were the three women in my life: my wife, Barbara; my stepdaughter, Betsy; and my granddaughter, Ella Francesca. The three all wore red, although Barbara and Betsy swear they didn't coordinate outfits.

My book tour began with a *Today* show appearance and continued on to twenty-five cities. After the US and Canada, I toured Europe. In Germany, I had the pleasant surprise of meeting a journalist who delayed our interview

Planet Barbecue—*traveling the world's barbecue trail through sixty countries on six continents.*

because she hadn't finished reading the book (a rarely heard qualm in this country). In Holland, I met the founder of a Steven Raichlen fan club. In France, I appeared on *France Info*, a radio show with the gravitas of NPR in the US. I listen to *France Info* every morning—I can't describe how thrilling it was for me to be a guest on the show.

How do you measure success?

Through bestseller lists? At the book party at Workman's offices, Peter presented me with a framed copy of *Planet Barbecue* bearing a brass plaque: "New York Times Bestseller." For the first time in my career, I made the list. It felt terrific.

Through the words of your colleagues? "Just when you thought Steven Raichlen taught you everything there was to know about grilling, he returns with *Planet Barbecue*," wrote *Top Chef*'s Tom Colicchio. "*Planet Barbecue* delivers," proclaimed Thomas Keller, while Francis Mallmann hailed it "an epic voyage."

But the ultimate measure of success of a book may just be how the author feels on reading it. The book captured the world of barbecue in the first decade of the new millennium. Even today, I'm not quite sure how I managed to make all those trips and write all those words (638 pages' worth). I reread *Planet Barbecue* recently, and it remains the book of which I'm most proud.

Of course, some of the grill masters I profiled have died since I wrote the book. Others have closed their restaurants. That's the bittersweet reality of writing an eyewitness cookbook. Suzanne Rafer and photo editor Anne Kerman have retired. Peter Workman passed away, and his publishing house now belongs to the multinational publishing conglomerate Hachette.

As for the three women in my life on the dedication page, today Ella is driving. By the time this memoir comes out, her two siblings will be driving too. Betsy still serves as Director of Sports Nutrition at the Miami Heat. And Barbara and I just celebrated our thirty-fifth anniversary.

Eventually *Planet Barbecue* suffered the fate of most books: In 2023, it went out of print. (You can still order the e-book.) But I'll always remember those five years of round-the-world travel and research as among the most exhilarating, exhausting, and rewarding of my life. I still can't believe I did it.

BARBECUE ALLEY LAMB KEBABS

Every city has one—a street lined with grill joints and cook stalls, where meat sizzles over open flames and the air is fragrant with barbecue. In Marrakech, Morocco, said barbecue alley is Bani Sadr Street—just off what may be the liveliest square in all of North Africa, the Jemaa el-Fna. (The square, with its elaborate pop-up restaurants, makes an awesome barbecue destination too.) And once again, my inner sensor goes off, buzzing with the thrill of finding authentic grilling the way the locals enjoy it. It's a thrill that has kept me traveling the world's barbecue trail for thirty years. The meat of choice in Morocco is lamb—here grilled simply on skewers, with salt and ground cumin as the sole seasonings, with a simple tomato relish by way of a condiment. I've jazzed up the recipe a little (I can't resist), interspersing the lamb chunks with onions and peppers. Cubanelles are light green peppers with a mild flavor and no heat—a close facsimile of the peppers you find in Morocco. Preserved lemons are pickled lemons. Look for them jarred in gourmet shops and of course at Moroccan markets. Or substitute lemon zest and lemon juice. Think of this as Marrakech shish kebab and don't think of firing up your grill without trying it.

Serves 4

1 large sweet onion

1 ½ pounds boneless lamb (preferably from the shoulder and not too lean), cut into ¾-inch cubes

2 cubanelle peppers or poblanos, seeded and cut into ¾-inch triangles

Coarse salt and freshly ground black pepper

Ground cumin

For the tomato relish:

1 large, luscious, ripe red tomato (or 2 small tomatoes)

3 tablespoons finely chopped onion

2 tablespoons minced preserved lemon *or* grated zest and juice of 1 lemon

3 tablespoons finely chopped fresh parsley

Coarse salt and freshly ground black pepper

You'll also need:

metal or bamboo skewers

1. Cut the onion in half crosswise, then cut each half into 6 wedges and break each wedge into segments. Thread the lamb onto the skewers, alternating with onion and pepper pieces (one or the other between each chunk of meat). Finely chop the onion pieces that are too small to skewer and set aside for the relish. Lightly season the kebabs with salt and pepper.
2. To make the relish, cut the tomato in half crosswise. Grate it, starting with the cut side, on the coarse side of a box grater. The skin will stay on the outside of the grater, which makes this a very easy way to peel tomatoes. Stir in 3 tablespoons chopped onion, the preserved lemon, and parsley, and season with salt and pepper to taste. The relish should be highly seasoned.
3. Set up your grill for direct grilling and heat to high. Brush or scrape the grill grate clean and oil it well.
4. Arrange the kebabs on the grate and grill until sizzling, browned, and cooked to taste, 2 minutes per side for medium-rare, 3 minutes per side for medium. (Moroccans eat their lamb more well-done than we do: medium to medium-well.)
5. Transfer the kebabs to a platter or plates. Sprinkle each with salt and cumin. Serve with the tomato relish for spooning or dipping.

Chapter Seventeen

PARLEZ-VOUS BARBECUE?

2008–2015

On the set of Le Maître du Grill *with sound engineer Simon and makeup artist Pascale.*

C*inq:* The food stylist arranges a pile of fiery red chilies in an Arcimboldo-esque still life composed of ingredients I'm about to use to make piri piri chicken.

Quatre: The makeup artist powders my forehead to cut the shine. *Zut,* it's hot standing next to all these grills.

Trois: The cameraman rehearses his move—close-up on the ingredient display, panning out to the grills and the worktable with me behind it.

Deux: The gaffer starts moving the camera dolly on the rails that curve around the front of the set.

Un: I take a deep breath and lock my eyes on the lens, trying to remember to smile, act animated, and look relaxed (which is harder than it sounds) while delivering my lines in a language that I have studied and loved since my first French class in high school, but that, ultimately, is not my own.

Bonjour! Je suis Steven Raichlen. Bienvenue au Maître du Grill!

There have been many improbable turns in my life as a food writer, but none, perhaps, so surprising as my TV career in Québec. Walking down the street in Montréal or Québec City, people would shout, "Bonjour, Steven!" Or, more often, "Bonjour, Monsieur Raichlen," the Québécois being more formal than people in my country. I would look over my shoulder to see if they were calling out to my dad.

My Québec grilling adventure had begun with my book *Miami Spice,* the translation rights for which were purchased by the Montréal-based publisher Les Éditions de l'Homme. Like many Québécois, publisher Pierre Lespérance had a winter vacation home in South Florida. We arranged to meet for lunch at the tony Bal Harbour shopping mall in North Miami. When Pierre realized I spoke French, he asked if I would be willing to do a book tour. Twist my arm! I flew to Montréal that spring, where radio and TV hosts were delighted—and not a little amazed—to be interviewing an American who spoke their language.

While in Montréal I made a prescient observation: There was not a balcony so narrow or a terrace so small that it didn't boast a barbecue grill. I guess after eight months of winter, the Québécois would grab any occasion to fire up their grills. Never mind that the menu was limited to sausage, chicken, or steak—charred to within an inch of its edible life. This was barbecue's promised land.

A few years later, *How to Grill* came out in French and it quickly became a one-hundred-thousand-plus-copy bestseller. That may not sound like a staggering number for the US (although it isn't chicken scratch). But keep in mind that at the time, Québec had a population of six million, so roughly one in sixty people bought my book.

At one of my book signings, a tall, young, good-looking guy named Sébastien Arsenault approached me. "I own a TV station called Zeste," he said. "How would you like to do a barbecue show?"

Mon œil (literally, "My eye"—a French expression for deep skepticism). Like this would really happen. But sure enough, nine months later, in 2009, I found myself on an outdoor TV set in the village of Knowlton (population 2,900), deep in Québec's Lake Country, introducing myself as *Le Maître du Grill* (the Grill Master).

The shoot took place on the estate of Seb's father, Serge Arsenault. In the 1980s and '90s, Serge was a popular French Canadian TV host, sportscaster, and promoter who launched the Montréal Marathon and brought competitive cycling to Québec. When I met him, he loved nothing better than traversing his estate on his tractor—to bring bushes and trees from his greenhouse to our set to create the illusion of summer. (This was, after all, a barbecue show.) Never mind that the temperature hovered around fifty degrees, which is certainly not summer weather for this Floridian. One day during the shoot it actually snowed.

The set overlooked a pond (that's how large Serge's property is), and the setup—rustic worktable flanked by grills—followed my American TV show model. The crew organization was similar too: field chef to cook backups and swap-outs, food stylist to ready the finished dishes for beauty shots, camera and sound crew, gaffers, stage manager, director—the whole nine yards.

But there were differences. For one, I had a makeup artist (in the US, my makeup—if you can call it that—was applied by the stage manager). Her name was Pascale Lanari and she went on to write a book called *Maquilleuse de Stars* (*Make-Up Artist of the Stars*). And there, among such Canadian luminaries as Céline Dion and Roch Voisine, was Steven Raichlen from Miami.

I also had a wardrobe person, which meant someone to spare me the angst of picking out my own clothes. (I hate clothes shopping, as you've probably noticed if you watch my shows.) At the same time, I often ran the risk of looking like someone I wasn't.

As we prepared for the first day of shooting, I still had two stumbling blocks to overcome. The first was the stand-up intros. The second was the lead cameraman's headgear. Back in those days, my intros to a particular show or segment ran a full paragraph. (Over the years, I've streamlined my delivery.) Talking to camera without a prompter in English is hard enough. In French, it could eat up an hour to get my lines right. So, our director came up with a strategy in which he'd shoot me one line at a time, moving the camera after each take. The result was a rush of staccato one-liners, which certainly gave the show a lively start.

As for the cameraman's offending headgear, it was a baseball cap with a large Yankees logo. Now, I'm a diehard Red Sox fan and I couldn't see staring at that for two weeks. He graciously agreed to cover it with a circle of cardboard. The shoot continued without incident.

The first season hewed closely to the menus I did on my *Barbecue University* TV shows in the US. This gained us time, as I had already worked through the staging and timing of the dishes.

We wrapped (finished the shoot) on a glorious day in May. The sun had finally come out; the temperature rose above eighty. I could scarcely believe I had done it: taped a thirteen-part TV series in French. At our wrap party, Seb grabbed a microphone and made the following farewell speech:

> *We have had the good fortune to work with an American who came to our country, spoke to us in our language, and showed us respect and kindness throughout the grueling hours of shooting. He arrived on the set early and waited for everyone to finish before he left. He didn't even complain about our Québec "spring" weather. Thank you, Steven. You are a true professional.*

They had a present for me: a Canadian Border Patrol baseball cap that would serve me well on my many future visits to Québec. (A border control agent would take one look and wave me through.) And I had a present for the crew: autographed copies of *How to Grill,* which had just come out in French.

I didn't know it then, but this was the first of more than a decade of French-language television in Québec.

Barbara tells me I'm better on TV in French than in English. I'm certainly more relaxed. You would think the opposite, that performing in a foreign language would add more stress, not less. But somehow, concentrating on speaking French correctly freed me from the internal censorship I applied to myself in my American shows. No more: "That sounds really goony" or "You said that in the previous show" or "Would an intelligent person really say that?" All the self-critical phrases that sabotaged my dialogue in the US were gone. (I would notice the same phenomenon when I taped my *Steven Raichlen Grills Italy* show in Italian.)

Come time for seasons two and three, I incorporated more Canadian ingredients and flavors into my menus. Ribs rubbed with maple sugar and glazed with Canadian whisky, for example. Chicken wings fired up with sriracha and maple syrup. Grilled quesadillas filled with tiny, supernaturally sweet Nordic shrimp from Gaspé, on Québec's far east coast. Maplewood-smoked blueberry crisp washed down with *cidre de glace* ("ice cider"), sweet, perfumed cider pressed from apples that had frozen on the tree. (Freezing concentrates the natural fruit sugars, just as it does for the grapes used to make Germany's *Eiswein.*)

My French publisher at the time, Pierre Bourdon, showed me the backwoods version of the ubiquitous cedar-planked salmon: trout on a log. His grandfather would stuff a freshly caught trout with sliced lemon and onion and set it on a split log in the middle of a campfire. As the fish roasted, it absorbed a powerful smoke flavor, and the presentation—a fire-seared trout served on a smoking log—was off-the-charts dramatic.

To make sense of all this gastronomic bounty, I would visit the Marché Jean-Talon—a world-class food market located in Montréal's Little Italy. The market was the home of one of the most popular morning TV shows in Québec: *Des Kiwis et des Hommes* ("Of Kiwis and Men," literally, with a wink to John Steinbeck's *Of Mice and Men*). I appeared on the show often to talk food and sometimes demonstrate barbecue for the cohosts, TV veteran Francis Reddy and Senegalese-born Boucar Diouf. The dialogue was fast-paced, with the Québécois accent thick enough to spread on toast. Sometimes I struggled to keep up. I mastered the art of saying *ben oui* ("obviously") and nodding with authority.

We taped four seasons of *Le Maître du Grill*. But Zeste wasn't done with me yet. Next came *Les Incontournables du Barbecue* ("The Musts of Barbecue")—shot on an outdoor set at the network's sprawling new studio in Longueuil on Montréal's north shore. The taping took place in April, which again to this Floridian seemed the very dead of winter. It hurt to be dressed in summer clothes (that's when the show would air) while the camera crew in front of me wore parkas and ski hats.

One night I got my revenge. The Canadiens, Montréal's beloved hockey team, were in the playoffs against the New York Rangers. We gathered at a bar to watch. They teased me mercilessly all evening until . . . the Rangers won. The chill on the set the next morning was as glacial as Montréal winter. Ultimately, I must have redeemed myself, because the day we wrapped, the crew gave me a nickname I cherish to this day: "The Wayne Gretzky of the Grill."

The next show—*La Tag BBQ* ("Barbecue Tag")—spoke volumes about the French Canadian character. The premise was simple: five local chefs participating in a round-robin grilling marathon presided over by me and my cohost, chef-turned-TV personality Martin Juneau. In each episode, we presented the contestants with a challenge: Grill a steak without a grill

With La Tag BBQ *cohost Martin Juneau.*

grate, for example, or make the best *guédille* (lobster roll) in Québec. The "tag" came at the end of each episode: Each participant handed off an ingredient to the next chef.

Meanwhile, Martin and I provided commentary, grilling tips, and recipes of our own. I focused on cocktails, demonstrating how to "grill" sangria—more accurately, grilling sugar-crusted orange, lemon, and lime halves over a screaming-hot fire to flavor the sangria. (Try it sometime—the caramelized fruit takes sangria to a whole new level.) In another episode, I showed off my "Smoky Mary," made by smoking tomato juice with maplewood sawdust from a handheld smoker. The Québécois have a fetishistic obsession with Bloody Marys: At some restaurants, the garnishes—shrimp, bacon, pickles, veggies, and more—come on skewers taller than the glass. The crew went crazy for that one.

I called the various chefs in the show "contestants," but I should have used the word "colleagues." What surprised me about the show was its spirit of collaboration, not competition. In the US, there would have been fierce rivalry and teams would have been voted off the set with malicious glee. Here, the chefs supported one another in an atmosphere of cooperation.

By now, between television and book tours, I had made yearly pilgrimages to Montréal and Québec City for more than two decades. That all crashed to an end with Covid. But quite amazingly, my French Canadian TV career continued. The Zeste producers came up with a new series tailored to the lockdown: *BBQ en Boîte* ("Barbecue in a Box"). Each week, they delivered a box of mystery ingredients to the home of a local chef, caterer, or grilling enthusiast—accompanied by a skeleton (and duly masked and socially distanced) camera crew. I recorded my segments from afar in Miami.

My cohost and I issued challenges based on the contents of the box: "Grill Two Amazing Tacos," for example, or "Say Cheese" (grill cheese three ways), or "Create a Camping Menu" (Canadians are fanatic campers).

Despite the distances (both social and physical in my case), the show had an intimacy I would never have thought possible during Covid. Again, it reflected the Canadian spirit in that it was cooperative rather than competitive. Perhaps our own society would be less polarized if we Americans took a similar approach.

My time in Canada brought opportunities I never would have imagined. I became a food columnist for Québec's largest newspaper, *Le Journal de Montréal.* I headlined a barbecue festival in Sept-Îles, a remote town on the far north shore of the St. Lawrence River, where forty-degree weather is considered springtime. I bicycled along Montréal's Lachine Canal and learned not to go anywhere in Montréal on *La Nuit des Vélos,* "Bicycle Night," when the entire city shuts down to clear the streets for twenty thousand bike riders. (Barbara and I once got caught in a three-hour traffic jam trying to reach our hotel.) I got to taste moose (prepared by one of our cameramen) and seal (dished up by one of our show guests). The former tasted like dry venison, the latter like briny rubber. And much to the hilarity of the crew, I got drunk on Caribou—hot mulled wine spiked with brandy—lots of brandy—and sweetened with, what else, maple syrup.

But my Québec adventures weren't solely culinary. In 2013, Les Éditions de l'Homme published *Refuge à Chappaquiddick* ("Refuge on Chappaquiddick"), the French translation of my novel, *The Hermit of Chappaquiddick*—more on that later. Québec's television book critic and premier mystery writer, Chrystine Brouillet, hailed it as "a charming novel, with a skillful marriage of *gourmandise* and emotion. Truly delicious, to be savored like a fine Burgundy." She loved to tell the story of how she read the galleys in Paris during a snowstorm. The first chapter made her skeptical: "Who is this American writer?" The second chapter piqued her interest. She wound up reading the whole manuscript in a single sitting on that snowy Paris night, and as she later confessed, growing *very* hungry in the process.

Chrystine is a terrific writer (think a cross between Sue Grafton and Agatha Christie—if you happen to read French, don't miss her Maud Graham series). She's also a formidable cook. Her dinner parties included a who's who of French Canadian writers, filmmakers, and media people. Thanks to Chrystine, I was adopted by Québec's literary community. I met the Vietnamese Canadian writer Kim Thúy, whose poetic books *Ru* and *Mãn,* about her experiences growing up as a refugee from Vietnam in Montréal, became prize-winning international bestsellers. (They're available in English, and you should read them.) You should also read Jocelyne Saucier's *Il Pleuvait des Oiseaux* (available in English as *And the Birds Rained Down*)—set during the devastating Matheson Fire of 1916, which burned five hundred thousand acres and destroyed whole cities in northern Ontario.

My book *La Bible du Barbecue* (*The Barbecue Bible*) even made a cameo appearance in a French Canadian novel—*Naufrage* ("Shipwreck") by Sébastian Fréchette, in which the protagonist establishes his grilling bona fides by having a copy of my book in his library. The fact is, I was taken much more seriously as a writer of more than cookbooks in Québec than I ever have been in the US.

When my favorite hotel in Montréal—the Saint-Sulpice in the heart of the old city—decided to publish an anthology of short stories written by "local" authors, they included one by an American: "The Man Who Invented (Québec) Barbecue." I'm not sure what pleased me more: seeing my story in print or being considered a local. (Guests will find a copy of the book in their rooms.)

While staying in Montréal, for breakfast I would walk around the corner from the Saint-Sulpice to Olive + Gourmando, a bakery-café that serves the world's best pecan sticky buns. (They also make a mean Cubano sandwich, the recipe for which I included in my book *Man Made Meals*.) For dinner, I would head to Griffintown, Montréal's once rough-and-tumble Irish district, today a gentrified neighborhood with cutting-edge restaurants and lively bars.

When I first visited Montréal in the 1990s, the city might charitably have been described as a culinary backwater. Today, it's one of the most exciting dining destinations in North America. The revolution began in 2004 at a seedy storefront in a Montréal neighborhood called Little Burgundy. The restaurateurs were an unlikely trio: an anglophone chef, David McMillan; a francophone chef, Frédéric Morin; plus Morin's then-girlfriend and now wife, Allison Cunningham. The restaurant? Joe Beef.

Joe Beef took its name from an infamous nineteenth-century Irish tavern keeper, Charles McKiernan (who earned this nickname doing a stint in the British army during the Crimean War). His Joe Beef tavern attracted a rowdy crowd of prostitutes, sailors, wharf rats, and other waterfront lowlifes. McKiernan kept a live bear in the dining room and a club for controlling unruly patrons. The modern Joe Beef's owners lived up to their colorful namesake: David McMillan, for example, was reputed to "throw busboys into dumpsters, drink magnums of Chablis nightly, and, in general, either terrify or completely charm everyone around him." (In 2021, he forswore alcohol and moved to a farm in the hamlet of Saint-Armand—population 1,239.)

I didn't know any of this when Barbara and I dined at Joe Beef for the first time. Dinner unfolded as it often does in restaurants where I'm recognized. I ordered a couple house specialties, including the foie gras "breakfast sandwich" (with slabs of foie gras standing in for the bread) and *pojarski de veau* (a giant porcini-flavored veal meatball cooked and served on a veal rib bone). David McMillan then proceeded to send us half the menu with his compliments, because Steven Raichlen couldn't leave Joe Beef without trying his *tartare de cheval* (horse steak tartare—it tastes better than it sounds), lobster spaghetti (it tastes exactly as it sounds, which was excellent), and *merveilleux* ("the marvelous"—an obscenely rich meringue, whipped cream, and chocolate dessert). We staggered out of the restaurant after midnight.

A few years later, David and Fred opened a wine bar-restaurant called Le Vin Papillon. They led me to the courtyard out back, where they had installed a wood-burning grill. There proceeded another belly-bludgeoning meal highlighted by the likes of wood-grilled razor clams, flame-seared maitake mushrooms, and wood-fire rotisserie cauliflower topped with crispy chicken skin. (In Yiddish, we call the latter *gribenes,* and my family members would fight over who would get the last bite.)

And so, the live-fire cooking revolution came to Montréal—inspired in part, I like to believe, by an American grill master who had the good

With David McMillan after a belt-loosening meal at Joe Beef in Montréal.

fortune to appear on Québec television. In 2010, Jonathan Nguyen opened Montréal's first barbecue restaurant, Le Boucan. (The name comes from a Franco-Caribbean word meaning "smoke"—the origin of our term *buccaneer.*) His success lay in marrying traditional American barbecue techniques with the foods beloved by French Canadians—for example, poutine (Québec's beloved dish of cheese-curd-and-gravy-topped French fries), here lavished with pulled pork.

These new kids on the live-fire cooking scene joined a much older tradition: Montréal "smoked meat." In 1926, Jewish Romanian immigrant Reuben Schwartz opened Schwartz's Deli, specializing in the French Canadian version of pastrami. Today, smoked meat is served at delicatessens and sandwich shops throughout Québec and beyond.

And while we're on the subject of Montréal's live-fire Jewish delicacies, I would be remiss if I didn't mention Montréal bagels—cooked in a wood-burning oven at such landmark bakeries as Fairmount Bagel, opened in 1919, and St-Viateur Bagel (1957). Said bagels are sweeter, cakier, and less chewy than United States bagels, but they quickly become addictive.

THE QUÉBÉCOIS ARE AN EXTRAORDINARY PEOPLE. I've always been impressed how they kept their language and cultural identity intact for more than four centuries—despite having lost to the British in the Battle of the Plains of Abraham outside Québec City in 1759. (The Band immortalized the French defeat in the song "Acadian Driftwood.") Local legend credits the persistence of French to the Catholic priests, who encouraged their parishioners to have large families. ("Five children? Try harder. Nine kids? Not bad," they would say. "Twelve? Now you're on the righteous path.")

I admire Québec's multiculturalism. I admire its warmth. I admire the fierce pride in the local heritage. (Every Québec license plate comes emblazoned with the words *Je Me Souviens*—"I remember.") I admire how open the Québécois were to having an American teach them how to grill.

I learned a lot about international relations during my two-decade commute to Québec. That cooperation sometimes trumps competition. That Québec's social cohesion sometimes bests the militant individualism of the United States. Canadians are astonished by the gun violence of their southern neighbors. Then again, most Canadian police don't even carry guns.

Above all, I learned that diplomacy doesn't always have to be executed with a cudgel. Sometimes it can take place cooperatively over a barbecue grill. The results are infinitely better.

MAPLE-SRIRACHA CHICKEN WINGS

I created this recipe for my *Le Maître du Grill* ("The Grill Master") TV show in Québec. You'll recognize it as a Canadian twist on the Buffalo wing, only here the glaze contains maple syrup, Canadian whisky, and sriracha instead of the traditional Tabasco sauce. I love how the sweet heat of the glaze counterpoints the smoke flavor of the wings.

12 large chicken wings (about 3 pounds)

For the rub:

1 tablespoon sea salt

1 tablespoon freshly ground black pepper

1 tablespoon smoked paprika or sweet paprika

½ teaspoon baking powder

1 ½ tablespoons extra-virgin olive oil

For the glaze:

3 tablespoons unsalted butter

¼ cup pure maple syrup

3 tablespoons sriracha, or more to taste

2 tablespoons Canadian whisky

2 tablespoons finely chopped fresh chives

You'll also need:

1 ½ cups smoking wood chips soaked in water for 30 minutes, then drained

1. Cut each chicken wing in half, into a drumette and flat, trimming off and discarding the wingtips. Place in a large mixing bowl.
2. Sprinkle the salt, pepper, paprika, and baking powder over the wings and stir to mix. Stir in the olive oil.
3. Set up your grill for indirect grilling and preheat to medium-high (400°F). Brush or scrape the grill grate clean and oil it well.
4. Arrange the chicken wings in a single layer in the center of the grill, skin side up. Add the wood chips to the coals. Cover the grill and smoke-roast the wings until the skin is crisp and nicely browned and the chicken is cooked through, 20 to 30 minutes. To check for doneness, make a slit in the largest wing; there should be no traces of pink at the bone.
5. Meanwhile, make the glaze: Melt the butter in a small saucepan over medium-high heat. Stir in the maple syrup, sriracha, and whisky and boil until syrupy, 5 minutes. Set aside and keep warm.
6. About 5 minutes before the chicken is done, brush each wing on all sides with the glaze and return to the grill. Glaze again for the last minute. Arrange the wings on a platter and drizzle with the remaining glaze. Sprinkle with chives and serve at once.

Chapter Eighteen

COOKING FOR MEN

2014

The legendary Peter Workman: publisher, mentor, and friend.

In the fall of 2012, Peter Workman summoned me to New York for a meeting. "Summon" was an odd word to use in connection with Peter. Usually, he hinted. Or intimated. Or gently requested. I had a hunch what he wanted to discuss, and I wasn't looking forward to it.

A few weeks earlier, an editor at Barnes & Noble had approached me with an offer to republish one of my early books, *A Taste of the Mountains Cooking School Cookbook*. "We'll modernize it, of course," he said, "but we love your technique-oriented content, not to mention those charming pen-and-ink illustrations."

It always thrills an author to give an old book a new life and a new audience. Besides, the money was good, and it didn't require much work. Of course, I notified my editor at Workman, Suzanne Rafer, who went uncharacteristically quiet.

When I sat down in Peter's office, he delivered both good news and bad. "You are a Workman author, Steven," he said. "It would be awkward to see a Raichlen book with another publisher." That was Peter's gentle way of saying no. No to Barnes & Noble. No to any other publisher. Period. The good news was that he had an idea for a new book, and he wanted me to write it. It was a book on cooking for men.

Peter's unfailing sense of what the public wants to read at a particular moment enabled him to build a four-person start-up into the largest privately owned publisher in the US. His right-book-at-the-right-time successes included *Steal Like an Artist* and of course *The Silver Palate Cookbook*. To that list I would immodestly add *The Barbecue! Bible* and *How to Grill*—both now displayed in a showcase in the lobby featuring Workman's million-copy bestsellers.

When Peter has an idea, you listen.

Admittedly, cooking for men was a departure from my barbecue books.

"Men who barbecue are likely to be men who cook," Peter reasoned. "As for men who cook but don't barbecue, they might be inspired to buy a grill—and one of our barbecue books."

When Peter has an idea, you say yes.

The more I thought about it, the more I liked the idea of a book on cooking for men. Much as I love barbecuing and grilling, after eight books on the subject, I was ready to write about something new.

The book also appealed to me on an emotional level, going back to my childhood.

WHEN I WAS YOUNG—maybe ten or eleven—my father and I instituted a "Men's Night." One Saturday each month, women (make that my mother) were barred from the kitchen. My dad and I would do the cooking, with a lavish meal to follow.

Our menus seemed the height of sophistication to us at the time (and totally dated today):

Caesar salad
Crab-stuffed mushrooms
Sirloin steak
Jack Tarr potatoes

I took charge of the salad. There were no salad spinners back in the Men's Night era, so I painstakingly dried each lettuce leaf with a dish towel. My dad and I would stuff white mushrooms with crabmeat and mayonnaise. (No one knew of shiitakes or morels in those days.) And nobody grilled vegetables back then, so we baked the stuffed mushrooms in the oven.

Likewise for the Jack Tarr potatoes—bakers we scooped, mixed

My dad and me—founders of the Men's Night Culinary Society—in 1966.

with bacon, sour cream, cheese (at the time we used Velveeta), scallions, and butter, and stuffed back into their skins for a second baking. We grilled the steaks on one of those old brazier-type charcoal grills with a crank to raise and lower the grate. (Invariably, the grate wobbled to one side.)

My father worked long hours in those days, so our Saturday Men's Nights were among the rare times when we got to do something together. They were indescribably precious, and remembering them still warms my heart.

THE MORE I THOUGHT ABOUT *Cooking for Men* (my working title for the book—that would change), the more excited I got. But first I had to address a few foundational questions: Does cooking have a gender bias? Do men and women really cook differently? Are there really such things as guy foods and gal foods?

The answer to the first question is of course not. Despite the age-old stereotype of the male chef, today women are Michelin three-star restaurateurs, venerated TV personalities, and Barbecue Hall of Fame pitmasters. Gender is not a requirement for excellence in the food world.

As for the second question, on a domestic level, Barbara and I definitely cook differently. I'm more adventurous, more willing to take chances, more apt to cook a dish for a dinner party I've never previously prepared. I like big, in-your-face flavors and all manner of ethnic foods. When I don't have a particular ingredient, I improvise. I'm an incorrigible multitasker, which drives Barbara crazy. I rarely follow a recipe—even my own.

Barbara is laser-focused and hyper-organized in the kitchen. She favors familiarity and predictability. She would rather spend four hours making one perfect meal than bang out four dishes in forty-five minutes. She finds me messy and disorganized (accusations I dispute—but only half-heartedly). Fortunately, most of my cooking takes place outdoors. We're still married after thirty-five years, so I guess we found a formula that works.

The question as to whether there are guy foods and gal foods is more nuanced. Most guys I know do not bake cupcakes or mix pink martinis. Most women I know do not shuck oysters, cook live lobsters, or smoke cocktails—at least not while there's a man around to do it. Guys delight in dangerous tools like razor-sharp knives and blowtorches. We love to play with fire and set stuff on fire, which, of course, gives us a natural edge at the grill.

As I started to plan the book, I drafted three lists. (There's that list maker again.) The first covered dishes I thought every guy should know how to make:

- Survival dishes, like omelets and grilled cheese sandwiches
- Sustaining dishes, like a perfect roast chicken or a properly grilled steak
- Impress-your-boss dishes, like a whole roast beef tenderloin (cooking and prep time: 30 minutes) or my "Big Kahuna" prime rib—eight monster pounds of meat that require only five ingredients (two of which are salt and pepper)
- Seduction dishes, like oysters on the half shell (and how to shuck

them without impaling your hand on the knife) and an irresistible chocolate dessert (in this case, Belgian beer brownies)

- Most important of all, impress-your-kid or -grandkid dishes, like made-from-scratch multigrain pancakes (when I was a kid, I was mesmerized when my dad made pancakes) and blowtorch oatmeal, which lends a breakfast plebe the gourmet aura of crème brûlée (the secret: Sprinkle the top with brown sugar and caramelize it with a torch)

My second list focused on aspirational dishes—the sort of food you'd prepare for your poker-game buddies, for a Super Bowl party, or for the inaugural barbecue at your new home. Here a man should know how to cook killer chicken wings, smoky baby back ribs, and a five-alarm chili that sends you lunging for your beer.

The third list concentrated on show-off dishes—recipes that involve flames, hardware, or alcohol (ideally all three), and no small dose of theatrics. Case in point, my "pitchfork steak"—an oversize slab of sirloin skewered on a pitchfork and cooked in a cauldron of hot oil. Or "ten-penny nail potatoes," in which you drive a metal spike through a spud to speed up the cooking time.

When it comes to cooking, I'm an unapologetic purist, and I encourage my readers to be the same. But I try to make it easy for them. You won't find bottled salad dressings in my refrigerator or in my book. But you will find my "Ball jar dressings," for which you add oil, vinegar or buttermilk, and other flavorings to a jar, screw on the lid, and shake like a demon: authentic made-from-scratch salad dressing with a preparation time measured in seconds. Or my mayonnaise "bearnaise," which has all the tarragon-shallot brightness of the original French sauce, but with none of the whisking and cooking of temperamental eggs.

By the time I had covered what I deemed every indispensable dish, I had 288 recipes. That's not including the final chapter on cocktails, because every guy should know how to stir a martini (never shake), make an old-fashioned (to which I add a spoonful of marmalade to pump up the orange flavor), or whip up a kitchen sink–size punch bowl of sangria.

Having been a cooking teacher (and wannabe academic) for so many years, I wanted the book to teach principles, not just recipes. (Teach a man to fish and all that.) I assumed my reader knew nothing, so I opened the book with a crash course on cookware, knifesmanship, and the essential cooking techniques. I also included a series of "Man's Best Friends"—essays on essential guy foods, from eggs to steak to shellfish.

That would cover the recipes and cooking techniques. But what about the big picture? I have always tried to write books that are more than collections of recipes. What else would a guy need to know to survive and thrive in the kitchen? I wanted a narrative that transcended the realm of cookbooks. I wound up writing a manifesto.

THE IDEA FOR HOW TO MAKE the project more than just a cookbook came from—you guessed it—a woman. That woman happened to be a publicist, not to mention the source of most of my brilliant ideas: my wife.

"You've filled the book with *your* ideas of what men should know how to cook," Barbara reasoned. "Why not ask some high-profile guys and well-known chefs what *they* think men should know about cooking?"

So off I went to interview chefs, actors, activists, and food-and-drink experts for a series of profiles called "Food Dudes." Some were friends. Some became friends, and they certainly broadened the book's perspective.

My Food Dudes had strong opinions on what men should cook, how they should cook it, and what your food should say to the world. Dudes like superstar chefs Thomas Keller (the only chef in the US to run two Michelin three-star restaurants). Activists like José Andrés (founder of World Central Kitchen and an amazing chef in his own right). TV personalities like the Italian food–obsessed Stanley Tucci and Andrew Zimmern (who once ate rotten shark in Reykjavik and giant fruit bats in Samoa).

I even channeled Thomas Jefferson through his historian, Thomas J. Craughwell (author of *Thomas Jefferson's Crème Brûlée*). Little-known fact about the drafter of the Declaration of Independence: He was America's first foodie, introducing our fledgling nation to French fries, macaroni and cheese, and, yes, crème brûlée.

I devised a questionnaire for each Food Dude. Almost everyone concurred on the first question: Name three dishes that every guy should know how to make. Every guy should know how to scramble eggs, roast a chicken, and grill a steak. Modernist cuisine visionary Nathan Myhrvold shared his secret to exquisitely creamy scrambled eggs: Use three yolks, but only two whites. Thomas Keller explained how to roast chicken with supernaturally crisp skin: "Let it sit, uncovered, in the refrigerator for a day or two to dry out the exterior. 'Temper' the bird—that is, let it come to room temperature before cooking, then roast it in a really hot oven [425°F]."

As for the perfect seduction dish (another question I asked all my Food Dudes), Keller got right to the point: "Champagne and caviar to start. Pasta with truffles. Chocolate for dessert." Stanley Tucci begged to differ: "Not pasta. A lot of women feel they shouldn't eat pasta. Make risotto instead. Let her watch your hands as you stir slowly and smoothly and leave the rest to her imagination . . ."

As to the question of why a man should know how to cook, Andrew Zimmern voiced a sentiment a lot of us can relate to (I certainly do): "As a guy, I'm lousy at expressing my feelings. Cooking is as touchy-feely as I get and it shows what's in my heart."

My Food Dudes had some great advice for guys just starting out in the kitchen:

"Spend money on your ingredients," said Tucci. "If you skimp on the quality, you'll never get great results." He went on to extol the virtues of sautéing—flicking the pan with your wrist to send the food sailing up in the air, then back into the pan. "It's controlled recklessness and women find it very sexy. Hell, *I* find it sexy," Tucci said.

"Work hot," suggests Zimmern. "A lot of guys fear heat, but unless your pan or grill is screaming-hot, you won't get a good sear."

South American grilling virtuoso Francis Mallmann made four trenchant observations (*trenchant* being the appropriate word for an activity that involves sharp knives):

- You will cut and burn yourself. Man up. It comes with the territory.
- You will rarely succeed the first time you try a dish. Learn from your failures.
- Learn to cook with three or four pans at a time. You'll look like a culinary god.
- Learn to cook a meal from start to finish using only ingredients you find in your refrigerator. *That's* cooking for men!

But it was José Andrés who best embodied the message of my book: "When a man knows how to cook, it's a sign of good breeding and culture. If you want to lead the tribe, you have to be able to feed the tribe." Amen.

BY THE TIME I FINISHED, in typical Raichlen obsessive fashion, my book had swelled to 630 pages. Which was 530 pages more than what most guys probably want. I followed Peter Workman's category killer model, which had served me so well in books like *The Barbecue! Bible* and *BBQ USA*. I might have been better off writing the Cliff Notes. In retrospect, one hundred dishes would have been less intimidating. Or fifty dishes, or twenty-five. I was still laboring in the big-book paradigm. In my obsession to explain everything, I forgot another age-old adage: "Sometimes less is more."

The art department came through with a dramatically different look for the book. No lip-smacking food photographs on the cover. Just brushed silver emblazoned with manly cooking terms, like "torch," "crush," and "smoke." A photo of me leaning against a black-and-red banner with the book's title. It was a tough look for a tough book. I loved it.

That left the title, and here my publisher and I disagreed. I thought *Cooking for Men* was the perfect title for the book. It said what it was, period. Suzanne Rafer, the Workman editorial department, and even Barbara felt

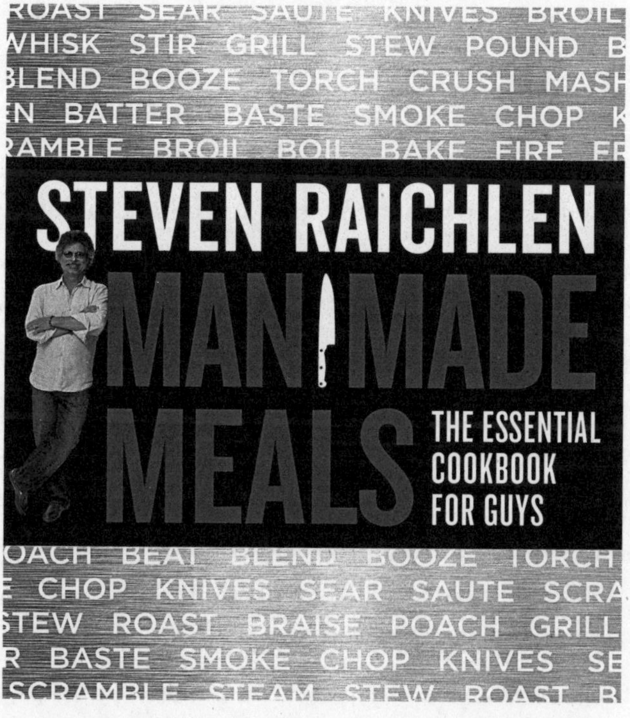

My first non-barbecue book in a decade. The original title was Cooking for Men.

differently. The book came out with an alliterative title: *Man Made Meals.* It was cute. It was clever. It was abstract. But ultimately, I believe, it failed to capture the spirit of the book or its potential audience.

Despite a twenty-five-city book tour and translations into three major languages, *Man Made Meals* was only a modest success. I still regard it as one of my best books.

Did Peter Workman cook? Most men of his generation didn't. But he certainly loved to eat. Whenever we came to New York, Peter would take us to dinner. He was always gracious enough to include Barbara. He favored bistros and trattorias—places that served excellent food with minimal pretention—for example, Da Silvano in the East Village and the Union Square Café. He had little use for the trendy hot spots. He usually ordered beef—*bistecca alla fiorentina* was a favorite—and a nice bottle of wine or two to wash it down.

One magical night, after dinner, Peter invited me back to his apartment for cognac and cigars. (Barbara preferred to go back to our hotel.) Along the way, we stopped at Barnes & Noble in Union Square. Peter took a quick look to make sure the latest Workman books were prominently displayed. It wasn't enough that they faced out. (If you ever want to show appreciation for your favorite author, when you go to a bookstore, make sure his or her books face out—including this one!) No, Peter also wanted his books at eye height. Of course, he also surveyed the competition, absorbing a million data points about covers, titles, artwork, authors, trends, and competing publishers. This took place in less than a minute, but you could sense that Peter registered everything worth knowing.

At the time, Peter and Carolan lived on Gramercy Park, a private oasis accessible only to people living in the surrounding buildings. The apartment was comfortable, but not grand. Then again, Peter himself was modest and unassuming. Not surprisingly, the walls were lined with books and record albums.

Peter loved jazz and put on Stan Getz. He filled two snifters with Hennessy and produced two Cuban cigars. I had never smoked a real Cuban before. The smoke was intense and pungent. I tried not to cough.

I took the opportunity to ask Peter how he got his start. "Was publishing always what you wanted to do? How do you manage to read the zeitgeist so accurately—to know what sort of book the public craves next before readers know themselves? Why do you make even serious books whimsical? And how do you manage to keep all your businesses straight?" (By this time, Peter had purchased four other publishing houses and ran them under the Workman aegis.)

On a more personal note, I asked how Peter found time for ski trips and family vacations. (Me, I hadn't taken a vacation in years.)

Curiously, I don't remember Peter's answers. He had a way of deflecting the spotlight away from himself and onto his authors. He did have some questions for me. What was I reading? (At the time, it was a French novel set during the Crusades called *Saint-Sépulcre!* by Patrick Besson. I guess French publishers like exclamation marks too.) Was I pleased with my book tour? (Beyond pleased and beyond exhausted.) What would I do once my book sales start to diminish?

The last question startled me. At the time, we were selling literally thousands of barbecue books each week. It never occurred to me that the Raichlen juggernaut would come to an end. In his own gentle way, Peter was trying to warn me to think about what came next. When we returned to Miami, Barbara and I paid off our mortgages. We've remained debt-free ever since.

Peter refilled our brandy glasses, and we continued to puff our cigars. It was well after midnight when I walked back to the hotel. I told a half-asleep Barbara: "This was one of the most extraordinary nights of my life."

Peter loved life and loved to celebrate its triumphs. The party for *Miami Spice* was a full-blown Caribbean carnival, complete with a steel band and limbo dancers. The launch party for *The Barbecue! Bible* took place at a newly opened lounge with a large outdoor terrace, B Bar in New York's East Village. When Peter turned seventy, he chartered one of those round Manhattan cruise boats and we celebrated with a starlit trip to the Statue of Liberty. What impressed me most was the presence of several of Peter's friends from childhood and college. Here was a man who knew how to make friends—and, more importantly, how to keep them.

Peter was frugal, but he wasn't cheap. He insisted his authors fly coach and he claimed to do the same. (Peter stood over six feet tall, so that was more of a hardship for him than for me.) "Instead of spending the money on first-class airfare," he would say, "I'd rather add two cities to your book tour." Yet another lesson from Peter Workman: Spend money to make money, not for luxuries that offer no return on investment.

One final memory: We gathered in Peter's office for a meeting. He was on the phone, arguing with Workman's landlord. The building management had removed the doorman's chair, so the poor man had to stand for the entirety of his eight-hour shift. Peter could have been on the phone with his banker or his lawyer or one of his bestselling authors. Instead, he took the time to right an injustice for a man who didn't even work for Workman.

One afternoon in the fall of 2012, Suzanne called, and I could hear uncharacteristic distress in her voice. "I have some bad news," she said. "Peter has a brain tumor." Apparently, his behavior at work had become erratic. "He would lose his train of thought in conversations," Suzanne said. "Or open his mouth, and no words would come out." His oncologist told him: "We can treat your glioblastoma but not cure it." The news crushed everyone at Workman—authors, editors, the whole staff.

Peter continued to show up at the office as long as he could. Then he didn't. He finished his days in a wheelchair. I asked several times if I could come to New York and see him. Suzanne told me the family didn't want visitors. I should have tried harder. A lot harder. On April 7, 2013, I got the call from Suzanne: Peter had passed away.

We flew to New York, where some of the old-timers gathered at Peter and Carolan's apartment. The funeral was for immediate family only. A few weeks later, a memorial service was held at Columbia University. Barbara and I joined the more than five hundred people in attendance. The CEO of Barnes & Noble reflected on Peter's enormous influence in the publishing world. Workman's celebrated children's book author Sandra Boynton started her eulogy with a list of things Peter Workman couldn't do. "He couldn't draw," she said. "He couldn't do ballroom dancing." She apologized for such a short list, because Peter Workman, she said, could do just about everything else.

But the most eloquent eulogy came from Peter's wife, Carolan. "The doctors told Peter his tumor was treatable, not curable. I'm afraid the same is true for a broken heart."

Peter Workman didn't live long enough to see the publication of the men's cookbook he had commissioned. He wanted a big book, full of actionable information and big-flavored food. I tried to infuse *Man Made Meals* with his big-hearted spirit.

The book's dedication read:

In memory of Peter Workman

Publisher. Mentor. Friend.

MORNING-AFTER HASH

Perhaps you invited someone home for your first-ever dinner together. Perhaps you grilled a steak and baked a potato—a meal perfect in its primal simplicity. Perhaps there will be leftovers—you should always cook enough food for leftovers. And perhaps you get lucky enough to have someone in your bed to cook breakfast for the next morning. Enter morning-after hash. You make it with the previous night's leftovers, which might include steak or prime rib or corned beef or pastrami (or even a chicken breast)—prepared by you or taken home in a doggie bag from a restaurant. That's where hash comes in, for it's the perfect way to resurrect these leftovers for breakfast. (Our word *hash* comes from the French *hâcher*, meaning "to chop"—also the derivation of our word *hatchet*.) You'll want to use a chef's knife, not a hatchet, to cut up said steak and potatoes, adding onion, peppers, Worcestershire sauce, and hot sauce for extra flavor. The morning after is starting to look as memorable as the night before.

Serves 2 but can be multiplied as desired

2 to 4 tablespoons unsalted butter, divided

1 small onion, finely chopped

1 clove garlic, minced (optional)

1 poblano chili or small green bell pepper, seeded and cut into ½-inch dice

1 jalapeño pepper, seeded if desired and minced (optional)

Cooked steak, prime rib, corned beef, pastrami, pork, chicken, ham, or other protein, cut into ½-inch dice (enough to make 1 ½ to 2 cups)

Cooked potato or sweet potato, cut into ½-inch dice (enough to make 1 ½ to 2 cups)

2 teaspoons Worcestershire sauce

½ teaspoon your favorite hot sauce

2 tablespoons chopped fresh parsley, chives, basil, or other herb (optional)

Sea salt and freshly ground black pepper

2 large eggs (optional)

1. Melt 2 tablespoons of the butter in a large skillet over medium-high heat. Add the onion, garlic (if using), poblano, and jalapeño (if using) and cook until nicely browned, 3 to 4 minutes, stirring with a wooden spoon.
2. Stir in the meat and potatoes and continue cooking until all the ingredients are aromatic and browned, another 3 to 4 minutes. Stir in the Worcestershire sauce, hot sauce, and fresh herbs (if using) and cook for 1 minute. Add salt and pepper to taste. Lots of pepper. The hash should be highly seasoned. Transfer the hash to plates and keep warm.
3. If using eggs, melt an additional 1 to 2 tablespoons butter in the same skillet over high heat. Crack in the eggs and fry until cooked to taste, 2 to 3 minutes for sunny-side-up, or flip the eggs to cook them over easy. Slide the eggs onto the hash and dig in.

Chapter Nineteen

THE HERMIT OF CHAPPAQUIDDICK

2000–2012

The Chappy ferry—a 527-foot crossing to a true Island Apart.

When I graduated from college, I never imagined I'd become a food writer. Given my love of books and languages, I imagined a career as a professor of comparative literature. I dreamed of writing fiction, of course, but so does just about everyone with a liberal arts degree.

The opportunity came many years later when my longtime cookbook editor, Suzanne Rafer, went on an extended leave. I had six months with no cookbook to write. I had an idea for a novel—a foodie love story set on Martha's Vineyard. I began writing what would become *The Hermit of Chappaquiddick.*

Chappaquiddick. If you're a baby boomer or a political junkie, you'll remember it as the site of a tragedy. On July 18, 1969, an Oldsmobile driven by Senator Edward Kennedy careened off a wooden bridge leading to East Beach into eight feet of rushing water. Kennedy survived. His passenger—a young woman named Mary Jo Kopechne—did not. The circumstances of her death and the senator's behavior have been debated ever since. Considerable alcohol was likely involved, and it took Kennedy ten hours and sixteen personal phone calls to get around to notifying the local police. (If you want to know more about the sad story, watch the 2017 movie *Chappaquiddick,* directed by John Curran, or read the novella *Black Water* by Joyce Carol Oates.)

I first came to Martha's Vineyard in 1977 on my very first out-of-town writing assignment. A lobster hatchery had just opened on the Vineyard; *The Boston Globe* assigned me to report on what it did. The hatchery produced roughly a half million baby lobsters a year, which were released into Massachusetts waters. That may sound like a lot of lobsters, but then again, only one in ten thousand juveniles would actually reach adulthood. The assignment came with an expense account—my first. I felt like a big shot. My survival rate as a journalist had improved considerably. In the following

Barbara on Chappaquiddick, with the Edgartown lighthouse behind her.

years I would return to the Vineyard to review restaurants for *Boston* magazine's annual summer travel issue.

Barbara often accompanied me, and in between restaurant reviews, we found time to explore Chappaquiddick. We were intrigued by this tiny island at the eastern edge of Martha's Vineyard. To get to Chappaquiddick, you first board a Steamship Authority ferry from Woods Hole on Cape Cod to the town of Vineyard Haven on Martha's Vineyard. From there, you drive to Edgartown, then take the Chappy ferry, a three-car barge called the "On Time." The journey across the harbor spans 527 feet and lasts all of two minutes.

There were no hotels or restaurants on Chappy (there still aren't) and only one paved road. Barbara and I walked across the small wooden Dyke Bridge, where the Kennedy tragedy took place. We toured a Japanese garden on Chappy called Mytoi. We rode out to the lighthouse at the end of East Beach—a beacon originally commissioned by Thomas Jefferson. We bought shellfish licenses and went clamming in Katama Bay. We loved Chappy's sylvan beauty, but most of all, we savored the quiet.

As we packed up the car to leave one year, I dropped to my knees and, with all the *Gone with the Wind* sentimentality I could muster, grabbed a handful of sand. "Someday we'll have a place of our own here," I told Barbara. And eventually we did.

When we returned to Martha's Vineyard in the year 2000—celebrating our tenth anniversary—Barbara thumbed through some real estate listings on our ferry crossing to Vineyard Haven. On a lark, we called the realtor, who took us on a tour of the island. We found a vacant lot on a wooded hillside in the center of Chappy. The seller had erected a wooden tower, and from the top I could see a snippet of ocean. I made a modest offer, never really expecting a response. Two days later, the realtor called back: "If you are still interested, the seller has agreed to your price." We became the proud owners of a three-acre parcel. Now what?

Our home in Miami is 1926 old Spanish. We've lived there for thirty-three years. We'd never built a house from scratch before, but we had done several renovations. For the Chappy property, we interviewed three architects. The first quoted an astronomic price. The second lost interest when she heard what we could afford. The third was a Yale architecture school graduate who had lived on Martha's Vineyard for decades. Bruce MacNelly didn't laugh at our budget. He set out to design us the nicest house he could for the money.

To take advantage of that water view, we decided to build an upside-down house, with living quarters and kitchen upstairs, and guest bedrooms and my office on the ground floor. We made many naïve mistakes along the way, including taking the contractor at his word for the completion date. When we arrived with a moving truck on our move-in day, there was no working stove in the kitchen, one working bathroom on the ground floor, and a barely working shower upstairs. The house would be full of workmen for another month. I was scheduled to leave on a six-week book tour in three days.

Barbara had never lived anywhere but Miami, and she had certainly never lived in the middle of the woods. The day I left, she came face-to-face with a deer in our driveway. I'm not sure who was more frightened: Barbara or the beast. It was a make-or-break moment: Either Barbara would love the sylvan majesty of our new home on Chappaquiddick or she'd tell me to sell the house and move us back to civilization. Happily, it was the former, and we've lived on Chappy for six months a year ever since.

All of which is a very long prologue to a discussion of my novel, *The Hermit of Chappaquiddick*, and I hope you'll forgive the digression. Up next: how a food writer came up with a love story set on our little island—with nary a whiff of wood smoke or drop of barbecue sauce.

HOW DO YOU WRITE A NOVEL? I had no idea. I had never taken a writing class. I had never previously attempted fiction. I knew that some novelists plan out the whole story ahead of time: the plot, the characters, the dialogue, themes, and message. Other writers focus on the characters and let them direct the story.

My process was a hybrid. I started with a title: *The Hermit of Chappaquiddick*. It popped into my head while we were building our house, staying at the Beach Plum Inn at the opposite end of Martha's Vineyard. The Hermit would be a recluse living off the grid and off the land, deep in the woods on Chappaquiddick. People would gaze at him without really seeing him. No one would know his real name, where he lived, or where he came from.

As we drove back to our building site, other characters popped into my head. I knew there would be a New York book editor named Claire Dohaney, who was recovering from a serious illness. She would be house-sitting for her boisterous friend Sheila Feinblatt, who, with her psychiatrist turned self-help guru husband, Elliott, owned an imposing home on tony North Neck Road. Claire would have a rebellious daughter named Molly. Molly would have a biker boyfriend named Wrench. Every story needs a villain, and that would be Claire's soon-to-be ex-husband, Maxwell.

I knew there would be kids—a baby named Samantha, a little boy named Nate. (I borrowed their names from the children of my friends Joe and Cindy Kropp.) There would be an eccentric fictional character named Ely writing a book about a very real-life figure, the iconoclastic psychotherapist Wilhelm Reich.

I've always been something of a history buff, and making Claire a book editor would allow me to incorporate other real-life figures into my story. The Roman statesman Cicero would make an appearance. So would the French philosopher Jean-Jacques Rousseau, the Italian librettist Lorenzo Da Ponte, and the Russian empress Catherine the Great. Each had a life trajectory that mirrored or counterpointed Claire's and the Hermit's.

Fiction writing is a mysterious process. In addition to my cast of characters, I somehow knew how the story would begin and how it would end. I had no idea what would happen in the middle. For this, I looked to the characters to lead the way.

I knew there would be a birth. I knew there would be a death. I knew there would be a murder and a trial and a terrible misunderstanding that would cost someone their family, friends, and career. I knew there would be food—lots of food—and the characters would connect through cooking. But I was adamant that there would be no recipes. I didn't want anyone to confuse my first novel with a cookbook.

I also knew there would be no barbecue in *The Hermit of Chappaquiddick*—not a single rib or brisket. In writing the book, I wanted to get as far away from my barbecue books as possible.

The novel would be my love song to Chappaquiddick. I'd end it with an apology to my fellow Chappaquiddickers in the event the book brought unwanted attention to our little island.

I began the book with an epigram—a line from a John Donne poem: "No man is an island." To that I appended a lyric from a Jefferson Airplane song: "He's a peninsula." For that would be the governing theme of the novel: a lonely man living in utter isolation who discovers that life is worth living only when connected to other people.

I went through nine drafts before the story was published. I certainly learned a lot about writing in the process. I painstakingly crafted the first two chapters, only to discard them in the final manuscript. They focused on the wrong protagonist. But those sixty pages got me to the real start of the story, so I didn't consider the time wasted.

I learned to use active verbs, rather than passive "to be" constructions—tip o' the hat to my writer friend Brian Rochlin (no relation) for that one. I learned that some terrible crimes are socially acceptable, and others are not. Thus, the crime and trial scenes in my novel changed several times. I learned how a medical examiner works and how a murder trial unfolds by interviewing real-life experts, who generously shared their time and knowledge with me. I even learned to have some fun with the writing. In the trial chapter, for example, I gave the experts obscure food names. The prosecutor is called Manzo (the Italian word for "beef"). The medical examiner is Dr. Pilz (the German word for "mushroom"). The surprise witness is named Thuringer (a sausage from the German state of Thuringia).

Above all, I learned to live with rejection. Most publishers seemed to want only cookbooks from Steven Raichlen, not novels. The rejection emails piled up. Finally, my agent, Jane Dystel, found a home for the book at Forge Books. At the time, Forge was best known for science fiction books, but they had started to branch out into other genres. One of my favorite historical fiction writers, William Martin, published with Forge, and made introductions. He also wrote a fine blurb for the book.

Read the fine print of most book contracts and you'll find that the publisher retains final say over the title and cover. The rationale for this is that the publisher has more to lose than the author. (All the latter stands to lose is the years it took to write the book!)

My editor at Forge hated my title. I tried to reason with him. There are seventy-some million baby boomers living in the US, and virtually all of them will remember the controversial Kennedy accident on Chappaquiddick. That's a lot of potential readers for *The Hermit of Chappaquiddick*. But Forge wouldn't hear of it, so we settled on a much blander title, *Island Apart*, which is what *Chappaquiddick* means in Wampanoag—the language of the Indigenous people of Martha's Vineyard.

For the cover, I provided a photo of the Chappy ferry emerging from the fog—an image full of beauty and mystery. That got rejected (although it appears on the inside cover), so I came up with an alternative—a photo of the Edgartown Harbor and lighthouse at sunset—a stunning image taken by amateur photographer and one of the Chappy ferry captains, the late Bob Gilkes. The publisher insisted on inserting a tiny silhouette of a hand-holding couple in front of the lighthouse. They were trying to make my story look like a damn romance novel.

Island Apart came out in spring 2012. *Booklist* called it "a sweet grown-up love story. A beach book for smart people."

Which brings us to the question most readers really want to know: How much of the story is autobiographical? Well, I'm not a hermit, and you'd never call a guy who's been on television for twenty years a recluse. But I am something of a loner, and when I'm not on camera or onstage, my personality tends to fade into the background. Like many people in my industry, I express my feelings through my writing and my food. In the first draft of the story, the Hermit's real name was David Stevens. My name is Steven David. I wonder what Drs. Freud or Reich would have made of that.

As for Claire, she's purely fictional, but her meticulousness as an editor was inspired by my longtime editor at Workman. Maxwell was modeled after the ex-husband of someone I knew; Molly was inspired by her daughter. I only wish I had friends like the Feinblatts.

Sheila's drug problem was inspired by what I experienced growing up with my mother. (The chapter dealing with that got cut from the first edition, but later I restored it.) Wrench would be the kind of son-in-law any parent would wish for his daughter—tattoos and Harley-Davidson notwithstanding.

Claire made her mark in the publishing field as a book editor, but earlier in her career, she wrote a novel called *Outside Looking In*. That novel, as well as the Thanksgiving chapter in *Island Apart*, was inspired by a poignant entry in one of my mother's journals:

> *Some people are born being part and substance of the whole. Others are always on the outside looking in. How very lonely it is being on the outside looking in. Cannot those who are on the inside extend a hand to those who are on the outside and bring them inside where it is warm and light and safe?*

As for Wilhelm Reich, his pioneering work paved the way for expressive therapies, like primal scream and psychodrama. For a brief time, I even did therapy sessions with Reich's disciple, Myron Sharaf, who wrote the definitive biography of Reich, *Fury on Earth*.

I had plenty of fodder for psychotherapy; I had never fully dealt with my mother's drug use or grieved for her suicide. For many years, I was too shut down ("armored against my feelings," Reich would have said) to contemplate therapy for myself. Eventually, I came to terms with my childhood. I joined a twelve-step program and sent lots of psychotherapists' kids to summer camp with my therapy fees. But mostly, I have found solace in writing, and writing *Island Apart* was certainly cathartic.

As first novels go, *Island Apart* was a moderate success. I earned out my advance and then some. The book sold well enough to warrant a paperback edition (with a ghastly romance-novel cover). My Montréal publisher translated it into French. But the book never reached Hollywood, which is a shame, because I had dreamed up a great cast at the time: Nick Nolte would play the Hermit; Meryl Streep, Claire; Wynona Ryder, Molly; Bette Midler, Sheila; and Art Garfunkel, Ely.

The French edition of my novel, The Hermit of Chappaquiddick.

Over time, the royalties dwindled, and like the vast majority of all novels, the book went out of print. I reacquired the rights and republished it through Amazon with its original—and in my opinion, much superior—title, *The Hermit of Chappaquiddick.* I added a bonus chapter, cut from the original manuscript—Sheila's backstory. I changed the cover art to a photo I actually like—a lighthouse with a portentous sky above it. I still cry when I read the sad parts of *The Hermit.* I hope you'll be tempted to read it too.

I had an idea for a second novel before I even finished my first: a foodie mystery set in Amsterdam called *In Rembrandt's Kitchen.* It turned out, for me at least, that a second novel is a lot harder to write than the first. Other, more lucrative cookbook deals came up, and I got busy with more TV shows. The first chapter of *In Rembrandt's Kitchen* still sits in my computer. I hope to get around to writing it soon.

KATAMA KIRS

This cocktail comes from my favorite chapter in my novel, *The Hermit of Chappaquiddick*. "Giving Thanks" (chapter 10) brings all the major characters in the novel together for the first time for Thanksgiving dinner—including one character who never quite makes it through the door. It's a dinner brimming with warmth, welcome, acceptance, and surprising character evolutions. Presiding over it is Elliott Feinblatt—psychiatrist turned self-help guru—who possesses a formidable knowledge of wine. Originally, the kir was a Burgundian aperitif—named for a resistance fighter and former mayor of Dijon named Félix Kir—a combination of crisp white Aligoté wine and crème de cassis liqueur. That gave rise to the kir royale (made with champagne instead of white wine), and that in turn inspired Elliott to add a Martha's Vineyard touch: blueberry syrup instead of crème de cassis. Blueberry syrup is available at specialty shops and online (good brands include Walden Farms and Stonewall Kitchen), but you could certainly substitute a spoonful of blueberry jam.

Serves 2 but can be multiplied as desired

3 tablespoons wild blueberry syrup

12 ounces (1 ½ cups) champagne or prosecco

6 fresh blueberries

1. Pour the blueberry syrup into the bottom of 2 champagne flutes. Gradually add the champagne or prosecco, gently swirling the glass to blend the ingredients. Add the blueberries and serve at once.

Chapter Twenty

STEVEN RAICHLEN GRILLS ITALY

2017

With photographer Paolo and director Stefano overlooking Portofino.

It all began with a selfie.

Some years ago, Barbara and I traveled to Modena, Italy—birthplace of balsamic vinegar—to dine at Massimo Bottura's celebrated Michelin three-star restaurant, Osteria Francescana. A man stopped me in the street to ask for a photo together. Then a couple stopped me. Then another.

It turned out that my American TV show *Primal Grill* was airing on Gambero Rosso (the Italian food network). Strangers would call out: "Buongiorno, Steven!" They'd ask for selfies and call me "Il Mago del Grill" ("The Wizard of the Grill")—the name of the Italian version of my book *How to Grill.*

Being recognized is a mixed blessing, and we certainly witnessed its downside at the Osteria. On the plus side, we were shown to the best table and showered with extra dishes from the kitchen. Some—like the "burnt edges of the lasagna" (the part everyone likes) and a deconstructed lemon meringue pie called "whoops, the dessert fell on the floor"—were pure genius. (Chef Bottura certainly has a sense of humor.)

In the not-so-sublime category: a minuscule sliver of duck breast served dried out and lukewarm. At $250 per person for a tasting menu, I would have been justified to send it back. But the flip side of being recognized is to never, ever complain. I said nothing and was glad I didn't because after the meal I was invited into the kitchen, where the chefs proudly showed off the newest addition to their kitchen: a Big Green Egg.

My next meal was a lot more satisfying—even though it was a clumsy pasta dish prepared by students at the cooking school at Gambero Rosso's headquarters in Rome. I went there to meet producer Bianca Perugia and director Stefano Monticelli to find out why people were stopping me in the street. Yes, it was true that my American TV show was running on their network. Yes, they had my book *La Bibbia del Barbecue* (*The Barbecue! Bible*), and yes, it had become something of a cult cookbook.

I suggested, half joking, that we should make a grilling show in Italy. We met with some higher-ups, then with higher higher-ups. By the time I left Rome, I had a new project, and Gambero Rosso had a new TV show: *Steven Raichlen Grills Italy*.

As a food writer, I'm sometimes frustrated by Italian grilling. On the one hand, Italy has given the world three of the most iconic dishes in the global barbecue pantheon: *bruschetta*, *bistecca alla fiorentina* (Florentine steak), and *pollo al mattone* (chicken grilled under a brick).

On the other, Italians prize simplicity to such a degree that the vast majority of their grill recipes limit the flavorings to olive oil, garlic, and salt (and rosemary or lemon juice if you're feeling fancy). If barbecue were mathematics, Italian grilling would boil down to the following equations:

Beef + salt + fire + optional olive oil = steak
Fish + salt + olive oil + lemon = seafood
Chicken + salt + herbs + plus olive oil = poultry

Italians fetishize simplicity to a degree that makes their grilling delectable, but a challenge to write about. So when the opportunity came to dive deeper into Italian barbecue—to learn what my equations were missing—I couldn't pack my bags fast enough.

We decided that this would be a very different sort of program than the how-to shows I do in the United States. Instead, it would be a two-way voyage of discovery. I would travel around northern Italy, meeting local grill masters and learning how they put food to fire. Then we'd rent a villa in Tuscany, where I'd fire up the grills to create Raichlen versions of the Italian dishes I tasted during our travels.

There was just one problem: I didn't speak Italian. So, I downloaded the Pimsleur Italian-language app. (In my opinion, Pimsleur is the best language-learning app—I use it often when I travel.) I also subscribed to another great language-learning app: *News in Slow Italian* radio, delivered weekly in Italian by native speakers. And I hired an Italian tutor.

By the time I returned to Rome four months later, I had a working knowledge of Italian. I didn't speak the language of Dante and Italo Calvino, but I could understand and make myself understood. We agreed that when the grill master spoke better English than my Italian, we'd conduct the interviews in English, providing subtitles for the viewers. When my Italian was better than his or her English, Lord help us, I'd exercise my limited Italian.

We set off from the Gambero Rosso studios in a caravan consisting of an imposing white Volvo SUV (complete with bilingual driver) for me, plus two vans for the crew and camera gear. We hadn't traveled an hour before we pulled into our first Autogrill, where the crew stopped for a coffee break. They lit up the inevitable cigarettes while I thumbed through *gialli,* Italian mystery novels (so named for the yellow covers of the Italian whodunits of the 1930s). It turns out that Italian highway rest stops double as surprisingly well-stocked bookstores.

Once back on the road, we stopped an hour later for another coffee break, this one highlighted by a midmorning snack of mortadella panini. *Delizioso!* I quickly learned that the coffee and cigarette break was an inviolable part of the Italian workday. And that typical American workaholism would not be tolerated.

We finally arrived at our first destination: Gorino—a fishing village in the Po River Delta on the Adriatic Coast south of Venice. If you've ever enjoyed *spaghetti con vongole verace* (pasta with "real" clams), this is where these thumbnail-size shellfish come from. (Later in the show, I would use them on a grilled pizza.) But we had come in search of a more esoteric local seafood: *Anguilla anguilla,* European eel.

By six o'clock the next morning, I was standing in a fishing boat, cutting through thick fog to a cove where the marsh meets the open water. Roberto, my guide and fisherman, hauled *cogoli,* handwoven basket traps, out of the water. A half dozen fat black eels slithered inside.

Eel was the specialty of a century-old restaurant called La Capanna di Eraclio in the nearby village of Codigoro. "Hercules's Hut," as the name means in Italian, is the sort of restaurant we food writers dream of—rustic with faded elegance, and totally off the tourist circuit. You'd never find it if you didn't know someone who lives in the area. And there to meet us was its third-generation chef-owner, Maria Grazia Soncini.

This sure didn't look like a grill restaurant, nor Maria Grazia, in her starched chefs whites, much of a grill master. Until, that is, she brought me to the rear of the restaurant, where a huge, raised, weathered metal hearth awaited our eels. She raked the embers, adding pinecones to flavor the fire.

Boarding a fishing boat at dawn in Gorino in the Po River Delta.

Preparing eel is one of my least favorite tasks on the planet. (We'd had to do it at La Varenne.) The sous chef pinned a slimy creature to a plank with an ice pick. He skinned it alive, eviscerated it, and cut it into six-inch sections. The sections continued to writhe while being trimmed and marinated, and even for the first few minutes on the grill. Maria Grazia seasoned the eel with sea salt, stuffed it with garlic and rosemary, then seared it over the fire. She basted it with olive oil, using a goose feather as a basting brush. She finished the eel *in umad*—simmered with dry white wine in a skillet. What emerged was rich, moist, flaky, and surprisingly delicate, subtly scented with rosemary and garlic. We washed it down with local Trebbiano Romagnolo wine.

OUR NEXT DESTINATION WAS a thirteenth-century castello near the town of Polesine Zibello in Emilia Romagna. Chef Massimo Spigaroli and his brother Luciano spent two decades restoring the imposing castle, which they run like their personal fiefdom. It houses a small hotel, a Michelin-starred restaurant, a casual bistro specializing in house-cured pork products, and a museum dedicated to another Spigaroli specialty: *culatello,* cured pork shoulder ham.

Massimo's *culatello* is famous the world over. He led me to a dank cellar where hundreds, perhaps thousands of hams hang from the ceiling. He pointed out hams with handwritten labels destined for King Charles of England, Prince Alberto II of Monaco, the Bulgari family, and more.

Culatello is one of the most exquisite hams I've ever tasted: imagine salty, fatty, velvety ribbons of the richest imaginable prosciutto melting on your tongue like butter. I could've gladly eaten it for the rest of our visit—hell, for the rest of my life—and never wished for another ham.

But tasty as it was, I was there for the grilling. Massimo led me to a fireplace in his Michelin-starred restaurant, where wild ducks spun on a five-hundred-year-old rotisserie, flanked by pears grown in Massimo's orchard. According to Massimo, the clockwork mechanism turning the rotisserie spit was designed by Leonardo da Vinci.

The chef had something different in mind for our on-camera grill session. He started with a young pig meticulously boned from snout to tail. (His hogs—the rare Black Parma breed—graze wild on the vast property.) Massimo marinated the meat with rosemary from his garden, red wine from his vineyard, and *mostarda* (a pear and quince marmalade) made, where else, in his restaurant kitchen.

The next step called for a technique I had never seen, and I've spent time with a *lot* of grill masters. Massimo reached for a bowl of soft black dirt dug from the nearby riverbank. He mixed in flour and beaten eggs and kneaded it into a sort of dough. He spread half of the mixture on a sheet of metal, lining the surface with fresh rosemary branches and dried tree leaves. He nestled the pork on top, covering it with more herbs, leaves, and the rest of the dirt crust. He set the pork, thus entombed, on its metal sheet over a wood fire. He let it cook for about an hour, adding sticks as needed to maintain a gentle flame.

The curious thing about chefs is that the more successful they become, the less time they actually cook. Watching Massimo work—the tentative quality of his gestures—I got the feeling he had never actually made this dish before. When the clay crust had hardened and whitened with ash, he hammered and chiseled it open. A blast of steam emerged—herbaceous, earthy, and pork-scented, with the fruity aroma of the *mostarda*. The meat was meltingly tender and ineffably tasty. Massimo looked surprised and delighted that his experiment had actually worked.

Our next stop introduced me to a grill found in the Fruili region of northern Italy and nowhere else on the planet: the *fogolâr*. Picture a raised stone hearth smack-dab in the center of the living room, where it functions as both fireplace and grill station. We were lunching at the Antica Osteria Stella d'Oro in the village of Verzegnis in a sparsely populated mountainous region in northeastern Italy called Carnia. I was joined by an old friend, Fabrizio Nonis, a village butcher turned Italian celebrity TV chef.

Earlier that day, Fabrizio had taken me to a butcher who makes an obscure local specialty called *varhackara*. It's a sort of pâté concocted from the trimmings of locally smoked pancetta, guanciale, and prosciutto, and he is the last butcher in Italy to make it. We toasted slices of dark, dense local rye bread over the *fogolâr* fire and slathered it with the smoky *varhackara*. Foie gras would pale in comparison.

Over the next few weeks, we crisscrossed northern Italy, going as far north as San Candido, a tiny Alpine village where the stone houses of Carnia gave way to the sort of wooden chalets you see in the Austrian Alps. Which is no surprise, as the Austrian border is only four kilometers to the north. I dusted off my rusty German to converse with our next chef, Markus Holzer. Markus told me about the history of this stunning region. How Italian artillery soldiers hauled cannons up sheer mountain cliffs with ropes to fend off the Austrian army during the "Great War" (as Italians call World War I). How the Austrian composer Gustav Mahler holed up in a cabin nearby to write his famous Ninth and Tenth Symphonies.

Come time for our grill session, Markus led me to the last piece of cooking equipment I would expect to find in this remote village: a massive steel offset barrel smoker in the finest Texas tradition. (It came from a forge in Germany.) In it he placed a venison loin, which he slow-smoked over beech and juniper wood. In true Austrian tradition, he accompanied it with spaetzle and braised red cabbage.

The mountains gave way to the sea as we arrived in Portofino. Once a quiet fishing village but today a magnet for moguls (the Armani family and Domenico Dolce of Dolce & Gabbana have villas here), Portofino has managed to retain its small-town charm despite the onslaught of international tourism. I was there to grill with a Ligurian pugilist-turned-chef named Mina Patti. He led me to a stone pier to meet the *Albatross*—a fishing boat piloted by a captain right out of central casting, complete with orange bib waders and a black wool cap. We left with wooden crates of *pulpo* (octopus), *seppie* (baby cuttlefish), and *gamberi rossi* (supernaturally succulent red shrimp).

The day's grill session required a bit of a hike. Actually, more than a bit of a hike—a mountain climb. Our producer had arranged for us to shoot at the Castello Brown, a castle occupied by a wealthy English diplomat in

Octopus doesn't get fresher than this.

the nineteenth century, and now a museum and culture center. The only way to get there is by foot. The crew hauled cameras, lights, sound gear, bags of charcoal, and two Weber kettle grills up a precipitous footpath. The exhausted host hauled himself. Forty minutes later, we arrived, sweating, hungry, and thirsty. The spectacular bird's-eye view of Portofino below helped compensate for the arduous hike.

Mina marinated the seafood in the inevitable olive oil, garlic, and rosemary. One note of originality: He flavored a vinaigrette with local Vermentino white wine. He grilled the seafood over charcoal, using a bunch of parsley as a basting brush—just long enough to cook it, but not so long to lay on the char marks so prized by American grill jockeys. It's some of the freshest, sweetest, briniest seafood I've ever tasted—utterly devoid of any of the spicing or seasoning you find so often on American grilled seafood.

In Florence, we connected with my old friend Luciano Ghinassi. Barbara and I have been dining at his restaurant, Buca Lapi, for twenty years. Luciano came to the hundred-plus-year-old Buca Lapi as a scullery boy, working his way up to chef and eventual owner. He's trod the stone steps down to the subterranean dining room, with its imposing barrel-vaulted ceilings, daily for more than fifty years.

We Americans are obsessed with newness—the hottest chef, the newest restaurant. Italians venerate history. Restaurants announce "founded in 1957 or 1963" with pride. It's as though their adherence to tradition makes them immune to trendiness.

Luciano took me around the corner to a walk-in meat locker, where he ages sides of Chianina, Marchigiana, and Romagnola beef for a full month. Luciano likes his steaks thick (three to four fingers thick), and his chefs have a singular technique for cooking these monsters through. They season the meat solely with coarse sea salt, then sear both sides over charcoal. Now comes the ingenious part: They stand the steaks upright, backbone to the grate, and continue grilling to the desired degree of doneness. The bone conducts the heat upward through the meat.

Of course, doneness is a relative term in Italy, with preference going to *al sangue* (literally "with blood"), which translates as very rare, make that still mooing. I ordered my steak *media al sangue* (medium-rare), which in Italy means warm but still blood-red in the center. Luciano sliced the steak, drizzling it with Tuscan virgin olive oil. It was about the best three ingredient steak (beef, salt, and oil) I'd ever tasted—even if it was barely cooked in the center.

Our ultimate destination? Venice! Where fire meets the water in the world's most beautiful city. Only, sadly, it no longer does. For years, we would lunch at a Venetian restaurant called Da Ivo. Signor Ivo claimed to own the last charcoal-burning grill in Venice, and on it he'd cook wondrous *tagliate* (sliced steak) and seafood. Ivo had a method for grilling shrimp I've never seen elsewhere. He'd brush it with olive oil, dredge it in breadcrumbs, then sizzle it on the grill. You'd expect the breadcrumbs to burn before the shrimp cooked, but they didn't. Ivo even went so far as to accompany the shrimp with a sauce: a piquant caper, anchovy, and parsley *salsa verde*.

Unfortunately, by the time our TV crew arrived—we on a *motoscafo* (one of those gorgeous wooden Venetian motorboats), our gear on a clunky motorized barge—the Venice municipality had outlawed all open-fire cooking. The only way we could move forward was to cook on an electric grill. Now, normally I don't consider electric grills grilling—even if Weber's Lumin electric grill can achieve temperatures of 650 degrees. But the setting was so spectacular, I set aside my scruples.

We set up our grill station on the top-floor terrace of the posh Hotel Danieli. Before us stretched the San Marco Basin, with its frenetic boat traffic and the magnificent white Santa Maria della Salute Basilica rising behind it. Earlier that morning, Danieli executive chef Dario Parascandolo took me to the Rialto Fish Market to buy the seafood for our grill session. With cameras rolling, we loaded up on swordfish, tuna, branzino, calamari, and my favorite, *cannolicchi* (razor clams slender as pencils)—each more ocean-fresh than the next.

By then I was used to the Italian seasonings: salt, pepper, and olive oil flavored with garlic and rosemary. By then I was used to the grill time: just long enough to cook the seafood (that is, hardly at all), with grill marks almost nonexistent. By way of an accompaniment, Dario served the grilled white cornmeal polenta for which Veneto is famous. By way of a sauce, he prepared a simple vinaigrette with olive oil, lemon juice, garlic, and chopped anchovies—the latter adding a rich umami flavor to the already briny seafood. I couldn't wait to try it at home on Martha's Vineyard the next time I grilled swordfish.

It had been an amazing journey, and it exposed me to aspects of Italian grilling I had never previously experienced. The work of the Italian grill masters was done; mine was about to begin.

THE PREMISE OF THE SHOW was that I would experience Italian grilling, then create my own interpretations based on what I saw. We rented a villa—a castle, really—in Bucine, a village thirty miles southeast of Florence. We set up our grills—charcoal kettles, gas grills, smokers—in the shadow of the imposing nineteenth-century edifice. I provided the food stylist with a shopping list, and the improvisations began.

For my twist on Maria Grazia's eel, for example, I borrowed a page from the sushi-ba playbook. I simmered soy sauce, sesame oil, honey, and Italy's beloved *vin santo* dessert wine together to make an Italo-Japanese teriyaki sauce. I grilled the eel over charcoal, lacquering it with vin santo teriyaki. The crew devoured it.

The Raichlen renditions followed in rapid succession: For Mina and our Portofino grill session, I improvised a grilled squid stuffed with breadcrumbs, capers, and raisins—a combination inspired by a previous trip to Sicily. For Fabrizio, I grilled rye bread sandwiched with *varhackara*, thinly sliced mountain cheese, and sauerkraut to make a sort of Italo-American Reuben sandwich. Markus's smoked deer became a spit-roasted saddle of venison marinated in red wine, juniper berries, and bay leaves, with a red currant barbecue sauce to go with it.

Massimo's clay-roasted pork became a *braciole* (traditional Italian stuffed meat roll), in this case a pork loin butterflied and pounded thin, stuffed with sliced provolone, sage, and his gorgeous *culatello*. As for Luciano's *bistecca alla fiorentina*, I grilled it caveman-style, directly on the embers. By way of a sauce (not that any self-respecting Florentine would put a sauce to *bistecca*), I fried sliced friggitelli peppers with garlic and parsley in olive oil. I poured the

On the set of Steven Raichlen Grills Italy *in Bucine, thirty miles from Florence.*

sizzling mixture over the *bistecca*. The crew was skeptical, but they managed to clean their plates. I still haven't had the courage to tell Luciano.

In general, the crew liked my versions of Italian grilling, although a couple of the cameramen complained of too much flavor. The protests became universal when I grilled homemade pizza dough, topping it with those *vongole verace*, baby clams. I took my inspiration from the clam pizza at Frank Pepe's in New Haven, Connecticut. My Italian friends didn't buy it.

It turns out that Italians are every bit as obsessed with live-fire cooking as we Americans are. But our approaches are radically different. What matters most to Italians is seasonality and tradition. Paramount is the respect for the raw materials—rich-flavored meats and impeccably fresh seafood. To preserve the pristine flavors, they do as little to the food as possible. In other words, when it comes to grilling, as it does for so much Italian cuisine, less is more.

Just the opposite is true where I come from. In America, we love fragrant spices, fiery chilies, pungent marinades, and bold sauces. When it comes to our grilling, the bigger the flavor, the better. I'm definitely a more-is-more kind of guy.

A JOURNALIST ONCE CALLED ME a "minor celebrity." For a moment, he hurt my feelings, then I realized that the observation—which is absolutely true—was a blessing.

Yes, I have the pleasure of being recognized at airports and shopping malls on occasion.

"Aren't you . . . ?"

"Yes, I'm the barbecue guy."

"Love your show."

"Thank you."

"I've learned so much from your books."

"That makes me really happy."

But I don't have the inconvenience of having to hide from my public, or book hotel rooms under aliases, like Emeril used to do. (One Emeril alias I loved was "Harry Covert"—a pun on the French green bean, *haricot vert.*)

But once—just once—during that Italian TV shoot, I felt like a bona fide celebrity. We were taping in St. Mark's Square in Venice, which Napoleon called the "drawing room of Europe." I strolled through the square—just strolled—with a cameraman rolling beside me.

An American came up to me and told me he loved my show.

An Italian approached to tell me how much he had learned from *La Bibbia di Barbecue.*

A fan from Montréal waved and shouted: *Vive le barbecue! Vive le Québec!*

For thirty seconds, I felt what a movie star must experience when he walks the red carpet at the Venice International Film Festival.

A year later, I checked in with some of the Italian grill masters who appeared on the show. Two had moved and three had closed their restaurants. *Sic transit gloria mundi,* the master of ceremonies used to say to newly elected popes at St. Peter's: "Thus passes the glory of the world." Italians put it in terms any barbecuer would understand: *Fama e gloria sono fumo*: "Fame and glory are just smoke."

THE BARBECUE HALL OF FAME

Unless you're a diehard baseball fan, you probably don't remember Sandy Koufax. He pitched for the Los Angeles Dodgers from 1958 to 1965. Koufax was Jewish, and in the 1965 World Series (between the

Dodgers and the Minnesota Twins) the first game fell on Yom Kippur, the holiest holiday of the Jewish calendar.

Despite the pressure and prestige, Koufax did what virtually no major league sports player would do today. He refused to play. This made him a hero at my Sunday school and to Jews around the world.

Koufax sat out game one, but he threw shutouts in games five and seven. The Dodgers won the World Series and Sandy Koufax is remembered as one of the greatest pitchers—and greatest Jewish athletes—of all time.

Incidentally, the following year the Dodgers battled my hometown team, the Baltimore Orioles, in the 1966 World Series. I remember watching from the bleachers at Baltimore's old Memorial Stadium. The Orioles won the series (go Birds!), and Koufax retired after an illustrious career.

But back to barbecue. In 2014, the American Royal Association (organizers of the World Series of Barbecue festival in Kansas City) invited me to be inducted into the Barbecue Hall of Fame. Naturally, I was honored; the Hall of Fame includes some of the greatest legends of American barbecue, from pitmasters like Myron Mixon to entrepreneurs like Joe Traeger (who invented the pellet grill). It was a huge honor—or it would have been had the awards ceremony not fallen on Yom Kippur.

It wasn't a hard decision. Mindful of Sandy Koufax, I explained that I couldn't accept. Next year, I'd be delighted—provided that the awards ceremony didn't fall on a Jewish holiday.

Well, the following year, I found myself onstage in front of a thousand people at the Kansas Speedway. Joining me were some of the industry people I most admired, from Big Green Egg founder Ed Fisher to Paul Kirk, whose grand championship barbecue competition wins were so numerous, most people—even Paul—lost count. The award itself was a bronze rack of ribs mounted on a marble pedestal. ("That goes in your office," said Barbara.) I held it high and proudly as I thanked the audience, the awards committee, and my fellow honorable inductees. I can't reconstruct my whole speech, but I do remember my closing line:

"Thanks to all you barbecuers and grillers out there, I have the best job on the planet."

My induction into the Barbecue Hall of Fame.

COLAZIONE AL BBQ

(Grilled Breakfast Eggs)

Leave it to Italy to turn a poultry farmer into a celebrity. His name is Paolo Parisi, and the eggs from his farm, Le Macchie, are so prized, each one bears his logo (not to mention a one-euro price tag). His chickens range free, of course, and their supernaturally rich yolks are the color of an orange sunrise. So when it came time to come up with a recipe based on our visit with Paolo—the last stop on my barbecue tour across northern Italy—I created a breakfast of smoke-grilled eggs. Think of it as a deconstructed frittata. The crowning touch: a topping of thinly shaved truffles. The wood smoke, although not particularly Italian, adds an interesting dimension to the eggs. You'll need to know about a couple special ingredients. Pancetta is Italian bacon—it's cured, but not smoked. Guanciale is cured pork jowls—again cured, but not smoked. Feel free to substitute American bacon, which is both cured and smoked. I've made the truffle optional too, but if you can find one, it will make an unforgettable breakfast even better.

Serves 2 and can be multiplied

2 tablespoons unsalted butter, divided

4 thin slices pancetta, guanciale, or bacon, cut crosswise into ¼-inch slivers

2 slices Italian bread

4 large eggs (preferably farm-fresh eggs)

Sea salt and freshly ground black pepper

3 tablespoons heavy cream

A 3-ounce chunk of Parmigiano-Reggiano cheese (you won't need all of it, but it's hard to grate a smaller chunk)

¼ cup toasted breadcrumbs (preferably homemade)

1 small white or black truffle (optional)

You'll also need:

an 8-inch cast-iron skillet; 1 cup hardwood chips or a wood chunk; a truffle shaver (optional)

1. Set up your grill for indirect grilling and heat to medium-high (400°F).
2. Melt 1 tablespoon of the butter in the skillet on your grill's side burner or on the stovetop over medium-high heat. Add the pancetta and cook until crisp and brown, 3 minutes, stirring often. Using a slotted spoon, transfer the pancetta to a small bowl.
3. Brush the bread slices on both sides with the fat in the skillet and set aside. These will become grilled toast.
4. Let the skillet cool to warm. Crack in the eggs, taking care not to break the yolks. Season with salt and pepper. Sprinkle the pancetta over the eggs and drizzle the cream on top. Freshly and finely grate the Parmigiano over the cream, and evenly sprinkle the top with the breadcrumbs. Dot the top with the remaining 1 tablespoon butter, cut into little bits.
5. Place the skillet with the eggs on the grill away from the heat. Add the wood chips to the coals or place in the smoker box of your gas grill. Indirect grill until the breadcrumbs are browned and the eggs are just set, 7 to 10 minutes. (The yolks should remain a little runny in the center.)
6. Meanwhile, toast the bread slices directly over the fire, 1 to 2 minutes per side.
7. Transfer the eggs in their skillet to the table. Thinly shave the truffle (if using) over the eggs. Serve with the grilled bread for dipping in the yolks.

Chapter Twenty-One

UP IN SMOKE

2017–2020

With Texas barbecue legend Aaron Franklin in Austin, Texas.

The year 2015 got off to a rough start. Peter Workman passed away before the publication of *Man Made Meals*. Sales were underwhelming—perhaps because Peter wasn't around to oversee the marketing. The book never made it to a second printing.

We stalled on the TV front too. After three seasons of *Primal Grill,* we were unable to secure the funding for a fourth season. I was uncertain when—or if—I would return to television. Book writing and television were the two activities that had defined my professional life for more than a decade. Like many men, my professional life defined pretty much my whole life. The future looked bleak.

Then a two-word title popped into my head—for a book, for a show, I wasn't sure. It played off a popular fashion TV show at the time called *Project Runway*. The words were "Project Smoke," and like a leaping flame, I was off and running again.

There was no shortage of barbecue shows. This one had to be different. But how? I brainstormed with my producer, Matt Cohen, and of course with my wife, Barbara. I'd base the show on a simple but not immediately obvious premise: All barbecue is smoked, but not all smoked foods are barbecue.

Smoked foods in the barbecue realm include Texas brisket, Memphis ribs, and Carolina pork shoulder. Among the more outlandish examples are pig shots (bacon-wrapped sausage disks topped with cream cheese and crab) and "blue balls" (smoked pork sausage wrapped around nuggets of blueberry muffin—tastier than it sounds).

But what about smoked foods that aren't barbecue?

Pastrami is smoked, and it originated where my forebears did—in the world's least likely barbecue region: Jewish Eastern Europe. Italians smoke *scamorza* (a mozzarella-like cheese) over smoldering hay, but they'd never call it barbecue. British kippers, kippered salmon, and finnan haddie are smoked, but they're certainly not barbecue. (In case you're wondering: The first are smoked herring; the second, hot-smoked salmon; the third, smoked haddock originally from the town of Findon, Scotland.) Then there are smoked spirits, like single-malt Scotch whisky—also from Scotland. And smoked beers, like Germany's Rauchbier from Bamberg in Bavaria.

Steven Raichlen's Project Smoke would focus on the world of smoked foods and drinks—not just barbecue—and that would set us apart. Grill and smoker companies liked the idea too. In short order, we lined up sponsors. We found a location in Tucson, Arizona. With luck, I'd be back on the air in time for barbecue season.

To produce *Project Smoke*, I teamed up with my long-standing partners, Resolution Pictures and Maryland Public Television. Our crew flew in from all over the country. Most of us had worked together for three seasons of *Primal Grill*, so the TV shoot felt like a family reunion. The long hours in often-trying conditions outdoors inspire a strong sense of camaraderie. It's part of what I like best about television.

My longtime assistant, Nancy Loseke, managed the logistics of the shoot from her home base in Cleveland. Nancy's organizational powers are formidable, and if you've visited my website, BarbecueBible.com (if you haven't, you should), you'll recognize her byline on many of our biweekly blogs and newsletters. She's also a meticulous editor—this book is the latest of the dozen of my books that she has fine-tuned with contentiousness and wit.

We built our set on a hillside overlooking Tucson. Our backdrop was the high desert with its saguaro cacti, piñon pine, and manzanita. It was an austere setting after the previous shows, but it seemed to fit *Project Smoke* perfectly. During our night shoots, Tucson stretched out before us like a million scintillating stars.

Meanwhile, our fire wranglers, Andreas Langley and Rob Baas, were busy setting up our grills and smokers. It was an awe-inspiring lineup, including massive offset barrel smokers from Horizon and a Kalamazoo Gaucho grill—an Argentine-style wood-burner with a grate raised and lowered by a giant flywheel that cost more than my first three cars combined.

Our fire wranglers play an essential role in the production, assembling grills and smokers and keeping them fired up and functioning. Some smokers weighed six hundred pounds, and we needed them wheeled on and off the set in minutes. Others had complex electronics that didn't always work, requiring MacGyvering to get them running.

Crew call was at 6:30 AM Everyone arrived on set at daybreak.

WE DECIDED TO WORK IN a more documentary style for the new series: no more long, wordy openings shot from a boom camera. Instead, I would walk on set, say a few words, and start grilling. (We'd fill in the backstory with another new feature of the *Project Smoke* series: fireside chats.)

On day one, the gaffers readied the silk. The stage manager clapped the slate, and we were off. We started with a simple dish to get everyone warmed up: cold-smoked scallops with smoked tomatoes and jicama salsa. In cold smoking, food is smoked without actually cooking it—accomplished by separating the heat source (smoldering wood) from the smoke chamber. Cold smoking is often used with seafood: Think Scottish-style salmon or Jewish-style Nova. It's perfect for delicate foods, like scallops and tomatoes, where you want to retain the pristine texture of the raw ingredients.

I "circumcised" the scallops—a technique I learned in Paris that involves removing the tough thumbnail-shaped muscle from the side of each shellfish. For seasoning, just sea salt and black pepper—to keep the focus on the scallops and the smoke. I served them on smoked tomatoes with a nod to our Arizona location: jicama salsa. We finished the segment in time for lunch—four hours of shooting for a six-minute segment!

The episode concluded with a true barbecue dish: baby back ribs with cactus pear barbecue sauce. I always try to tailor my shows to our shooting location. Cactus dominated our backdrop—what better to base a barbecue sauce on than its sweet, musky fruit?

In planning the menus for *Project Smoke,* I tried to present smoke cookery in all its manifestations—from traditional American barbecue (hence our "Barbecue Trinity" and "Smoking the Competition" episodes) to international smoking ("Global Smoke"). Several episodes focused on iconic smoked foods (like "Bacon 24/7" and "Thanksgiving Comes Early"). We even did an episode entitled "How to Smoke When You Don't Have a Smoker," showcasing techniques for smoking food indoors. Over the course

On the set of Project Smoke *with fire wrangler Rob Baas.*

of thirteen episodes, I demonstrated forty-one individual dishes. I'm not going to enumerate them all here (you can stream them from my website), but I would like to highlight three that represent the spirit of the show:

- Smoked Gazpacho: I cold-smoked halved tomatoes, cucumbers, onions, peppers, and garlic on a tray of ice, then pureed them in a blender with olive oil and vinegar, as legions of Spaniards do in summer. If smoke is the umami of barbecue, this chilled soup makes you feel like you are tasting gazpacho for the first time—familiar, yet otherworldly.
- Smoked Shrimp Cocktail: In my opinion, shrimp cocktail is one of the worst dishes in the American repertory. Boiling is a surefire way to remove flavor from food. (That's why we boil bones to make beef stock.) For the *Project Smoke* version, I marinated the shrimp with cilantro, hot pepper flakes, and cumin prior to a slow smoke over smoldering mesquite. The sauce riffed on a shrimp cocktail I experienced in Campeche, Mexico, where chipotle chiles, diced onion, and fresh orange zest and juice turbocharge the traditional ketchup and horseradish. To paraphrase Raymond Chandler, the *Project Smoke* version beat traditional shrimp cocktail hollow.
- Smoked Ice Cream: It began as a joke—you can't really smoke ice cream. Or can you? To keep my smoked ice cream from melting, I froze water in a large metal bowl, then unmolded a pint of vanilla on top. I added hickory chips to a screaming-hot fire, generating thick clouds of fragrant smoke. The ice cream emerged two minutes later with dark, dreamy swirls of wood smoke, tasting uncannily like a fire-toasted marshmallow, only frozen. It's one of my coolest creations.

Making television shows always takes longer than you'd think. Invariably we fell behind—sometimes due to a camera or sound glitch, more often to a tongue-tied TV host. We even once had a windstorm that blew over the tent housing our control room. I was smoking a brisket for our "Barbecue Trinity" episode when the silk flew off and the tent collapsed. Matt kept the cameras rolling. If you watch that episode, you'll see the chaos unfold on-screen.

Matt had one more innovation up his sleeve: bloopers. Watch to the very end of each episode and you'll see me stumbling over lines (and stumbling on the set, literally), dropping tongs, burning food, and otherwise mis-performing. When I meet fans at airports or in the street, they all tell me how much they love the bloopers. Ouch.

Project Smoke premiered on June 27, 2015. Three months later, we had 95 percent carriage—meaning that 95 percent of the 350-plus PBS stations across the country carried the show. *Project Smoke* proved the viability of a TV show dedicated to smoking. Once season 1 was in the can (a reference to the flat metal containers film used to be stored in back when shows were shot on celluloid), it was time to write the book.

First stop: London, where I set out in search of the "smoked salmon whisperer." He wasn't easy to find. An hour and two changes on the London Underground brought me to a shabby neighborhood of workshops and warehouses. After several wrong doors and an "I don't know who you're talking about, mate" or two, I came face-to-face with a tall man in red waders and boots, his hair swept back, his features decidedly Nordic.

"Pleased to meet you. I'm Ole Hansen," he said. "Welcome to Hansen and Lydersen."

I wanted *Project Smoke* to be more than a collection of recipes. I wanted to bring readers on the journey I took along the world's smoke trail. So, I did what I always do when researching a new book: I packed a suitcase.

I often say that people buy my cookbooks for the recipes, but I write them for the prose. What fascinates me is not just how to smoke the best brisket, salmon, or mozzarella. It's the role smoke plays in human history and culture—why smoked foods loom so large on the world's food scene. Why people smoked food in the first place, and why we do it with such enthusiasm today.

On my desk sits a clumsy clay figurine—a bust of a Neanderthal I made in elementary school. Like most boys, I was fascinated by cavemen and dinosaurs. I'm still obsessed with the prehistoric roots of barbecue today.

Why we started smoking is easy: It keeps food from spoiling and makes it taste better. I imagine a prehistoric campsite. Early human ancestors—perhaps *Homo erectus,* perhaps *Homo neanderthalensis*—gather around a fire. They use it for cooking—an innovation that would turbocharge human evolution.

One of the cave dwellers notices fewer flies in the smoke downwind of the fire. She hangs meat on a stick downwind, and sure enough, the smoke keeps the bugs at bay. The smoked meat turns out to be less prone to spoilage (we'll get to the chemistry behind that in a minute). More importantly, it tastes better. We've just witnessed the birth of proto–beef jerky.

Someone else—living near a salt deposit or the sea—tries salting and then smoking wild boar belly or fish, which makes it taste even better. He just paved the way for bacon and smoked salmon. Smoked foods became not just safe-to-eat staples, but delicacies. As our prehistoric ancestors spread across the globe, so did their smoked foods. Which explains why I've come to this rickety smokehouse to sample what's supposed to be the best smoked salmon in all of England. For months I'd been hearing about a man whose fish was so spectacularly savory, top restaurants compete to serve it.

Ole came to London as a musician but found it difficult to make a living. He turned to the trade of his Norwegian forebears and improvised a smokehouse on the city's outskirts. An old potbelly stove burns the wood, and an ordinary room fan circulates the smoke. "My working capital was thirty-three pounds," he says. A single side of his fish sells for twice that today.

There was one additional ingredient I've never seen in a smokehouse before or since: music. An old upright piano sits next to the smokehouse; Ole serenades the fish as it smokes. "The music, the movement, give the smoked salmon energy," Ole says. "They make it taste alive."

I certainly can't argue with the result. This is extraordinary smoked salmon: sea-salty and bacon-crisp on the outside, giving way to creamy, velvety, gently smoke-scented flesh that's oily-rich yet incredibly delicate.

FAST-FORWARD TO MY NEXT DESTINATION on the world smoke trail: central Mexico, where I was to meet a guy you might call the "Still Seeker." Since 1995, Ron Cooper has scoured the hill towns around Oaxaca in pursuit of a smoky spirit called mezcal. If mezcal now rivals tequila at top-shelf craft bars, Ron is largely responsible. He may even have dispelled the myth that the Spanish introduced the art of distillation to the New World. Trailing Ron around means enduring bone-jarring rides over bad or nonexistent roads for hours.

Mezcal, like its cousin tequila, starts with the hearts of the agave cactus. At our first stop, we witnessed what makes it so unique. The distillers—local farmers—had dug a giant pit, which they lined with river stones and firewood. They burned logs to ashes, piled in the piñas (cactus hearts), then buried the whole shebang under a thick layer of dirt. Thus entombed, the piñas roasted for five days, acquiring a haunting smoke flavor. Miraculously, they retained that smoke flavor through the processes of mashing, fermenting, distilling, and bottling.

Ron handed me a clay cup—the size and shape of the tastevins that sommeliers once wore at swanky restaurants. I couldn't vouch for its cleanliness—then again, I was drinking a liquid that's 100 proof. It would take a damn strong microbe to survive that.

The liquid in the cup was as clear as water and as potent as moonshine, with a soulful smoke flavor that overlaid the herbaceous tang of agave. I sipped another cup, then another. Maybe I'd sleep on the bone-jarring ride back to the hotel.

Ron's genius was to recognize that mezcals from each small distillery and microregion possess a unique character. He pioneered the single-village mezcal and remains one of its fiercest advocates.

So what makes me think the Aztecs practiced distillation before the arrival of the Conquistadors? Our last stop was a distillery where *campesinos* pounded the roasted agave hearts in a stone trough with a pestle the size of a tree trunk. The "still" was a clay bowl heated by a wood fire. The "pipes" were sections of bamboo tubes, the "condenser" a clay bowl filled with cold water. What resulted was some of the best mezcal I've ever tasted—and not one piece of metal was required for its production.

Laphroaig makes the smokiest single malt in Scotland. I went there to learn how they do it.

A different scene with a similar ethos awaited me on Islay, a windswept island in Scotland. I'd come here, to the Laphroaig distillery, to learn how the whisky makers get so much smoke into their single-malt Scotch. It starts with the peat—ancient plant matter that time and the elements have transformed into a combustible fuel (think waypoint in the process of making coal). I was handed a wooden rake and shown how to spread the malted barley on the stone floors of a giant kiln, drying and smoking it with smoldering peat. The smoke flavor was as powerful as that of mezcal, but utterly different in taste.

I spun the globe again. Next, I was in Bolzano in the Italian Alps, where farmers developed a unique method of curing ham over the centuries. They massage the raw pork with a mixture of mountain herbs, salt, and juniper berries. They cure it for several months—originally in caves, now in concrete warehouses with vents to channel the mountain air. Then they slow-smoke it over beechwood and juniper. The result is speck—smoked prosciutto, if you will—and if you think Italy's raw cured ham tastes great, speck will leave you speechless.

A day's drive south brought me to the ancient city of Paestum, where cheesemakers flavor fresh mozzarella with smoke from smoldering straw. Unlike the slow, patient smoke required for speck and other smoked hams, *scamorza* (for such is the name of the smoked cheese) smokes for the two minutes or so it takes to turn the straw into ash. The flavor is herbaceous and smoky, but utterly different from that of wood smoke.

Next, my *Project Smoke* research took me to Bornholm, Denmark—an island in the Baltic Sea that was once the epicenter of Europe's smoked-fish trade. The landscape is dotted with tall white-brick chimneys—the island once boasted more than one hundred smokehouses. Today, a dozen are still active, turning out smoked salmon, smoked shrimp, and smoked herring—the latter used to make a typical Bornholm specialty: *Sol over Gudhjem* (fried smoked herring topped with onions, radishes, and a raw egg). The herring tasted strongly fishy; you probably need to be Danish to enjoy it.

Of course, I visited smokehouses and barbecue joints in the States too, from Georgia to the Texas Hill Country. In Austin, I spent a day with legendary brisket master Aaron Franklin. A former drummer and nail banger, Aaron got his start cooking barbecue on a pit he fashioned from an old propane tank. Today, customers wait for up to three hours outside his aquamarine cinderblock restaurant for his monster beef ribs, peppery "hot guts" (beef sausage), and brisket so luscious, it squirts when you cut into it.

Up in New York, I interviewed John Stage of Dinosaur Bar-B-Que in Rochester, and Joe Carroll of Fette Sau in Brooklyn. Their backgrounds were as intriguing as their barbecue. Stage was a hardcore biker who started cooking at Harley-Davidson meetups to earn some extra cash. Today he presides over an empire of six Dinosaur Bar-B-Qs, including a popular outpost in Brooklyn.

Carroll was a musicologist and bartender when he got the idea to open a barbecue restaurant in Brooklyn. This was back in 2007—long before the current barbecue renaissance—and his location, a former auto body repair shop, seemed as outlandish as his irreverent name for the restaurant: Fette Sau (literally "fat pig" in German, but with the connotation of a woman with loose morals). Carroll was the first to turn Jewish pastrami into barbecue (it was amazing) and assembled a world-class collection of bourbons.

If a biker and a musicologist could become titans of barbecue, I guess it's not so strange that a former French literature major could answer the call of smoke and fire.

It's one thing to gallivant around the globe documenting smoke cultures and gathering recipes. It's quite another to organize that information into a coherent narrative that allows readers not just to execute recipes, but to understand the techniques and science behind them. We all know smoke when we see it, but what exactly is it? And how does it preserve food and make it taste so good?

My first chapter would have to explain the science of smoke. There was just one problem: A scientist I am not. I still wince when I think of the frog I had to pith in my high school biology class (scramble its brains with a needle so it won't feel pain when you dissect it alive). The only way I made it through calculus was by memorizing long theorems by brute force.

To help me understand the science of smoke, I turned to Modernist Cuisine visionary Nathan Myhrvold. Nathan took early college enrollment at the age of fourteen and became the first chief technology officer at Microsoft. He holds more than nine hundred patents and has a life-size *Tyrannosaurus rex* skeleton in his living room. A passionate foodie, he graduated from La Varenne in Paris, where I began my culinary training years earlier. His six-volume *Modernist Cuisine* is simply the most exhaustive and beautiful book on the science of cooking ever written.

According to Myhrvold, there are more than four hundred different compounds in wood smoke—solids like soot, liquids like tar and oils, and gases like carbonyls (responsible for the inviting brown color of smoked foods). Different compounds are released at different temperatures, and each adds its own unique flavor. On the lower range (390°F), for example, smoke contains formaldehyde, which kills bacteria and acts as a preservative. At high temperatures (570°F), smoke releases isoeugenol (responsible for clove and other spice flavors), furans (which add caramel notes), and all-important vanillin.

I like to say that smoking food is easy, but it isn't simple. A grill is a grill in the sense that all of them cook food on a grate over fire. But smokers come in a bewildering array of shapes, sizes, and functionalities—water smokers, barrel smokers, offset smokers, handheld smokers, electric and gas smokers—and that's before you get to smokehouses. The next chapter will explain the various types of smokers and the fuels associated with each.

Which brings me to a question hotly debated on the barbecue circuit:

How much does your choice of wood matter? To find out, I smoked eight identical pieces of salmon with different woods, then submitted them to a blind taste test. Heretical as it sounds, our tasting panel could detect no appreciable difference between the smoke flavors of apple, cherry, hickory, or oak. Mesquite delivered a stronger, slightly bitter flavor that makes it a popular smoking fuel in the Southwest, and also in Hawaii, where it's known as kiawe.

Pitmasters can go on for hours about which woods to pair with which meats and precisely when to add them. It's part of the palaver that gives barbecue its mystique. Pretty much everyone agrees you shouldn't use woods from evergreen trees, like fir, spruce, or pine, which produce a resinous, sooty smoke. But I've learned over the years that in barbecue—as in life—there's an exception to every rule. Years ago, I attended a street fair in Nuremberg, Germany, where vendors grilled bratwurst over pinecone fires. Far from resinous and sooty, the sausage was smoke-scented and delicious.

By the time I covered the various smoking techniques (hot smoking, cold smoking, hay smoking, leaf smoking, etc.), smoker ignition, cleaning, and maintenance, I'd spent two months writing fifty-two pages on the introduction and appendix. The hundred-plus recipes in the book would take another year to write, test, and retest. Which proved once again the warning I give aspiring writers who want to write a book: It's much harder and it takes much longer than you could ever imagine.

Overall, I tried to strike a helpful balance between the traditional smoked and barbecued recipes people expect and the offbeat—dare I say revolutionary—recipes that excited me. For that reason, I included icons like Texas-style brisket, Kansas City–style spareribs, and Carolina pulled pork alongside foods you'd never expect to see, like smoked hard-boiled eggs (smoked deviled eggs are a Raichlen classic) and smoky cocktails, like "mezcalinis."

I particularly enjoyed writing the dessert chapter, because most people don't think of smoking, say, bread pudding, flan, or apple crisp. The fact is that smoke has the mystical quality of giving you a new perspective on commonplace dishes—even desserts. I'd put my smoked cheesecake up against any at a New York deli.

The photo shoot for the book took place at the Hudson Valley farm and studio of photographer Matthew Benson. Our food stylist was Nora Singley, who also worked on several of my TV shows. (Nora trained with Martha Stewart, which is about the toughest food-stylist graduate school in the world.) My role was to appear in the how-to shots—how to set up a water smoker, for example, or load logs into a "stick burner" (barbecue speak for an offset barrel smoker), or just generally try to look cool standing in front of big hunks of meat and smoky fires.

I was less effective when it came to styling the actual "beauties" (finished food shots). I've always been something of a control freak; it took me a few days to realize the shoot would go better if I let Matthew and Nora do their jobs. I learned an important lesson in management: Tell people the result you want, then leave it to them to figure out how to get there.

Project Smoke came out on May 10, 2016, and quickly became a *New York Times* bestseller. To date, we're at four hundred thousand copies and counting. It was definitely the right book at the right time—and later helped by a global pandemic. With the whole world in lockdown, people turned to food arts they hadn't had time for before. The rise of sourdough is well documented, but barbecue and smoking boomed too. My royalties were larger during Covid than when *Project Smoke* first came out.

I remain an avid smoker, myself. My wok-smoked salmon often accompanies our Sunday-morning bagels for breakfast, and smoked rotisserie chicken is a weekly Raichlen family dinner. What I love about smoke is how it seems to make every food taste more like itself—only better.

PAC-RIM SHORT RIBS WITH HOISIN BARBECUE SAUCE

This recipe starts with a cut of meat much beloved in Korea: beef short ribs. But the cooking method itself—slow-smoking over cherry wood—comes straight out of Texas, with an Asian-inflected spice rub that leans heavily on Chinese five-spice powder. The latter may remind you of anise or licorice—no surprise here, as its primary ingredient is star anise. (The other spices are fennel seed, cinnamon, ginger, and white pepper.) Five-spice powder is available in Asian markets, of course, and at well-stocked supermarkets (including Whole Foods) and online. Incidentally, the alphanumeric rub recipe is easy to remember: just think 5-4-3-2-1. If you like your beef sweet, spicy, and smoky, with haunting anise overtones, these short ribs are for you.

Serves 4

For the rub:

5 tablespoons brown sugar (light or dark—your choice)

4 tablespoons coarse salt

3 tablespoons freshly ground black pepper

2 tablespoons five-spice powder

1 tablespoon granulated onion

4 pounds beef short ribs

½ cup sake or mirin, in a spray bottle (or in a bowl brushed on with a pastry brush)

Hoisin Barbecue Sauce (recipe follows)

You'll also need:

hardwood chips or chunks (preferably cherry). If using chips, start with 4 to 5 cups and soak them in water to cover for 30 minutes, then drain. No soaking needed for chunks. To cook the ribs, you'll need a smoker, pellet grill, kamado grill (like a Big Green Egg), or charcoal grill. It's hard to achieve the proper smoke flavor on a gas grill.

1. Combine all the rub ingredients in a bowl and mix well, breaking up any lumps in the brown sugar with your fingers.
2. Place the short ribs on a rimmed baking sheet. Generously season the ribs on all sides with the rub—you'll need ⅓ to ½ cup rub. (Store the excess in a sealed jar away from heat and light. It comes in handy for all manner of smoking and grilling.)
3. Set up your smoker or pellet grill following the manufacturer's instructions and heat to 250°F. If using a kamado or charcoal grill, set it up for indirect grilling and heat to 250°F. Add the wood to the coals—you'll need about 1 cup chips or 1 chunk every hour.
4. Arrange the ribs, fat side up, on the grate.
5. Smoke the ribs until very tender, spraying or brushing them with sake every hour. The total cooking time will be 5 to 6 hours. When cooked, the meat will have shrunk back from the ends of the bones by ½ to 1 inch. The internal temperature of the meat will be around 205°F.
6. At this point, you can serve the ribs with the Hoisin Barbecue Sauce on the side for dipping or spooning. Or, if you'd like to go a step further, increase the grill heat to high. Brush the short ribs with the barbecue sauce and grill them to sear the sauce into the meat, 1 to 2 minutes per side, then serve.

HOISIN BARBECUE SAUCE

Hoisin sauce is a Chinese condiment based on soybeans. It's sweet and salty, with an aromatic anise flavor to finish. I think of it as Asian ketchup.

Makes 1 ½ cups

1 cup hoisin sauce

3 tablespoons toasted sesame oil

3 tablespoons brown sugar (light or dark—your choice)

3 tablespoons sriracha

1 teaspoon black pepper

1. Combine all the ingredients in a saucepan set over medium heat and whisk to mix. Gently simmer the sauce for 5 minutes to blend the flavors.

Chapter Twenty-Two

PLAYING WITH FIRE

2018–2022

Fire meets water in Steinhatchee, Florida.

I've always had a fascination with fire. When I was eight, my friend Maurice and I filled a paper cup with gasoline. (My dad kept gasoline around for the lawn mower and, more recklessly, to light our charcoal grill. As I warned earlier, do not try this at home.)

We set the paper cup on the sidewalk in front of a third friend's house and lit it with a match. Instantly, the cup erupted in flame and disintegrated, engulfing the sidewalk around it with fire. I don't know what Maurice did, but I ran back to my house as fast as my young legs would carry me. Heart pounding, I hid under my bed.

My mother answered the door to a policeman dressed in black, inquiring about a young neighborhood arsonist. Bless her heart, she denied any knowledge of the event. When the policeman departed, she coaxed me out from under the bed and told me never, ever to play with fire again.

I didn't listen. When I was ten, I loved to build model airplanes and battleships. I'd stuff them with cherry bombs and douse them with lighter fluid. I'd set them ablaze and watch a week's worth of work explode in a matter of seconds.

When I was fourteen and upset about my mother's hospitalization for a nervous breakdown, I would make paper airplanes. I'd set them on fire and send them sailing down the steps from the bedroom level of our house to the living room. I'd rush down the steps to catch them before they'd land on any furniture or the carpet.

One day, my father came home from work early and intercepted one of my flaming bombers. Oddly, he didn't yell at me or punish me. It was as though he could feel the hurt in my heart and understood that burning things helped me relieve it.

Freud would have called it sublimation—channeling a harmful urge into something positive and socially acceptable. I would call it barbecue.

Like many fathers and sons, my dad and I had a complicated adult relationship. He didn't understand the decisions that led me from a cerebral Reed College education to a precarious career as a freelance writer and cooking teacher. I don't think he got my work, period. He wanted me to call and visit more often and have a closer relationship with my stepmother, Cecille.

On my side, I hungered for more praise and acknowledgment for my writing. I was disappointed that he scheduled overseas vacations over my fortieth and sixtieth birthdays. Barbara had planned a Bob Dylan–themed surprise party for the latter with an invitation that riffed on "The Times, They Are a-Changin'." Friends and family flew in from as far away as Boston and California. I felt bad that my dad wasn't among them. He never saw me teach or lecture and never came to Barbecue University. Another hurt: To this day, I don't know if my father ever read my novel. He never mentioned it and I never asked. Communication wasn't one of our strong suits.

But the last six months of his life were some of the closest in our relationship. At the time, my father and Cecille were living in Naples, Florida. One day, I drove over to meet him for lunch. He talked about his childhood, which wasn't easy (the grandfather I loved so much was an overbearing man to grow up with). He lamented his family's lack of understanding when it came to dealing with my mother's mental illness. "I was all alone," he said sadly. Until then, I had focused on my pain; now I understood how painful the marriage must have been for him.

In 2016, Barbara and I returned to Miami from a trip to find a burst pipe and major roof leak that required a complete renovation of our house. We checked in to the East Hotel in the newly opened Brickell City Centre for six weeks. I spoke to my dad every day as I bicycled back and forth between the hotel and the house. I ended each call with "I love you, Dad." Every Father's Day, I post a photo of the two of us on my social media platforms. The best advice I can give anyone with a father still living is to tell him you love him. Do it often. The same holds true for your mom. Do it before it's too late.

In September of that year, my father came to Miami for a heart-valve replacement—a once-radical procedure that is now considered safe and routine. The hospital released him a few days later for the two-hour ride back to Naples. The doctor told him to resume his daily walks, which he did despite the fierce heat of a Florida fall. Halfway through his first walk, he tripped or fainted and hit his head on the sidewalk. His brain started hemorrhaging, and by the time the ambulance arrived, he had lost consciousness.

We rushed to Naples. Barbara had the foresight to tell me to bring a suit. When we arrived at the hospital, my father lay in a coma, breathing with the help of a respirator. His chest rose and fell, almost like he was sleeping. He never regained consciousness and died three days later—just as Hurricane Nate was descending on Florida. The airport closed; his sister and nephews and out-of-town-friends couldn't fly in for the funeral. It was a lonely funeral for a man much beloved by his friends and patients.

My father didn't live to see the publication of what would be my twenty-ninth book, *Project Fire*. I think he would have liked the dedication. There was a photo of the two of us—taken at the restaurant where we had our last deep conversation. The inscription reads:

In loving memory of my father
Sonny Raichlen
1929–2016

All of which is a lengthy introduction to my next book and TV show. When it came time to find a title, the answer should have been obvious. Only I toyed with tediously wordy titles—for example, *New Fuels, New Tools, and New Ways of Grilling*. Finally, Barbara came to the rescue. "Your last book was *Project Smoke*. This one should be called *Project Fire*."

Suzanne Rafer at Workman loved it. So did Maryland Public Television. I had a new book contract and TV show.

I began the *Project Fire* book with a question: "After thirty books, seven TV series, two decades of Barbecue University classes, hundreds of articles in publications ranging from *The New York Times* to *Esquire*, and literally thousands of TV and radio interviews, what more could I possibly have to say about grilling?"

It turned out, a lot. Barbecue continues to evolve—exponentially, I would add—so *Project Fire* would focus on the new foods, new grills, new techniques, and new taste preferences that had come to captivate a new generation of grillers. New cuts of steaks, like the baseball and the tomahawk. (Believe it or not, there was a time when no one had heard of a tomahawk steak.) New grills, like braseros and pellet grills. (For those of you not in the barbecue world, the former are pedestal grills with a wood fire in the center surrounded by a round or square plancha for griddling. The latter burn compressed sawdust pellets.)

I'd explore the new grilling techniques revolutionizing outdoor cooking, like reverse-searing (slow-roasting steaks at a low temperature first, then flash-searing them right before serving). You can cook really thick steaks perfectly every time using this method.

In fact, there was so much to say about the new fuels, tools, and grilling techniques, it took me forty-three pages to get to the first recipe. I called that introductory chapter "The Seven Steps to Grilling Nirvana," and I like to think that even a raw beginner could follow those steps and wind up a confident griller.

I opened the recipe section with an unusual chapter: Breakfast on the Grill. "It's 6 a.m. on Chappaquiddick Island—my favorite time of the day," I wrote. "So I do what any barbecue-obsessed guy would do at daybreak. I fire up the grill."

There followed a half dozen grilled breakfast dishes, from candied bacon to a perennial Raichlen family favorite: grilled eggs with Parmesan and prosciutto "bacon."

I closed the book with a chapter on Desserts and Drinks. I'd written about grilled desserts in previous books, starting with *The Barbecue! Bible,* but I don't think anyone had previously seen the likes of a dessert quesadilla stuffed with bananas, dulce de leche, and queso fresco. As for drinks, the *Project Fire* bellini contained, what else, prosecco and caramelized grilled peaches.

Project Fire *the book—with a caveman T-bone on the cover.*

In opening and closing the book this way, I tried to show that *Project Fire* was not just another grill book. It wasn't even another Raichlen grill book. This was live-fire cooking on the edge.

Project Fire got great reviews but did not do as well as *Project Smoke.* "No one really knows what sells a book," Peter Workman once told me. "You publish the best book possible, but only the public can make it a bestseller."

If the book sales were less than optimal, the *Steven Raichlen's Project Fire* TV show went gangbusters.

Curiously, the most challenging part of bringing a show to public television isn't the concept, host, or content. No, the greatest challenge—the only real challenge—is raising the money. If you bring money to public television and agree to follow their rules, you're almost guaranteed to find a station to run your show. Unfortunately, the rules of public television seem perversely designed to dissuade potential sponsors from underwriting.

Because public television shows have no commercial breaks, the sponsor gets a spot (ad) at the top and the bottom of the show. In that spot, there can be no claims of greatness ("We make the world's best grill") and no calls to action ("Rush out and buy our charcoal today"). The sponsor can't advertise prices or discounts. And we can't take money from liquor companies, although they have some of the largest advertising budgets.

We're not allowed to show product logos or mention products by brand name during the actual show, which requires strategic shooting on the part of the camera crew or even masking logos with duct tape. You can imagine how sponsors react to logo masking—especially in a world where product placement is such an integral part of commercial television.

The theory behind these restrictions is that making a PBS show noncommercial will give it greater credibility with the audience. Indeed, according to a survey by Marketing and Research Resources, Inc., PBS ranks "#1 in Public Trust"—above commercial broadcast television, cable television, the United States government in general, and Congress (no surprise about the last two).

Back in Julia Child's day, public television had an aura of high prestige: Just being associated with PBS was reward enough for an underwriter. I remember one episode with Julia and Jacques Pépin—a show underwritten by a California winery—in which Jacques offered to pour Julia a glass of wine as the show concluded. "No, I think I'll have a beer," said Julia. She adhered rigorously to the separation of "church and state," as it were, but sponsors flocked to her show anyway. These days, underwriters want product placement and even free public appearances on their behalf.

We shot season 1 of *Project Fire* at the Alisal Ranch in Solvang, California, where we had done the last season of *Project Smoke.* Our set overlooked a stream, a horse-filled meadow, and the rolling hills of the Santa Ynez Valley behind it. It was gorgeous. The Alisal is now home to my Barbecue University cooking school.

We also introduced a cool new feature: the mystery box. At one point in the show, I'd walk on set to find a large wooden box on my worktable. I'd lift it to reveal a mystery ingredient, which ranged from the unexpected (lamb ribs, for example, or chicken livers) to the downright weird (jumbo squid or a giant sunflower). My task was to invent a recipe on the spot, augmenting the mystery ingredient with some basic staples I found on the set.

I gave the lamb ribs the Greek treatment, smoke-roasting them with oregano, and served with a yogurt-cucumber relish. I smoked the chicken livers prior to turning them into my grandmother's chopped liver, accompanied by grilled pita. For the squid I made a stuffing with the tentacles, breadcrumbs, and capers and grilled them over mesquite. I tried grilling the sunflower with garlic, lemon, and olive oil as I would an artichoke. I'm not sure I'd make that one again. The mystery boxes were my favorite part of the show—I loved how they sparked my creativity and forced me to be spontaneous.

Three unusual occurrences took place during the series: an explosion, an encounter with a dangerous animal, and a trip to the City of Angels. The explosion took place on a frigid night in an episode we called "Extreme

Grilling." I was grilling a chocolate dessert on one of those newly fashionable salt slabs—mined from a salt mountain in the Pakistan Himalayas. Pastry chefs everywhere were adding salt to counterpoint a dessert's sweetness. The salt slab would serve the same purpose and would look unbelievably cool. And as I always say, never underestimate the power of looking cool at the grill.

I slowly preheated the salt slab as recommended by the manufacturer. When I opened the grill, the icy air caused the slab to explode like a hand grenade. Tiny shards of salt slab flew everywhere. Happily, no one was hurt, not least the host, which was a miracle when we reviewed the videotape.

The dangerous animal turned up at the Fess Parker Winery in the nearby town of Los Olivos. (Parker was a film and TV star of the 1950s, renowned for his portrayals of Davy Crockett and Daniel Boone.) We traveled there to meet chef John Cox, who had devised a wondrous way to cook strip loin. A month earlier, John wrapped a strip loin (the primal cut from which strip steaks are cut) in cheesecloth, then soaked it in bourbon. He aged the strip loin in a meat locker, soaking it with more bourbon at regular intervals to keep it moist. The day we arrived, he unwrapped the loin and cooked it in a mammoth smoker.

Around the time we arrived, so did Bubba, a 2,200-pound Wagyu steer, and if he took offense to the strip loin from one of his compatriots smoking away, he didn't seem to show it. He was smaller than I imagined a Wagyu steer to be (but still huge) and a lot more docile. Bubba's handler, a rugged cowboy, asked if I wanted to mount him. Sensing a once-in-a-lifetime opportunity, I climbed aboard, and Bubba stood calmly while I sat for photographs. The cowboy was not so lucky. When he climbed on Bubba, the steer bucked and threw him, and let me tell you, that cowboy fell hard. Someone—the God of Barbecue?—was looking out for me.

As for the Wagyu strip loin, it turned out to be remarkable. The month in the walk-in gave the beef a dry-aged funkiness, while the bourbon imparted a boozy sweetness. Thanks to the slow-smoking over smoldering oak, the steak was extraordinarily tender and flavorful. While I normally don't drink when working, I couldn't pass up a Fess Parker pinot noir. I gave Bubba a wide berth.

The trip to Los Angeles (said City of Angels) was to visit some of the city's top grill restaurants—my favorite being Chi Spacca (roughly translated as "he who wields a cleaver"). Brainchild of Cal-Ital culinary diva Nancy Silverton, Chi Spacca is a turbo-charged Italian chophouse specializing in massive *bistecce* (porterhouses) and *costate* (bone-in strip steaks) that tip the scales at thirty-six ounces. But I was there for a steak I'd never before seen: a pork tomahawk. It starts as a double-thick pork chop, with the entire rib bone attached and a generous slab of the pork belly at the bottom. The chef at the time, Ryan DeNicola, cured it in brine, seasoned it with fennel rub, and

Night shoot on the set of Project Fire.

grilled it over blazing almond wood. The sweet-salty rub and haunting smoke flavor made it the most extraordinary pork chop I've ever tasted. I liked the chef's philosophy even better: "Grilling is all about the imperfections: some spots burned; some spots less cooked. It's alive," Ryan said. Amen.

PROJECT FIRE WENT ON TO BECOME my most successful TV series. The second year, we shot in Steinhatchee, Florida—a tiny Old Florida town on the Steinhatchee River just south of the Florida Panhandle. For a liberal East Coaster, it was an interesting experience. A life-size photo cutout of Donald Trump stood in the dining room of our hotel, and MAGA hats were everywhere. But the riverfront setting was spectacular (my favorite of all my shows), and where else would I have had the chance to grill fresh swamp cabbage (Florida heart of palm) and "redfish on the half-shell" (a superb local fish grilled directly in its unscaled skin)? The people of Steinhatchee couldn't have been more hospitable, which just goes to show how barbecue transcends politics.

Season 3 found us at the Pearlstone Center—a Jewish retreat center in Reisterstown, Maryland—just north of my hometown Baltimore. By a bizarre coincidence, this wasn't the first time I had been here. Forty years earlier, a Milford Mill Day Camp existed on this site. I was one of the campers. Our shoot took place at the height of the Covid pandemic, so we followed strict rules of social distancing. Happily, my shows take place outdoors. No one got sick on our show, but the following week, another PBS production got shut down on account of an outbreak.

Our fourth season featured our first urban setting: St. Louis. We chose Union Square Station, once the largest railroad station in North America but today an urban entertainment center complete with a walk-through aquarium. I had my reservations about the location, but the rippling arched metal roof and crowds of passersby lent a dynamic energy to the show. We had a great roster of guests, who showed me how to grill everything from Bosnian *pljeskavica* (an oversize burger from a great local restaurant called the Balkan Treat Box) to turkey "ribs" (actually cut from the wing—an African American barbecue specialty) to St. Louis ribs and pork steaks from the landmark restaurant Pappy's Smokehouse.

In fact, we'd probably still be taping seasons of *Project Fire* if I hadn't had another idea. It was time to get around to taping a show I had dreamed of a quarter century earlier.

MY FATHER

My father and I had a fraught relationship. We loved each other, of course. But sometimes that love was tempered by disappointment and recrimination. We grew closer toward the end of his life, and I like to think he left this world at peace with our relationship. By way of a eulogy at his funeral, I shared seven things about my father most people didn't know. I list them here to honor a man I'm not sure I ever properly thanked while he was alive.

1. His name wasn't really Sonny; his real name was Isador, after his paternal grandfather. To say he wasn't crazy about the name Isador is putting it mildly, and his parents didn't offer him the consolation of a middle name. The first person to call him Sonny was his grandmother. He briefly changed his name to Marc. It didn't stick.
2. My father was a ventriloquist. He had a dummy named Oscar—I still have it. Every Saturday, he and Oscar would perform at the

old Hippodrome Theater on Eutaw Street in Baltimore. Asked to demonstrate this skill, he would say "Peter Piper picked a peck of pickled peppers" without moving his lips. He could do this well into his eighties.

3. My dad was cool before dads were cool. My friends loved him when I was growing up. My girl classmates all had a crush on him. Other dads were called Mr. This or Mr. That. My friends always called him Sonny.
4. My dad was an expert handyman. He knew how to solder copper sheets to make flower boxes. One summer, when I returned from Camp Saginaw, he had constructed an entire wall of bookcases in my bedroom. Another time, he built me a robot costume for Halloween, complete with dryer-vent hose arms and a rotating pie-pan antenna on the head. As a child, I clambered up to awesome tree houses he built and rode terrifyingly fast go-carts he assembled from old lawn-mower parts and plywood. I came home with skinned knees to show for it.
5. My dad was *not* a longhair. One of our worst disputes when I was growing up concerned hair length. I wanted mine long. He wanted it crew cut. Our battle came to a head when I was fifteen. One Saturday afternoon, he chased me around the block and dragged me to the local barbershop. We arrived just in time to watch the owner lower the blinds and put up a "Closed" sign. My dad never gave me grief about my hair again, and when I finally cut it six years later, I mailed it to him. Guess which one of us wound up wearing an earring. (My dad.)
6. My dad was an inadvertent pot farmer. When I was a teenager, I

decided to grow some pot plants in our yard on Ronis Road. My dad claimed ignorance but gamely mowed and weeded around the plants and watered them. Later that summer, we went to France with my Uncle Fred and Aunt Judy. We read a news headline explaining how the DEA had started aerial surveillance flights to look for illegal pot. No one on the trip knew why I got so pale and quiet.

7. My dad was a Frank Sinatra kind of guy. I rocked out to The Doors and Jefferson Airplane. But damn if he didn't buy me my first electric guitar and fuzz box, and gave me a gift certificate for a Höfner "fiddle" bass for my tenth birthday. He drove my gear to rehearsals and even attended—make that suffered through—some of my performances.

Rest in peace, Dad. We miss you.

The author with his father, Sonny Raichlen.

GAI YANG GAME HENS

(Game Hens Grilled with Thai Seasonings and Coconut Milk)

Gai yang, grilled chicken, is one of Thailand's most popular street foods. And no one makes it better than the Isaan, a people of Lao descent living in the northeast. The marinade plays salty against sour—the former in the form of soy sauce and fish sauce, the latter in the fresh lime. This being Thailand, there are aromatics—lots of aromatics—like ginger and lemongrass, with black pepper and Thai peppers to kick up the heat. Don't worry if you can't find all the ingredients; lemon zest makes a credible substitute for lemongrass, for example, and you can use additional soy sauce in place of the fish sauce. In Thailand, ingredients for the marinade would be pounded to a paste in a mortar and pestle. A blender or food processor does the job here. Note: You will need to master a special technique—spatchcocking—which involves cutting out the bird's backbone and opening it like a book so it lies flat for grilling.

Serves 2

2 (1 ½-pound) game hens

For the marinade:

3 cloves garlic, peeled and rough chopped

1 ½ inches fresh ginger, peeled and roughly chopped

2 lemongrass stalks, trimmed and roughly chopped

¼ cup chopped fresh cilantro, plus 2 tablespoons for serving

1 Thai or serrano chili, seeded if desired and roughly chopped

1 tablespoon sugar

1 tablespoon freshly ground black pepper

½ cup canned coconut milk

2 tablespoons soy sauce

2 tablespoons fish sauce

2 tablespoons vegetable oil, plus more for basting

Grated zest and juice of 1 lime, plus lime wedges for serving

For serving (optional):

¼ green or savoy cabbage, thinly sliced

6 ounces long beans or green beans, cut into 2-inch lengths

½ cup celery leaves or more fresh cilantro

1. To spatchcock the game hens, place them on a cutting board, breast side down. Using poultry shears, make a lengthwise cut on each side of the backbone. Remove the backbone (save it for stock). Separate the halves to open the bird like a book. Using a sharp paring knife, cut out the breastbone so the game hens lie flat. Cut off the tips of the wings. Turn the birds over and pull the legs down (away from the wing end). Place the game hens in a baking dish.
2. To make the marinade, place the garlic, ginger, lemongrass, cilantro, chili, sugar, and pepper in a food processor or blender and puree to a coarse paste. Work in the coconut milk, soy sauce, fish sauce, oil, and lime zest and juice. Pour the marinade over the game hens, coating both sides. Cover and marinate in the refrigerator for at least 6 hours, or ideally overnight.
3. Set up your grill for direct grilling and heat to medium (350°F). Have a fire-free safety zone where you can move the game hens if they start to burn. Brush or scrape the grill grate clean and oil it well.
4. Arrange the game hens, skin side up, on the grate. Grill until the undersides are sizzling and darkly browned, 10 to 15 minutes, basting with oil occasionally. If they start to burn, lower the heat or move the game hens over to the safety zone for a few minutes.
5. Flip the game hens and grill skin side down. You'll probably need to lower the heat and you may need to move the birds if flare-ups

occur. Grill the game hens, basting with oil, until the second side is browned and the hens are cooked through, another 10 to 15 minutes. Use an instant-read thermometer to test for doneness: Your target temperature in the thickest part of the thigh and the deepest part of the breast is 175 to 180°F.

6. Serve the gai yang with the cabbage, long beans, and celery leaves.

Chapter Twenty-Three

THE LAST PICTURE SHOW

2023

On the set of Planet Barbecue *in San Antonio, Texas.*

In November 2023, my production team and I converged on San Antonio to tape a new TV series: *Steven Raichlen's Planet Barbecue.*

The occasion was bittersweet.

Sweet because a book I had written fifteen years earlier—my most ambitious—was about to come to life as a TV series.

Bitter, because the show didn't quite live up to my original vision—traveling the world's barbecue trail with a camera crew in tow.

Sweet because it reunited a TV crew I'd worked with for more than a decade, giving a grueling shoot the benevolence of a family reunion.

Bitter because this would be my last TV show on public television, and possibly the last I would ever host.

Planet Barbecue. Two simple words that sum up my career. *Planet Barbecue* has been my beat. *Planet Barbecue* has been my mission. It has defined my professional life. Hopefully, my global approach to live-fire cooking will be remembered as my contribution to the art of the grill.

I'm the first to admit that I don't barbecue the world's best Texas brisket. Or grill the best Italian *bistecca alla fiorentina* or Thai satay. I don't possess the technical prowess of an Aaron Franklin or Rodney Scott. My social media presence pales in comparison to that of Derek Wolf of *Over the Fire Cooking* or David Olson of *Live Fire Republic.* Yes, I've done twenty years of public television. It's time to make way for new blood.

But I believe I did one thing no one else in the field of live-fire cooking has done before or since: I logged the miles. I've visited more than seventy-five countries on six continents in the single-minded pursuit of documenting how people grill, smoke, and barbecue in different cultures. I've written thirteen books on live-fire cooking—all with a strong travel component. (Number fourteen, *Barbecue University,* will be out in 2027.)

I've been a student of global grilling for thirty years now, traveling the world's barbecue trail with my readers. I've spent my adult life spreading the gospel of grilling literally around the planet. If once-unfamiliar dishes like Indonesian satay, Italian *pollo al mattone,* Turkish *adana kebab,* Nigerian *suya,* and Mexican *tacos al pastor* are now part of the North American grilling vocabulary, I like to think I helped.

IF YOU HAD TO TAPE A GLOBAL barbecue show without leaving the United States, San Antonio makes an excellent location. The city belonged first to Spain and then to Mexico, until Texas won its independence in 1836. (Texas became part of the US nine years later.) More than half the locals speak Spanish as their first language, and the Mexican border is only 150 miles away. But San Antonio is home to people from all over the planet—Brazilians, Venezuelans, Jamaicans, Thais—and all have contributed to the city's culinary melting pot.

We set up operations in the historic Spanish Governor's Palace, built in 1722. The tree-shaded cobblestone courtyard became our set, with the white adobe building in the background. String lights and brightly colored sarape blankets draped over the stone walls added local color. Tents went up for our control room, field kitchen, and food-styling studio. Grills were wheeled in and assembled. A day later, we were ready to shoot.

With Nicola Blaque, chef-owner of The Jerk Shack, for a segment on Jamaican grilling.

We brought global grilling to our set through a roster of

international guests. Buenos Aires–born Al Frugoni, for example, wheeled a huge wood-burning Argentine *asado* grill onto the set and used it to cook a magisterial ten-pound rib roast hung high over a mesquite fire. Mexican grill master Alejandro Gutiérrez, founder of the *Sociedad Mexicana de Parrilleros* (an association of Mexican grilling enthusiasts with six million followers), drove up from Monterrey to show us his unique take on grilled snapper. Andrew Ho, the Vietnamese American co-owner of Curry Boys BBQ, demonstrated his "Good Luck Cluck"—smoky Texas barbecued chicken thighs simmered in a coconut-rich Thai curry.

Which brings me to our field trips. These location segments took us deep into San Antonio's barbecue culture and brought my original vision for *Planet Barbecue* to life. Our first stop was one of my favorite barbecue restaurants in Texas, Two Bros. BBQ Market. Founded by classically trained chef Jason Dady and his brother Jake, Two Bros. has a vintage roadhouse dining room and sprawling courtyard on San Antonio's East Side. The pitch-perfect barbecue and live music draw crowds of up to two thousand on weekends. The beating heart of Two Bros. is a series of stone pits with smoke-blackened metal lids that raise and lower on pulleys. Here, pitmaster Laura Loomis smokes salt-and-pepper-crusted briskets for fourteen hours and glazes slow-smoked baby back ribs with cherry syrup. This being Texas, of course, there are poppers (cheese-stuffed, bacon-wrapped jalapeños), not to mention house-cured pickles and creamy banana pudding for dessert.

Our last stop brought us to the new cocktail lounge of an old friend, Johnny Hernandez. A philanthropist and Mexican food authority, Johnny runs restaurants across San Antonio, including La Gloria and La Frutería Botanero. When Johnny built his latest venture, Casa Hernán, he installed a *barbacoa* pit in the backyard. He prepared for us a dish he cooks every weekend: *barbacoa de borrego*—lamb swaddled in agave leaves and roasted in an underground pit. What emerged from underground was so insanely tasty, I had to force myself to stop eating so I could talk to camera and close out the show.

Chef Johnny Hernandez shows off his Mexican barbacoa *(pit-roasted lamb).*

When you watch *Planet Barbecue,* you'll see many of our openings shot on the tour boats that ply San Antonio's canals. (The city lives up to its nickname: the Venice of Texas.) Had you been there the last week of February 2024, you would have seen a bespectacled, bearded guy followed by a camera crew say: "Welcome to *Planet Barbecue.* I'm Steven Raichlen."

Steven Raichlen's Planet Barbecue launched the following spring and became one of the most popular cooking shows on public television. The plan was to turn it into a four- or five-season series. But politics got in the way. President Trump and the Republican Congress ended federal support for public television. Fundraising—never easy—became one challenge too many.

At this point, I had been on PBS for two decades. I still didn't consider myself a TV natural, but I had come to enjoy being in front of the camera. Did I want to give it up? Not really. Was it time to move on? Probably. The TV shoots were the most difficult two weeks of my work year. But they were also the most fun. I loved bringing my books alive on television.

But I'm not done with TV completely. As I write this, I'm working on a documentary on the history of barbecue—a subject that has fascinated me since my Watson Fellowship. Will we find a platform for the series? Stay tuned!

MEAT PIZZA (REALLY)

Leave it to an Argentinean to come up with this one. His name is Al Frugoni and he came on my *Planet Barbecue* TV show armed with his own mammoth wood-burning grill. We wanted to show how our southernmost neighbor grills beef, which is pretty much a weekly if not daily activity in Argentina. Al's scheduled dish for the show was a ten-pound rib roast, which he smoke-roasted over a wood fire, cut into steaks, then set ablaze with flaming bourbon. The meat pizza came as an afterthought, but, oh, what an afterthought! A butterflied flank steak stood in for the traditional pizza crust—topped with the traditional tomato sauce, olives, pepperoni, and cheese. Think of this as the ultimate gluten-free pizza.

Serves 3 to 4

1 (1 ½-pound) flank steak

Sea salt and freshly ground black pepper to taste

1 clove garlic, minced

1 ½ cups tomato sauce (preferably homemade)

12 pitted black olives

4 ounces pepperoni, thinly sliced

6 ounces fresh mozzarella, thinly sliced

Dried oregano, for sprinkling

Hot pepper flakes, for sprinkling

6 to 8 fresh basil leaves (optional)

Extra-virgin olive oil, for drizzling

1. Set up your grill for direct grilling and heat to medium-high (400°F). Brush or scrape the grill grate clean and oil it well.
2. Meanwhile, butterfly the flank steak: Lay it flat at the edge of the cutting board. Using a sharp, slender knife, carefully cut through one

long side almost to the far end, taking care not to pierce the top or bottom. This will feel a little awkward at first, but you'll soon get the hang of it. Open the steak up like a book and pound it with a meat mallet or the bottom of a cast-iron skillet to give it an even thickness. Season the meat on both sides with salt and pepper and sprinkle with the garlic.

3. Place the steak on the grill and grill until the bottom is sizzling and browned, 3 to 4 minutes. Flip the steak onto the flat side of a baking sheet so the cooked side is up. Spread the tomato sauce over the steak. Arrange the olives, pepperoni, and mozzarella slices on top.
4. Return the steak to the grill and lower the lid. Continue grilling the steak until the bottom is sizzling and browned and the meat is cooked through (it should be medium to medium-well), 3 to 4 minutes. The cheese should be melted and the tomato sauce hot.
5. Transfer the "pizza" to a cutting board or platter. Sprinkle it with oregano, hot pepper flakes, and basil leaves (if using). Drizzle with olive oil, slice, and dig in!

Chapter Twenty-Four

FAMILY MATTERS

2025–2026

SR, Ella, Mia, Julian, and Barbara in Jerusalem (left to right).

"Blood makes you related. Barbecue makes you family."
SLOGAN SEEN AT A BARBECUE FESTIVAL

Up to now, I've told you about my books, my TV shows, my classes—in short, my work. I haven't told you about what matters most to me: my family.

My grandfather, Dear, used to say a family is like a hand. Push on the center and the fingers come together. They grasp what's important in life. And if need be, they form a fist to fight whatever threatens one of its members.

True, some of my professional successes might have been possible without the support of my family. None would have been worth it. At the end of the day—and the end of my life—I'd trade my professional accomplishments for extra time with the people I love.

You've already met my wife, Barbara, and witnessed how she has shaped my career and my life. Barbara can size up the pros and cons of a situation before I'm even aware of it. She makes decisions in about ten seconds and she's almost always right.

So here's what else you should know about Barbara. She was born on Miami Beach back in the days when Miami Beach was a world unto itself. Everyone knew their neighbors. No one locked their doors. When hurricanes swept through (not an infrequent occurrence), Barbara and her siblings, Marty and Iris, would paddle on rafts through the streets.

Her father, Phil Seldin, was an ex-Marine who founded one of the most famous delis on Miami Beach, Raphil's. (Ray was his partner.) He taught Barbara many life lessons she still follows today:

- "You can say anything you want, provided you say it like a lady."
- "When you earn a dollar, or ten or one hundred, spend half of it

as you like and put the other half in your savings account." (Her father retired when he was in his forties, so this turned out to be very good advice.)

- "There's no such thing as *can't*."

Unfortunately, Barbara's father died young, and I never got to meet him. But through Barbara, I feel like he watches over our shoulders every day.

Barbara had a varied career in the food world, including a pioneering radio show in which her guests cooked on air. She would position a microphone next to a cutting board and an electric skillet. Listeners could hear the clatter of knives and the sizzle of steaks as Barbara interviewed the likes of baking diva Maida Heatter, Benihana founder Rocky Aoki, and a rising-star chef from Los Angeles, Wolfgang Puck.

But her biggest accomplishment, as I'm sure she would tell you, are my step-kids: Betsy and Jake. Both went into food, but at opposite ends of the spectrum. Jake is a chef. Over the years, he's worked in Miami, the Hamptons, Hong Kong, Singapore, and his current hometown, New York. Betsy is the Director of Sports Nutrition for the Miami Heat, flying from game to game with the team. When texts buzz on her phone, it's often a Heat player. For this reason, I can't enforce the no-cell-phones-at-the-dinner-table rule—much as I hate people staring at phones while we're eating. (I also hate televisions in restaurant dining rooms—even when what's on the screen is a Heat game.) But more important, Betsy gave us three fabulous grandchildren: Ella and the twins, Mia and Julian.

Ella is the oldest. The day she was born was the second happiest day of my life. (The first was when I married Barbara.) She seems to have inherited both the cooking gene and the writing gene. As I write this, she's baking an olive oil cake for a holiday dinner. She's well on her way through writing her first novel. (It's a spy story set in France during World War II.) When Ella was born, we celebrated with a big backyard barbecue. Ditto for the twins. But the little girl who used to stand on a stepladder to "help" me grill now drives and is looking at colleges.

I remember Ella's first taste of a milkshake at the age of two at our house. Her eyes widened as if to say: "Why was I not notified about this earlier?" During the Covid lockdown, "Basha" (short for Batsheva—Barbara's Hebrew name) gave Ella a crash course on French pastry. Once a week, we'd send over a shopping list. Basha taught Ella how to make madeleines, éclairs, chocolate soufflé, petits pots de crème, and more via Zoom. When they were young, Ella and her siblings ran a pretend "restaurant" at our home in Chappaquiddick. Although the food was imaginary, "PopPop" (that's how I'm called) had to fork up hard cash to pay the bill.

Mia is the family fashionista, currently enrolled at a Miami design high school called DASH. Even at age three, she insisted on picking out her own wardrobe and festooning her hair with colored chopsticks. Lots of colored chopsticks. She now consults with Basha on mood boards, hem stiches, and sewing machines. She's driven and decisive. I have no doubt she'll make waves in the fashion world.

Barbara, Betsy, and baby Ella pose for their dedication photo in Planet Barbecue.

Her twin brother, Julian, is the family soccer star, traveling all over the country for games and tournaments. It's rare—make that impossible—to find

Julian without some sort of ball in his hand. (The bouncing drives Basha and PopPop crazy.) Julian is an academic wunderkind with a penchant for science. He can also hear a song one time and play it on the piano. Despite his busy schedule, he manages to bring home straight-A report cards every quarter.

All three kids have studied French since kindergarten and speak it fluently. Once a month we have French night, dining at a restaurant and conversing in French the entire meal.

Given my volatile childhood, I never wanted kids of my own. Barbara gave me a ready-made family. I delight in the role of grandfather—even though it still shocks me to realize the term actually refers to me.

I've traveled the world over the course of my barbecue career, but not one of those journeys rivals the trips we've taken with the grandkids. On

Bound for home on the Chappy ferry.

their first big family trip, to Los Angeles some years ago, we asked each kid what they wanted to visit. For Ella, deep into magic at the time (another skill she learned via Zoom), we visited the Magic Castle. Our fashionista, Mia, requested a stroll on Rodeo Drive (no Barbecue Bus visible this time). Julian asked to see the La Brea Tar Pits, where we all witnessed, spellbound and heartbroken, as a reconstructed mastodon stood trapped in sticky tar while her plaintive infant looked on. I won't mention the climb to the Hollywood sign, although I suspect that trespassing and the subsequent hovering police helicopter made it the high point of the kids' trip.

Another journey took us to Israel, where Mia and Julian executed their *b'nai mitzvah* (the plural of *bar mitzvah* and *bat mitzvah*) with passion and aplomb. The Dome of the Rock shimmered in the distance. The ensuing meal at Jerusalem's Machneyuda was as dazzling as it was loud.

Last year, we convened in Paris. We bicycled to the Orsay Museum and along the Seine. We took the family to some of our favorite restaurants, including La Cordonnerie, where chef Hugo Wolfer cooks meals for the entire dining room in an open kitchen by himself. If you go, don't miss the *escalope de veau français à la normande* (veal with cream sauce). Tell Hugo that Steven and Barbara sent you.

In the Loire Valley, we stayed at a medieval castle impeccably renovated by an heir to the Schlumberger fortune. The playground had built-in trampolines (you can imagine how much the kids liked that!). From there it was on to Cap Ferret (like Cape Cod, only tonier), where we gorged ourselves on *fruit de mer* platters. Two kids are diehard ostreophiles (oyster lovers); there's aways hope for the third.

Meanwhile, we have yearly reunions in Chappaquiddick. I half dread the day when the kids tell Basha and PopPop to move into the guesthouse so that they, their friends, and eventual spouses can have the roomier main house.

When we're in Miami, we have barbecues in the backyard or gather on our sailboat. The kids quickly figured out how to put meals and Shirley Temples on my account at the Coconut Grove Sailing Club. (Smart kids.) I suspect that Ella will be the one to take the helm.

For a guy who never contemplated having children, I feel I've been triply blessed.

SMOKE-ROASTED VEGGIES

Call it supreme irony. Call it cosmic payback. The man who pioneered caveman T-bone, lamb on a shovel, and big, bad beef ribs—that would be me—is surrounded by non-meat eaters. Stepdaughter Betsy is a vegetarian. So is a close cousin. My wife, Barbara, has strong vegetarian leanings. So whenever we get together, I make sure we have plenty of meatless barbecue. Like these smoke-roasted vegetables, which we eat at least once a week. What varies are the veggies themselves: potatoes and garlic one week, brussels sprouts and cauliflower the next, or sometimes a half dozen different vegetables at a time. The key is to use dense vegetables, cut all the pieces to the same size, and cook them in a single layer. There are several ways to cook the vegetables: The safest are by indirect grilling or roasting in the oven. For even crisper vegetables, you can do direct grilling.

Serves 4

4 to 5 cups cut-up vegetables (1-inch pieces), such as fingerling potatoes, carrots, broccoli, broccolini, cauliflower, brussels sprouts, beets, etc.

1 head garlic, broken into cloves but unpeeled

3 tablespoons extra-virgin olive oil and/or melted unsalted butter

3 rosemary sprigs and/or 6 fresh sage leaves

Coarse sea salt and freshly ground black pepper to taste

You'll also need:

a 10- to 12-inch skillet or 9- by 13-inch aluminum pan; hardwood chips (soaked in water to cover for 30 minutes, then drained—optional) or 1 to 2 wood chunks

1. *To indirect grill:* Set up your grill for indirect grilling and heat to medium-high (400°F). Add wood chips or chunks to the fire if you desire a smoke flavor. *To direct grill:* Set up your grill for direct grilling and heat to medium-high (400°F). *To roast in the oven:* Preheat the oven to 400°F.
2. Arrange the vegetables in the skillet. Add the garlic and oil and stir to coat the vegetables. Stir in the herbs and plenty of salt and pepper.
3. *To indirect grill or roast in oven:* Place the vegetables on the grill away from the heat or in the oven. Cook until sizzling, browned, and crisp, 45 minutes or as needed, stirring often with a wooden spoon so the veggies roast evenly. *To direct grill:* Roast the vegetables as previously described, stirring every 3 to 5 minutes to keep the veggies from scorching. Cooking time here will be about 20 minutes. Serve at once.

EPILOGUE

At the helm of Barbacoa.

As I come to the end of this book, I'm filled with emotion. Relief that I got to the end. Surprise at what I've accomplished. Regret for what I haven't done. And impatience for the next project. I'm disappointed that my parents never got to see me in action. I'm sad to have lost my mother at such an early age. (Sad for her and sad for me.) And I'm sorry, unimaginably sorry, I never took my mother to see that movie.

But mostly I'm filled with gratitude. I've been incredibly lucky in this life. I married the girl of my dreams, who gave me a wonderful family. I live in two places where it's always barbecue weather, and I get to work mostly outdoors. I've been able to play with fire and turn it into a career that has spanned the globe. I've never had a boss, and I've never had to report to an office. I write about a subject that's infinitely fascinating, and get paid to eat and travel in the process. I've met some of the greatest chefs and grill masters of our era and had the good fortune to eat some of the best food on the planet.

Partners for life in marriage and grilling.

More importantly, I've gotten to meet readers and fans all over the world who tell me I've made a difference in their lives. I've tried to put my time on Earth to good use. I hope I've helped make the world a better—or at least a tastier—place.

I got to write this memoir, and I'm grateful for that too.

So, as Jed Bartlet used to ask in our all-time favorite TV series, *The West Wing*, "What's next?"

Well, first, there's sailing.

Barbacoa may not have been a great title for a book, but it's a fine name for a sailboat. Mine is a thirty-eight-foot Jeanneau Sun Odyssey, which we keep moored at the Coconut Grove Sailing Club. Sometimes Barbara and I set sail for the Florida Keys. More often, we just anchor in Biscayne Bay, where I'll pull out my laptop and work. Much of this book was written on *Barbacoa,* so I guess I should also be grateful for her too.

I've been sailing most of my life, but I still have much to learn and explore. I dream of cruising the Caribbean, or maybe Italy and the Greek islands.

Until then, I'll leave you with the words I write when autographing a book:

Grill On!

Steven Raichlen

Coconut Grove, Florida

January 5, 2026

GRAMMIE ETHEL COOKIES

I've saved the best for last. These crisp, buttery, vanilla-scented cookies were one of the great delights of my childhood (as they were for three generations of Raichlens)—stored in a red Snyder's of Hanover pretzel tin that never seemed to go empty. Grammie Ethel, née Ethel Lee Fribush, blended the ingredients in an ancient Sunbeam mixer and forced the dough through an antique cookie press into ridged ribbons. She baked them on a time-blackened cookie sheet and cooled them on a wire cake rack. The cake flour gives them exceptional crunch.

Serves 4

1 cup plus 1 tablespoon unsalted butter, at room temperature, divided

1 cup granulated sugar

1 large egg, lightly beaten with a fork

2 ½ cups cake flour (Grammie used Swans Down)

1 teaspoon vanilla extract

A pinch of salt

You'll also need:

a cookie press with a ridged extrusion plate

1. Preheat the oven to 375°F. Using 1 tablespoon of the butter, grease 2 rimmed baking sheets.
2. Place the remaining 1 cup butter and the sugar in a mixer and beat at medium speed until light and fluffy, about 3 minutes. Add the egg and beat until the mixture is smooth. Add the flour, vanilla, and salt and beat at low speed just until the batter is again smooth, 1 to 2 minutes.
3. Using a spatula, transfer the batter to the cookie press. Pipe it out in long, ridged ribbons running from the top to the bottom of the baking sheets, leaving 1 inch between each ribbon.
4. Bake the cookies until golden brown, 8 to 12 minutes, rotating the baking sheets halfway through (so the cookies cook evenly). Remove the baking sheets from the oven and cut the cookies crosswise on the diagonal into 2-inch lengths. Using a spatula, transfer them to a wire rack to cool. Once cool, store in an airtight container. They'll keep for at least a week, but I doubt they'll last that long. They sure don't in our house.

ACKNOWLEDGMENTS

The most fun part of writing a book is thanking the people who helped make it possible.

My agents, Stacey Glick and Jane Dystel at Dystel, Goderich & Bourret

My editor, Rebecca Pillsbury

My assistant, Nancy Loseke

My webmaster, Jared Reiter

Team Barbecuebible.com: Daniel Hale, John White, Steve Nestor

Team Barbecue University®: Craig Reed and Joe Archey

Team Television: Matt Cohen, Gwenn Williams, Ryan Kollmorgen, and Resolution Pictures

Frank Batavick, Stuart Kasanow, and the crew at Maryland Public Television

Field chef and food stylists: Chris Lynch, Nora Singley, Erika Martin

The crew at BenBella Books:

Glenn Yeffeth, CEO

Adrienne Lang, publisher

Claire Schulz, editorial director

Susan Welte, sales manager

Alicia Kania, vendor content manager
Madeline Grigg, senior publishing associate
Morgan Carr, designer
Monica Lowry, production director
Aaron Edmiston, designer
Karen Wise, copyeditor
Kellie Doherty, marketer

Roger Porter, Reed College
Sasha Burshteyn, The Thomas J. Watson Foundation
Susan Orlansky
Ken Winokur
Matt Morse
Susan Mattmann

My family: Ella, Mia, Julien, and Betsy, Amenya, and Jake

And last, but certainly not least, a huge thanks to my amazing wife, Barbara, without whom none of this would have been possible.

NOTES

Portions of this book appeared in or were inspired by my previously published writing. Most of the photos come from my family's collection, but a few were shared with permission. I've noted those here.

Chapter 1: The Battle of the Barbecue Gods

The chapter opener was inspired by "Clash of the Barbecue Titans" by Steven Raichlen. *The New York Times* (March 10, 2004). Adapted with permission.

Chapter 2: Growing Up On Coddies and Crab

A small portion of this chapter appeared in *Healthy Jewish Cooking* by Steven Raichlen (Viking, New York, New York, 2000).

Chapter 3: The Worst Day of My Life

Portions of this chapter appeared in Mom's Secret Recipe File by Christopher Styler, copyright © 2004. Reprinted by permission of Balance, an imprint of Hachette Book Group, Inc.

Chapter 4: James Beard Was Also an Alum

Portions of this chapter appeared in *Thinking Reed*, edited by Roger Porter and Robert Reynolds, Reed College, Portland, Oregon, 2011. Reprinted with permission.

The engraving of Christine de Pisan on page 45 is in the public domain and was sourced from Wikimedia Commons.

Chapter 5: Alimentary, My Dear Watson

Portions of this chapter appeared in *Thinking Reed,* edited by Roger Porter and Robert Reynolds, Reed College, Portland, Oregon 2011. Reprinted with permission.

Watson reunion photo printed with permission from the Watson Foundation.

Chapter 7: Hungry in the Hub

The description of my cooking classes in Cambridge comes from a story by Ken Winokur in *The Boston Phoenix.* Reprinted with permission.

Photo of SR wearing a mask by Ken Winokur.

Chapter 8: "You'll Never Make a Living Writing Cookbooks"

Booklet cover photos printed with permission from Anne Willan of La Varenne.

The *A Celebration of the Seasons* book cover is printed with permission from Simon & Shuster.

Chapter 9: A Taste of the Tropics

Some of the content in this chapter was inspired by *Miami Spice* (Workman Publishing). Adapted with permission.

The *Miami Spice* book cover is printed with permission from Workman Publishing.

Chapter 10: Follow the Fire: The Birth of *The Barbecue! Bible*

Portions of this chapter—write-up of Jamaica (Sufferer), grilled escargots, babi gulig, and Thai barbecue—were adapted from *The Barbecue! Bible.* Adapted with permission from Workman Publishing.

The Barbecue! Bible book cover is printed with permission from Workman Publishing.

Chapter 12: Teaching the World How to Grill

The *How To Grill* cover is printed with permission from Workman Publishing.

Chapter 13: Lights. Camera. Panic.

Barbecue University DVD cover printed with permission from Maryland Public Television (MPT).

Chapter 15: Primal Grill

Primal Grill poster printed with permission from Maryland Public Television.

Chapter 16: Travels on the World's Barbecue Trail

Planet Barbecue book cover printed with permission from Workman Publishing.

Chapter 17: Parlez-Vous Barbecue?

Portions of this chapter appeared in *Thinking Reed,* Edited by Roger Porter and Robert Reynolds, Reed College, Portland, Oregon 2011. Adapted with permission from Reed College.

Quebec book poster printed with permission from MédiaQMI INC.

Chapter 18: Cooking for Men

Man Made Meals book cover printed with permission from Workman Publishing.

Chapter 19: The Hermit of Chappaquiddick

Hermit of Chappaquiddick book cover: French edition published with permission from Groupe Livre Québecor; photo by Steve Dunwell/First Light.

Chapter 21: Up in Smoke

Portions of this chapter adapted from "The Still Seeker" in *Project Smoke* (Workman Publishing, 2016). Adapted with permission from Workman Publishing.

Project Smoke book cover printed with permission from Workman Publishing.

Chapter 22: Playing with Fire

Project Fire printed with permission from Workman Publishing.

Photo on page 292 by Frank Batavick.

ABOUT THE AUTHOR

Author, journalist, lecturer, and TV host Steven Raichlen is the man who launched the barbecue revolution. He has hosted many popular TV shows, like *Planet Barbecue, Project Fire, Project Smoke,* and *Primal Grill* on PBS. His thirty-five books include the international blockbusters *The Barbecue! Bible* and *How to Grill,* and *The New York Times* bestselling *Planet Barbecue* and *Project Smoke.* Raichlen's books have won five James Beard Awards and three IACP–Julia Child Awards and have been translated into seventeen languages. He is a member of the Barbecue Hall of Fame and Taste Awards Hall of Fame.

An award-winning journalist, Raichlen has written for *The New York Times, The Wall Street Journal, Esquire, GQ,* and all the major food magazines. He has appeared on numerous major TV and radio shows in the US and abroad, from *Oprah* and the *Today* show to *Fresh Air with Terry Gross* and *Howard Stern*. A one-time French literature major, Raichlen hosted eight years of barbecue TV shows in French in Québec and a ten-part series in Italy. He battled—and defeated—the Iron Chef in a Battle of the Barbecue Gods on Japanese television. Raichlen is the founder of Barbecue University—currently at the Alisal in Solvang, California. He and his wife, Barbara, split their time between Miami and Martha's Vineyard.